Echoes of Exclusion
and Resistance

Hanford Histories

Volume 3

Michael Mays, Series Editor

Titles in the series:

Nowhere to Remember: Hanford, White Bluffs, and Richland to 1943 (2018), edited by Robert Bauman and Robert Franklin

Legacies of the Manhattan Project: Reflections on 75 Years of a Nuclear World (2020), edited by Michael Mays

Echoes of Exclusion and Resistance

Voices from the Hanford Region

Edited by
Robert Bauman and Robert Franklin

WSU
PRESS

Washington State University Press
Pullman, Washington

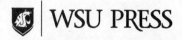

WSU PRESS

Washington State University Press
PO Box 645910
Pullman, Washington 99164-5910
Phone: 800-354-7360
Email: wsupress@wsu.edu
Website: wsupress.wsu.edu

Library of Congress Cataloging-in-Publication Data

Names: Bauman, Robert, 1964- editor. | Franklin, Robert R., 1981- editor.
Title: Echoes of exclusion and resistance : voices from the Hanford Region
  / edited by Robert Bauman and Robert Franklin.
Description: Pullman, Washington : Washington State University, [2020] |
  Series: Hanford histories | Includes bibliographical references and
  index.
Identifiers: LCCN 2020025624 | ISBN 9780874223828 (paperback)
Subjects: LCSH: Hanford Engineer Works--Employees--Interviews. |
  Minorities--Washington (State)--Tri-Cities--Social conditions--20th
  century. | Segregation--Washington (State)--Tri-Cities--History--20th
  century. | Race discrimination--Washington
  (State)--Tri-Cities--History--20th century. | Nuclear facilities--Social
  aspects--Washington (State)--Hanford. | Tri-Cities (Wash.)--History. |
  Tri-Cities (Wash.)--Race relations. | Tri-Cities (Wash.)--Ethnic
  relations. | Hanford Site (Wash.)--History.
Classification: LCC F899.P37 E34 2020 | DDC 305.8009797/51--dc23
LC record available at https://lccn.loc.gov/2020025624

Cover image courtesy of the Franklin County Historical Society and Museum.
Cover design by Jeff Hipp.

Contents

Illustrations

Tables

Acknowledgments

This volume would not have been possible without the support and contributions of a number of individuals and institutions. In particular, AACCES, the Afro-American Community, Cultural and Educational Society, has been a true partner in the oral histories collected for this volume. Vanessa and Leonard Moore, Edmon and Vanis Daniels and Tanya Bowers, through sharing their knowledge and expertise, and by sharing the oral history collection of AACCES, were especially vital to the creation and completion of this volume. We offer them our wholehearted thanks and appreciation.

Thank you to our friends and colleagues at Northwest Public Broadcasting—particularly Tom Hungate, Lori Larson, and Victor Vargas—who recorded all of these interviews for us. Their professionalism and cooperation has been a tremendous benefit to the project. Sarah St. Hilaire provided invaluable research that was vital to this volume's introduction.

In 2017, the Hanford History Project began a two-year undertaking with the National Park Service, Pacific Northwest Cooperative Extension Unit, to document African American migration, segregation, and civil rights at Hanford during and after the Manhattan Project. This generous funding from the National Park Service made three chapters of this volume possible and helped the Hanford History Project collect and preserve this important history. Special thanks go to Chris Johnson and Elaine Jackson-Retondo at the National Park Service for their guidance and patience.

This volume, and the Hanford Series as a whole, would not be possible without the efforts and support of Jillian Gardner-Andrews who took over the scheduling of oral histories in 2017, and participates in every Hanford History Project outreach event. A special thank you to the oral history transcriptionist, Evelyn Moos, who has watched and re-watched every AACCES and Hanford Oral History Project video to create and edit the transcripts used in the publication of this book. Transcription is a time-intensive task, often taking three to five times the length of the interview to create a transcript. Evelyn's attention to detail and knowledge of Hanford history has been an invaluable asset to the Hanford History

Project. The oral histories with full transcripts are found online at www.hanfordhistory.com.

Bob Clark, former editor-in-chief at WSU Press, believed in this project from the beginning and enthusiastically advocated for it. Indeed, this volume and the series of which it is a part, would not have happened without him. We also are particularly grateful to Linda Bathgate, who took over as editor-in-chief of WSU Press in 2019. Her vision has helped shepherd this volume to completion. Also, a special thanks to Beth DeWeese for her editorial guidance and expertise, and to the Editorial Board of WSU Press for their belief in this project. To Mike Mays, the series editor, our thanks for your unwavering support.

The authors and co-editors have presented versions of the material in this volume at a few different academic conferences. We would like to thank commenters and audience members at the Oral History Association Conference in Tampa, Florida, in 2015 and Salt Lake City, Utah, in 2019, the Northwest Anthropological Conference in Kennewick, Washington, in 2018, and the Western History Association Conference in San Antonio, Texas, in 2018. Questions and comments at those gatherings have made this volume richer and fuller.

The co-editors would like to especially thank our friends and family members who have provided so much support and inspiration over the past couple of years. Bob Bauman would like to offer special gratitude to Stephanie, Robert, and Rachel Bauman; and Robert Franklin to his wife, Evelyn Moos, and baby boy, Lanis William Franklin, the newest member of the Hanford History Project team. And, of course, huge props to our co-authors, Laura Arata and Tom Marceau, whose contributions go well beyond their expertise and excellent chapters in this volume.

Finally, we would like to thank all of the individuals whose interviews provided much of the background for the content of this volume. In particular, we would like to thank the members of the Yamauchi family—Brenda Kupfer, Roy Satoh, Linda Yamauchi Adkinson, and Bruce Yamauchi—for not only sharing their stories, but also for contributing family photographs to help share their family's experiences. The stories of all of the interviewees in this volume demonstrate the importance of oral history and preserving the memory of places like Hanford and the Tri-Cities. It is to those interviewees that we dedicate this volume.

Abbreviations

The following abbreviations for manuscript collections and newspapers are used throughout the notes.

HCRL   Hanford Cultural Resources Laboratory Oral History Program

HHP   Hanford History Project

The Four Deaths of Henry Williams[1]

Constructing Racial Narratives in the Tri-Cities

Robert Bauman

In its June 26, 1908, issue, the *Kennewick Courier*, one of two local weekly newspapers in Kennewick, Washington, a small, rural town on the dry, eastern side of the state, reported the following, under the heading "Dies in Jail":

> Charles Williams (colored), an old Roslyn miner, but more recently from White Bluffs, died in jail last night. He was taken in charge by Marshal Ellis in the rear of the Kennewick Bar and in complete intoxication and was hauled in a rig to the jail, where he was locked up. When the Day Marshal came on duty this morning he was found dead in his bed. There are no marks on him or indications of foul play or violent handling.[2]

What was apparently a simple case of a man dying of extreme intoxication, however, turned out to be not as straightforward as it initially appeared. Indeed, the events of Charles (Henry) Williams' death would be told in at least four very different narratives over the several months following his demise. And, over the next half century, Williams' death served as the foundation to the construction of the racial narrative in Kennewick, a town that prided itself on being "lily-white" well into the 1960s.[3] Each of the narratives constructed about Williams' death was wrapped in constructions of race and class in early and mid-twentieth century Kennewick. Those constructions of race and class raise questions about the place of African Americans in Kennewick and in the region of the American West as a whole. And they raise questions about the place of all nonwhites in the mid-Columbia region in the early twentieth century.

1

Two of the three cities that now make up the Tri-Cities, Washington (the third is Richland), Kennewick and Pasco were both founded in the late nineteenth century. Pasco was founded in 1884 with the completion of a railroad bridge over the Snake River, largely as a railroad town serving the workers building the Northern Pacific Railroad. The town was officially incorporated in 1891. The railroad would remain important to the economic and social fabric of Pasco for decades. By 1910, Pasco had over two thousand residents, with many being Chinese railroad workers.[4]

The town of Kennewick was primarily an agricultural hub for farmers in the region. Located across the Columbia River from the town of Pasco, the two towns were connected by a railroad bridge that brought the Northern Pacific through Kennewick as well as Pasco. By the early twentieth century, at the time of Henry Williams' death, Kennewick housed about one thousand residents.[5]

I.1. Downtown Kennewick circa 1905. Courtesy of the East Benton County Historical Society in Kennewick, Washington.

The town of Richland, like Kennewick also located in Benton County, was founded in 1905 by W.R. Amon and his son, Howard. Incorporated in 1910, Richland remained less populated than its neighbors of Pasco and Kennewick. Indeed, as of 1920, its population was only 279. That population remained small until the onset of World War II and the development of the Hanford Nuclear Reservation Site.[6]

Clearly, the initial narrative of Charles (Henry) Williams' demise was told to a representative of the *Kennewick Courier* by either Marshal Ellis or the unnamed "Day Marshal," Deputy Marshal Calhoun, and the *Courier* reported the incident as it had been told to them. It was a story of a severely inebriated "colored" man who drank himself to death. While the newspaper accepted the official law enforcement line, it left a bit of room for doubt. At the end of their brief article, the editor noted that "an inquest will be held this afternoon and evidence may be introduced there that will explain the cause of his sudden death." Thus, while "complete intoxication" was the apparent cause, the *Courier* article left the proverbial door slightly ajar for another possible explanation for Williams' death.[7]

One week later, in their July 3 issue, the *Courier* told another narrative of the death of Williams—and this story differed greatly from the first. In this account, rather than being the perpetrator of his own demise, Williams was, instead, the victim of a violent attack. According to this narrative, a number of witnesses testified at the coroner's inquest, and "all agreed" that a man named Tim O'Brien, described by the paper as a "blanket stiff," hit Williams and knocked him to the ground. Then William Howell, the bar's proprietor, grabbed Williams by the throat, dragged him out of the rear door of the bar and left Williams "propped up against a barrel" on the sidewalk. In addition to the witnesses' testimony, two local physicians, Drs. Crosby and Coone, had conducted an examination of the deceased Mr. Williams. They concluded that "Williams [sic] death was caused by concussion of the brain or by strangulation or both." Together with the witnesses' testimony, it appeared that Howell and O'Brien, not alcohol, had caused Williams' death. As a result, Marshal Ellis arrested Howell with bond set at $1000 (over $28,000 in today's money). O'Brien had "skipped" the railroad camps where he was living and working and could not be found.[8]

So, in this second narrative, constructed by the newspaper just a week after its initial version, Williams was no longer a debauched, "colored" drunk, but a helpless, raceless victim of a brutal attack. Indeed, Williams' race is not identified in this story at all when he is portrayed as a victim, but in the first narrative, when his demise was his own fault, the newspaper identified Williams' race as "colored," immediately in the first sentence of the article. Instead, what stands out in the newspaper's account after the coroner's inquest, is the term "blanket stiff" used to describe Tim O'Brien. Blanket stiffs were itinerant laborers who carried their blanket roll with them from town to town, from job to job. Since O'Brien was one of the perpetrators of the crime in this second version of the story, the fact that he was working class and poor is what is important. His race, one would assume white, is not identified; but his class is.[9]

The *Courier's* competitor, the *Kennewick Reporter*, told a more comprehensive version of this second narrative in its coverage of Williams' murder. First, the *Reporter*, which identified the victim as "Henry Williams, colored," published the full text of the coroner's jury decision which concluded that the combination of a blow to the head from Tim O'Brien and William Howell constricting Williams by the throat had caused the victim's death. The *Reporter* also included a thorough description of Williams' murder, based on the testimony provided by witnesses at the coroner's inquest. Apparently, Williams had arrived in Kennewick on a ferry from the town of White Bluffs, approximately thirty miles up the Columbia River from Kennewick. Williams first entered the Kennewick Bar sometime in the afternoon. At some point he got in an argument with Howell, who evicted Williams from the tavern. Williams returned to the bar about 5:30 in the evening and got in another argument with some of the patrons. One of them, O'Brien, punched Williams, knocking him unconscious. Howell, who had been in the bar's back room, came to the front of the tavern, grabbed Williams by the throat and dragged him out of the bar, choking him in the process, and left him propped on some barrels outside the bar. Several individuals testified that they saw O'Brien later that evening with his hand wrapped in a cloth, saying that he had "hurt it on a nigger."[10]

William Howell's version of the events of June 25, 1908, differed slightly. According to Howell, he and a few others were having lunch at the Kennewick Bar when Williams came in. Howell asked Williams to join them, which he did. Howell then claimed that Williams "acted in an ungentlemanly manner" and Howell kicked Williams out of the bar. When Williams returned later, Howell was in the back room. He heard a commotion and came to the front room to see Williams lying on the floor. He admitted to dragging Williams out the back door and propping him against some barrels.[11]

Though intoxication was no longer officially part of the explanation for Williams' untimely demise, a number of Kennewick citizens demanded regulation of saloons in the city, and in particular, demanded the revocation of William Howell's saloon license. To those citizens, liquor clearly was the primary reason for Williams' demise, and they chose his death as the catalyst to move forward with their anti-liquor agenda. The City Council arranged for the transfer of Howell's business license to others. Several citizens had also petitioned the city council to require all saloons to close at midnight and not re-open until six in the morning, and also to remain closed on Sundays. This was too much for the council. Rather than blaming liquor for Williams' demise, they chose to blame Howell and O'Brien. All saloons in Kennewick would stay open and unregulated.[12]

A third narrative of Williams' death emerged at the murder trial of William Howell and a man named John Shafer a few months later, in October 1908. In an article titled, "Howell Acquitted," the *Courier* wrote about the trial in the following manner:

> The trial of Wm. Howell and John Shafer charged with murder in the first degree for the killing of the negro Williams was held yesterday in Prosser and both men were acquitted in short order. The evidence failed to connect either man definitely with any act that would cause death.[13]

A number of items stand out in this third narrative of the death of Charles (Henry) Williams. First, a man named John Shafer, not Tim O'Brien, was charged with murder along with Howell. O'Brien, as noted in the second account, had apparently gone missing. And, for whatever reason, Shafer, who was not mentioned in the first two versions of this narrative, had been identified as Howell's accomplice. Either way, Howell and Shafer had stood trial for first degree murder and had been acquitted because of what the jury saw as a lack of evidence directly linking either man to Williams' death. Indeed, the newspaper emphasizes this by noting that the men "were acquitted in short order." This account, though, directly contradicts the second version of Williams' death narrative which explicitly detailed how Howell had grabbed Williams by the throat after O'Brien had punched Williams and noted that, according to the coroner's inquest, Williams had died of concussion or strangulation or both.

Perhaps the most significant detail in this third account is that Williams is, as he was in the first account, identified by his race, this time as "negro" instead of "colored," and this time with no first name. Perhaps the editor was confused by the fact that court documents identified Williams with the first name of Henry, while the paper had always identified him as Charles, and opted to omit Williams' first name due to their uncertainty. For whatever reason, he is simply "the negro Williams" in this account. The helpless, raceless victim of the second *Courier* narrative is no longer raceless and, apparently no longer a victim. For, if Shafer and Howell had not caused Williams' death, who had? O'Brien? He had not been officially charged and, apparently, could not be found. In this third account, Williams again appears to be held responsible for his own demise. And, as in the first account, he was explicitly identified by race, thereby linking his demise and his accountability for it due to his race. In the second account, when he was the victim, he was raceless. In the first and third narratives, when he was responsible for his own demise, he was "colored" or "negro."

Finally, one additional note about this third account—Howell and Shafer are not identified in any way other than as two men who were acquitted, and the suggestion is, wrongly accused, of murder. They are raceless and classless. In the second account, when the newspaper faulted Howell and O'Brien for Williams' death, it emphasized O'Brien's poverty and itinerancy. When the newspaper wrote about their acquittal, neither man's class was noted.

This third account, though, differed dramatically from the official narrative presented by J.W. Callicotte, the prosecuting attorney for Benton County. On July 15, just a few weeks after Williams' death, Callicotte filed the official charges against Howell and Shafer in Benton County Superior Court. Callicotte argued that Howell and Shafer with "deliberate and premeditated malice" beat and strangled Henry Williams to death. Importantly, Callicotte's account is also raceless. None of the individuals mentioned—Williams, Howell, or Shafer—are identified by race. In a narrative that matched the second account told by the *Courier*, Williams was a raceless, helpless victim, killed in a brutal and premeditated fashion by William Howell and John Shafer.[14]

Notably, William Howell had been involved in a similar episode a few years earlier. In the early hours of Christmas morning, 1905, Howell shot two customers at his bar, the Steamer Saloon in Tacoma. The following May, Howell was found guilty of assault, but upon appeal his conviction was overturned with his attorney successfully arguing that Howell had shot the men in self-defense. It was not long after his conviction was overturned that Howell arrived in Kennewick and he brought his history of violence with him.[15]

Although he was acquitted of the murder of Henry Williams, the case did impact William Howell's life. First, he lost his business. He also left the town of Kennewick. In its January 1, 1909, issue the *Courier* noted that Howell and his wife had moved to Spokane. Six months later, the Howells returned to the area, but this time to Pasco. Shortly thereafter, he lost his life. William Howell died in July of 1909 of typhoid pneumonia just over a year after Henry Williams' death.[16]

So, Howell and Shafer were acquitted of the murder of Henry Williams and Howell was now dead. It seemed as though the Henry Williams murder case was over. But it wasn't. This strange case took one more fascinating turn. Remarkably, almost three years after Williams' death, in February 1911, Tim O'Brien, living under the alias of Tom Cahill in Prince Rupert, British Columbia, confessed to Canadian authorities to having killed Williams. Following Howell's 1908 acquittal, Marshal Ellis had continued to work on the case intermittently, determined to pursue the case against O'Brien who apparently had fled Kennewick the day after Williams was killed. Eventually, after much dogged detective work, Ellis located O'Brien in Prince Rupert and brought him back to Benton County to stand trial for Williams' death.[17]

Importantly, in its story on the 1911 capture of O'Brien, the *Courier* noted that Howell had been tried and acquitted in the case in 1908, "but it was generally supposed that he was guilty. The confession of O'Brien will remove the stigma from Howell's name as well as bring to justice the guilty man." As far as the editor of the *Courier* was concerned, Howell, dead for almost two years, was now exonerated and O'Brien clearly guilty.[18]

O'Brien told his version of the events of June 25, 1908, the fourth narrative of Henry Williams' death, in his confession to Canadian authorities. According to O'Brien, he was having lunch in the Kennewick Bar with Howell and several others when "a coloured man" entered the bar and sat down next to the men, apparently uninvited, and began eating some of the lunch. When he took a glass of beer, Howell "hit the coloured man on the jaw and knocked him out." When Williams came to, he was ready to fight. O'Brien then claimed that Williams, who O'Brien referred to repeatedly in his confession as a "coon," attacked him. O'Brien declared that he then hit Williams twice in self-defense, knocking Williams unconscious. The next morning the bartender informed O'Brien "that the coon had died in jail. This bartender also told me that I had killed the coon, and that I had better hit the grit. I left immediately."[19]

The case came before the Benton County Superior Court in March 1911, but before the case actually came to trial, the Benton County Prosecutor, Lon Boyle, who had replaced Callicotte the previous year, submitted a formal request to the court that the charges against Tim O'Brien be dismissed. In his request to the court, Boyle reiterated many of the particulars of the events of June 25, with the key details being that Tim O'Brien had struck Williams after Williams had apparently threatened him, and that Howell and the bartender, Guy Shelton, had dragged Williams out of the bar. In his account of the events, Boyle noted that "all the eye witnesses were more or less intoxicated, and it is my opinion that none of them have a very clear recollection of the matter." In addition, Boyle argued that the case could not be successfully prosecuted because, as he put it, "this matter occurred nearly three years ago, and all the witnesses are gone, and for the most part it is impossible for this office to learn of their whereabouts." Boyle went on to conclude that "I feel certain that a crime of murder or even of less degree could not be sustained against Tim O'Brien....It is my opinion that an attempt to force O'Brien to trial would work an injustice upon him, and would likewise cause the County a great amount of unnecessary expense without the least possible chance of obtaining a conviction. In my opinion, the ends of justice would be better attained, and likewise a saving of a great amount of expense and trouble would be accomplished by dismissing the charge." So, remarkably, even though O'Brien had confessed to the murder of Henry Williams to Canadian authorities, Boyle decided not to try him. In response to Boyle's request, on March 24, 1911, the presiding judge dismissed the case against Tim O'Brien and discharged him from the county jail. There would be no further investigations into the murder of Henry Williams.[20]

The four narratives of the death of Henry Williams and the ensuing court case surrounding the circumstances of his death leave the modern reader less than satisfied. For what remain unclear reasons, Tim O'Brien never served any prison sentence for the murder of Henry Williams, even though he confessed to the crime. Because of time and distance, a lack of sources exists to fill the holes in these narratives. We will never know what became of O'Brien, nor do we know any of the particulars of Williams' life prior to his death in Kennewick, other than that he had been a miner in Roslyn and had lived briefly in the town of White Bluffs, about thirty miles northwest of Kennewick, prior to arriving in that town.

Williams' connection to the town of Roslyn, though, is an important clue. Located in central Washington, at the eastern base of the Cascade Mountains, Roslyn was an important coal mining town from the 1880s to the 1920s. When white miners in Roslyn went on strike over wages and working conditions in 1888, company officials called in strikebreakers, including approximately 300 African American miners from Kentucky, Virginia, and North Carolina. The arrival of the miners, many who brought their families, created the largest increase in the Black population in the history of the then territory of Washington. In 1890, African Americans comprised 22 percent of the population of Roslyn. Although initially significant tensions surfaced between white and Black miners, eventually those conflicts subsided as the strike ended and enough work existed for all miners, regardless of color. Henry Williams undoubtedly was one of the 300 miners who migrated to Roslyn in the late 1880s. As such, he represents an early migration of African Americans out of the south to the north. The Great Migration of African Americans, which involved over six million African Americans leaving the south, was still a couple of decades away. The Great Migration would have a profound impact on the mid-Columbia region and the town of Kennewick.[21]

But, beyond knowing that Williams was part of this group of Black miners in Roslyn, we have little detail about his life. What is clear, though, is that he was murdered and his killer did not pay for Williams' death. Unfortunately, this is not unusual in U.S. history. Thousands of African Americans, mostly, but not exclusively, men, have been lynched throughout the history of the United States, and not just in the south. And, of course, recent events in places like Ferguson, Missouri, Baltimore, and New York City have brought to light all too often that the killing of African American men, often by law enforcement, remains a central and ugly part of the United States. The white men who have committed those crimes have largely gone unpunished. The story of the death of Henry Williams, and the racial narratives constructed around his murder, reflect that violent history.

In addition to reflecting the history of violence against African American men, the incident of Williams' death also serves as a prelude to this history of race in the region that became known as the Tri-Cities. For much of its history, the mid-Columbia region has reflected the broader history of race in the American West. As many scholars have demonstrated, the American West always has been the most racially diverse region in the United States since early in U.S. history. Similarly, from its early history, the Tri-Cities region has been a diverse, multiracial place. From the thousands of years of Native peoples calling the region home to the arrival of Chinese immigrant miners in the 1860s to the internment of Japanese Americans during World War II to the arrival of thousands of Black migrants for wartime and Cold War jobs, the racial history of the region aligns well with much of the American West. But, of course, there are unique aspects to its history as well. Most of that uniqueness is connected to the Second World War and the construction of the Hanford Nuclear Reservation in 1942-43. The war and the construction of Hanford led to the removal of Native peoples, particularly the Wanapum, from their ancestral lands, the internment of local residents of Japanese descent, and the arrival of African Americans from the south to help build Hanford.[22]

This volume attempts to tell the story of the various nonwhite groups who have lived and worked in the mid-Columbia region. In so doing, it is important to understand race and racial formation as social and historical constructions. In other words, nonwhite racial groups were defined differently at different times in American history. In addition, in telling the stories of these groups, we borrow the term and idea of "racial scripts" from the historian Natalia Molina. According to Molina, the term racial scripts highlights both how different nonwhite racial groups have been "acted upon by a range of principals from institutional actors to ordinary citizens... [and] the ways in which the lives of racialized groups are linked across time and space and thereby affect one another, even when they do not directly cross paths." Although those groups' lives may or may not have crossed paths, and despite occurring in different time periods, Molina argues that "what once served to marginalize and disenfranchise one group can be revived and recycled to marginalize other groups."[23]

The stories of the various groups discussed in the following pages sometimes overlapped in time and space and at times did not. Regardless, their experiences impacted one another and linked them together in ways they likely did not know. The death of Henry Williams, and the narrative told about his death, directly influenced racial practices in Kennewick and gave that town the reputation, well-earned, of a place nonwhites should avoid. Indeed, for decades after Williams' death, residents of Kennewick prided themselves in the fact that their town was "lily-white." In addition, the segregation of Chinese railroad workers to East Pasco in the late 1880s began the practice of segregating all nonwhite residents of the town to east of the railroad tracks. From Japanese Americans who arrived in the early twentieth century to African Americans who migrated to Pasco during World War II and the early years of the Cold War, to Mexican Americans who began arriving in Pasco in the late 1950s and migrated in significant numbers beginning in the 1980s, all nonwhite groups were either formally or informally segregated to the east side of town. This volume explores the ways in which the lives of nonwhite racial groups in the mid-Columbia connected directly and indirectly and the ways in which the narratives of those lives affected each other. It also examines efforts to marginalize those nonwhite groups and the ways those efforts at marginalization used toward one group were used in turn to attempt to marginalize others.

This volume uses oral histories conducted for the most part for the Hanford History Project as the primary sources for its chapters. The exceptions to this general rule are oral histories of Native American informants conducted by the Atomic Heritage Foundation that inform much of chapter 1, and oral histories of African Americans conducted by members of the Afro-American Community Cultural and Educational Society (AACCES) that supplement the Hanford History Project oral histories in chapters 3, 4, and 5.

In addition, this volume is focused on the experiences of nonwhite groups whose lives were greatly impacted by the Hanford Site. Our volume includes chapters on Native Americans who were evicted from their traditional lands as a result of the construction of the Hanford Site, African Americans who migrated from the South to work at Hanford and transformed the region as a result, and Japanese Americans who were interned during the war, in part because of their proximity to Hanford. As a result of this focus, and because of a lack of oral histories with Latino/as, this volume does not include an extensive exploration of the significant Latino population in the Tri-Cities. Latinx migration to the Tri-Cities was not connected directly to Hanford, but to the region's agricultural growth. Our conclusion does, though, include a brief summary of this history of Latinos in the region. That story deserves a much broader and deeper examination in its own volume.

The first chapter in this volume, written by Tom Marceau, uses oral histories conducted by the Atomic Heritage Foundation in 2003 to explore the history of the Native peoples of the region. Native Americans resided in the Hanford area for thousands of years. The Yakama, Umatilla, and Nez Perce people had been removed from the region by treaties signed in the nineteenth century. The Wanapum, who did not sign a treaty with the federal government, continued to live in the region until World War II. Marceau's chapter describes how Native Americans interacted with the ancient landscapes of the region and the ways their lives relied on the natural resources of the region. Marceau's story of the Native Americans includes the impact of the construction of the Hanford Nuclear Reservation on the Wanapum and their removal from their traditional lands. This chapter also features the voices of other native peoples who tell the stories of their people and their responses to dislocation and forced evacuation from their native land. Finally, Marceau discusses the current relationship between Native Americans, the federal government, and their former lands.

In chapter 2, Robert Bauman examines the experiences of Asian Americans in the region, specifically through the lens of the Yamauchi family. Early arrivals to Pasco, the Yamauchis built the American dream—including establishing several successful businesses and sending several of their children to college—only to see that dream challenged, diminished, and damaged by internment during World War II. The stories of Asian Americans in the Tri-Cities area in many ways fit well with the broader narratives of Chinese and Japanese immigrants in the American West. But their location in a small town instead of a major urban area, and in a place far removed from the Pacific coast, highlight some of the unique characteristics of their experiences. This chapter uses an oral history conducted with members of the Yamauchi family, as well as other primary sources, to tell the story of Asian Americans in the Tri-Cities.

In the third chapter, Robert Franklin investigates the migration of thousands of African Americans to the Hanford area for wartime jobs. In many ways, these migrations mirrored the larger migration of Blacks to cities in the American West during World War II. Blacks at Hanford, though, found some unique circumstances in regard to their work and living conditions. Blacks were segregated both at Hanford and in available housing in the region. This chapter expands on Robert Bauman's previous scholarship by exploring the experiences of African Americans through the use of oral histories with Blacks who migrated to the area during the war.

In chapter 4, Laura J. Arata explores the special and unique experiences of Black women who came to work at Hanford during World War II and the early years of the Cold War. Utilizing several oral histories from the Hanford History Project collection, Arata highlights the stories of Black women, most of whom migrated from East Texas, and their stories and recollections about employment, discrimination, family, and faith. Arata situates her story firmly in the larger narrative of the Great Migration, but also notes some of the unique aspects of the narratives of Black women who came to the Tri-Cities area during World War II and the early years of the Cold War.

Chapter 5 continues the story of the experiences of Black workers at Hanford in the Cold War. African Americans migrated in significant numbers to the Tri-Cities from the late 1940s to the early 1960s, and they continued to face discrimination on the job and through segregated housing in the surrounding area. This chapter explores efforts by African Americans to challenge both job and housing discrimination through negotiations, demonstrations, and protests. This chapter, co-authored by Robert Bauman and Robert Franklin, places oral histories with African Americans at the center of this story.

The conclusion of this volume, co-authored by Robert Franklin and Robert Bauman, focuses on the experiences of Mexican American and Latinx migrants and the ways that migration has influenced and built on the already existing racial narratives. The conclusion also explores the ways in which the story of the multiracial Hanford region reflects the story of the American West in general. The American West has always been a diverse region, and the Hanford story reflects that. From native peoples to Chinese and Japanese immigrants to African American war workers, the Hanford region's diverse populations mirror those of the American West in general. In addition, the racial segregation and discrimination experienced by these groups in the Hanford region fits seamlessly with recent narratives of the American West. Each of the groups discussed in the following chapters challenged the segregation and discrimination they faced, and, in the process, they challenged the dominant racial narratives of the region. As part of the Atomic West, however, the story of Hanford's diversity is also unique. The oral histories in this volume both support the narrative of the multiracial west and add some important nuances to that story as well. In addition, the conclusion uses the idea of racial scripts to highlight the ways in which the narratives of these various groups, even though happening at different times, are directly connected. Those narratives and experiences have constructed a prominent racial narrative of the Tri-Cities region.

Notes

1. The title for this chapter was inspired by the film, *The Three Burials of Melquiades Estrada*. Tommy Lee Jones, Director, Sony Pictures Classics, 2006.

2. *Kennewick Courier*, June 26, 1908. Williams is identified as Charles Williams in the *Courier* accounts, but as Henry Williams in all court documents.

3. For the continuity of this local narrative, see Martha Berry Parker, *Kin-I-Wak, Kenewick, Tehe, Kennewick*, Fairfield, WA: Ye Galleon Press, 1986.

4. David W. Harvey, "An Oasis in the Desert? White Bluffs, Hanford, and Richland, The Early Years," in *Nowhere to Remember: Hanford, White Bluffs, and Richland to 1943*, edited by Robert Bauman and Robert Franklin, Pullman: Washington State University Press, 2018, 21–22.

5. Ibid; Ted Van Arsdol, *Tri-Cities: The Mid-Columbia Hub*, Chatsworth, CA: Windsor Publications, 1990, 42.

6. Harvey, "Oasis," 22–23.

7. *Kennewick Courier*, June 26, 1908.

8. *Kennewick Courier*, July 3, 1908.

9. Ibid.

10. "William Howell Held on Charge of Manslaughter," *Kennewick Reporter*, July 3, 1908. The White Bluffs ferry started operations in 1858. For more on the early history of the town of White Bluffs, see Robert Bauman and Robert Franklin, eds., *Nowhere to Remember: Hanford, White Bluffs, and Richland to 1943*, Pullman: Washington State University Press, 2018, especially chapters 1 and 2.

11. "William Howell Held on Charge of Manslaughter," *Kennewick Reporter*, July 3, 1908.

12. "License Transferred," *Kennewick Courier*, July 3, 1908.

13. "Howell Acquitted," *Kennewick Courier*, October 9, 1908.

14. Benton County Superior Court, Criminal Case File 44, 1908.

15. "Two Probably Fatally Shot in Christmas Morning Saloon Row," *Olympia Daily Recorder*, December 25, 1905; "Convicted of Assault," *Seattle Daily Times*, May 2, 1906.

16. *Kennewick Courier*, January 1, 1909, and June 4, 1909; Washington State Department of Health, Washington State Death Certificate Index, 1907–1960, Office of the Secretary of State, Washington State Archives, Digital Archives, www.digitalarchives.wa.gov. Accessed May 31, 2013.

17. "O'Brien Makes Confession," *Kennewick Courier*, February 17, 1911.

18. Ibid.

19. "Statement of Tim O'Brien," in Benton County Superior Court, Criminal Case File 98, 1911. O'Brien's trial was held in the town of Prosser, which was the county seat.

20. Benton County Criminal Case File 98, 1911.

21. Trevor Goodloe, "Roslyn, Washington." Retrieved from www.blackpast.org/african-american-history/roslyn-washington November 10, 2019.

22. For two classic works on the promises and limitations of the multiracial American West, see Richard White, "Race Relations in the American West," *American Quarterly* 38:3 (1986), 396–416; and Patricia Nelson Limerick, *The Legacy of Conquest: The Unbroken Past of the American West*, NY: W.W. Norton, 1987.

23. Natalia Molina, *How Race is Made in America: Immigration, Citizenship, and the Historical Power of Racial Scripts* (Berkeley: University of California Press, 2014), 6 (first quote) and 7 (second quote). On the social and historical construction of race, see Michael Omi and Howard Winant, *Racial Formation in the United States: From the 1960s to the 1980s* (New York: Routledge, 1986), and George Lipsitz, *How Racism Takes Place*

(Philadelphia: Temple University Press, 2011). See also, Veronica Martínez-Matsuda, "For Labor and Democracy: The Farm Security Administration's Competing Visions for Farm Workers' Socioeconomic Reform and Civil Rights in the 1940s," *The Journal of American History* 106:2 (September 2019), 341.

CHAPTER ONE

The Ties That Bind
Hanford's Ancient Landscape And Contemporary Native Americans

Thomas E. Marceau

INTRODUCTION

The Indian is part of the land, you know. The Indian is the land. And that's just the way it is. There's no difference about it. You know, that's just how it is. That's how the connection is—we are part of this land. Our people are here, generations upon generations, we're put here and we're always going to be here.[1]

Rex Buck Jr., a spiritual leader and Elder of the Wanapum people, whose traditional homeland includes the Hanford Site, had asked that he be interviewed in a setting that was important to him. So, the video of his oral interview shows Rex sitting on a camp stool between the 100-D and 100-H Areas of the Hanford Site with the White Bluffs of the Columbia River behind him as a backdrop. About six minutes into his 2003 interview, Rex was interrupted by the passage of a dust devil. During the time the camera was turned off, as we all grabbed our belongings and held on tightly as the fast-moving wind vortex engulfed us, Rex and I locked eyes, smiled, and said almost simultaneously "Bobby," referring to a recently passed Wanapum Elder, Bobby Tomanawash, who had been a long-time mentor to Rex and a patient friend to me. No other dust devil occurred that afternoon. This was a single event that literally touched us all. Even though the area in which we sat was very expansive, the dust devil had formed just a short distance away, passed only through the location in which the interview was being conducted, then quickly dissipated. Bobby, Rex assured me, had come by to make sure he "got it right" in his interview! Such is their world, a world in which the physical and metaphysical coexist seamlessly; a world in which spirits are not only present but interact freely with the living—often of their own volition. Theirs is truly a living world.

Tribal worldviews are older and more fundamental than those based on Western, empirical science. Tribal worldviews establish man's place within the universe, and define and perpetuate lifeways that have existed "since time immemorial." For example, from birth Native people are taught that they are responsible to care for the land and its resources, entrusted to them by the creator. Elders instruct the youth to take care of the soil so the soil will take care of them, to take care of the plants so the plants will take care of them, to take care of the animals so the animals will take care of them, and so on for all resources that contribute directly to the group's cultural identity and survival. In the words of Native writers, "American Indians believe they have the responsibility to protect with. care and teach the young... a non-destructive life on Mother Earth... Everything is considered to be interrelated and dependent on each other to sustain existence."[2] Human's relationship to the land and its resources and, equally important, their relationships to humans are essential elements within Native American traditional lifeways. If used with respect, "plants and animals for food, medicinal plants for continued health... and water to drink and use in ceremonies of all kinds" will continue to sustain not only them but also their children and their children's children.[3]

This covenant between man and land is particularly powerful with respect to the land within which "the people" were created. Anthropologist Richard W. Stoffle has worked with Indigenous communities on a variety of projects and summarizes their relationship to their homelands in very explicit terms: "A holy land is created by a supernatural being who establishes a birthright relationship between a people (however defined) and that portion of the earth where they were created. This relationship provides the people with special rights to use and obligations to protect resources on that portion of the earth." Specifically addressing the central theme of this chapter, he continues: "The relationship between a people and their holy land cannot be broken, even by a diaspora. **Forced relocation by another ethnic group will not break a relationship created by the supernatural.**[4] In traditional communities, one's ties to the land are inherited at birth and strengthen with age as elements of the cultural landscape are internalized.

It is equally important to understand that time is not viewed as linear in many traditional societies; rather time is perceived as an unbroken and unbreakable circle. Each ceremony performed in furtherance of one's current stewardship obligation to the land and its resources is a simultaneous acknowledgment to the ancestors and a commitment to the unborn that their way of life has continued and will continue unaltered; one honors tradition by passing it forward as it was received. But the words must be spoken; the ceremonies must be performed at the right time and in the right place. To do otherwise places not only the people but also the world in danger. This is precisely the condition that contemporary Native American communities now find themselves in with respect to the Hanford Site and their inability to freely access these lands.

In this chapter, the close ties between traditional people and the world in which they live will be examined as part of a case study focused on the effects of enforced removal on Indigenous communities with ancestral ties to the Hanford Site. As background, the antiquity of human use of the landscapes that comprise the Columbia Basin, and the ways in which landforms become meaningful elements within the cultural world of Indigenous communities will be considered. Subsequent to that discussion, the desire of contemporary Native communities to retain their connection to this land, as well as the consequences suffered through their continued loss of access, will be presented as expressed through oral histories recorded with local tribal members in 2003 by the Atomic Heritage Foundation. Though seventeen years have passed since these interviews, the sentiments and grievances articulated then remain the same today. Stated quite simply, their world is "out of balance" and endangered while these lands remain off limits.

How Old is the Columbia Basin Landscape?

Hanford was literally formed from fire and ice—fire from the combined volcanism and tectonism that created the surficial landforms of the Columbia Basin and surrounding uplands; ice from a continental glacier whose meltwaters fed the Missoula Floods that sculpted the basin just prior to, or maybe coterminous with, man's entry into this area.

"Flood basalt volcanism occurred in the United States' Pacific Northwest between 17.5 and 6 million years ago, when over 300 basaltic lavas of the Columbia River Basalt Group were erupted from fissures in eastern Washington, eastern Oregon, and western Idaho."[5] The flood basalts, cumulatively 12,000 to 15,000 feet thick, are overlain by younger sedimentary rocks of the Ringold and Hanford Formations.

"Concurrent with these massive basalt eruptions, was the folding and faulting of the basalt in the western part of the Columbia Basin and development of generally east-west trending anticlinal ridges and synclinal valleys collectively known as the Yakima Fold Belt."[6] Easily discernible on the modern surface, named portions of these anticlinal ridges or "folds" on the Hanford Site include Rattlesnake Mountain, Gable Mountain, Gable Butte, Umtanum Ridge, and the Saddle Mountains. Structurally, Robert Yeats explains that these ridges were "forced up by compressional faults in the rigid crust beneath the basalt." More visually, he describes the folds as a once level surface that has been "crumpled like a heavy carpet after a sofa has been pushed over it."[7]

It is instructive to note that the tectonic processes that created the landscape of the Columbia Basin continue today, albeit with significantly less visual impact. Reidel and his coathors remind us "that ~2400 ft of uplift has occurred on Rattlesnake Mountain since ca. 8.5 million years ago," while within the intervening valleys "subsidence has been occurring over a long period of time. The area continues to subside but at a very slow rate."[8] In line with a central theme of this chapter, one may interpret this to mean that the land is still "alive."

FROM TIME IMMEMORIAL

How far into the past can a connection to this land by contemporary Native Americans be made? In answering this question, we first look at the archaeological information for the greater Columbia Plateau, then focus more specifically on the Hanford Site itself.

The Columbia Plateau

A thorough review of the archaeological record of the Columbia Plateau was undertaken in response to a seemingly unrelated event that made world-wide headlines. In late July 1996, a skull and a few pieces of bone were found in the shallow shoreline waters of the Columbia River at the western end of Columbia Park in Kennewick, Washington. Once the find came to the attention of authorities, Dr. James Chatters, then the consulting archaeologist for the Benton County Coroner, was hired to examine the find spot. As he describes the event, the Kennewick Man's "remains were disarticulated and scattered, clearly having eroded from a collapsed portion of the cut bank, and were distributed along more than 30 m [98.5 ft] of beach." Chatters would make ten trips to the discovery area to search for additional materials; as a result of these efforts "approximately 350 fragments representing at least 143 elements" of the skeleton were recovered). When dated, the nearly complete skeleton returned a $\delta^{13}C$ corrected age of 8410 ± 60 radiocarbon years before the present (BP).[9]

Given the conditions surrounding the discovery of Kennewick Man (referred to as "the Ancient One" [*Pips-Me-Maw-Winch*] by the Tribes), as well as the age of the skeleton, the National Park Service (NPS) contracted with Dr. Kenneth M. Ames to conduct "a study that would focus on the possible cultural affiliation of the remains with present-day Indian tribes." In conducting his review of the extant archaeological record for continuity or discontinuity in human occupation of the Columbia Plateau, as evidence of cultural affiliation between the Ancient One and modern Native Americans, Ames considered the following lines of evidence: radiocarbon dates; land use; mobility patterns; subsistence (for example salmon, roots); houses; chipped and ground stone artifacts (for example projectile points, microblades, small hand milling stones, edge-ground cobbles, net weights); bone artifacts (for example needles, awls, harpoons, antler wedges); and trade and exchange.[10]

In summarizing this information, Ames makes the following points regarding cultural continuity: "While we do not have strong control over the human demography of the Plateau, it is clear from the evidence... that people have shifted around on the Columbia Plateau landscape during the Holocene. However, **there seems to be no evidence of a major Plateau-wide break in occupation during that time.**" In fact, Ames did not see populations moving into or exiting the Plateau as explanation for population dynamics or settlement over the 9,000 years separating the Ancient One from modern Indigenous people. "As far as I am aware, no one has invoked major population incursions to explain periods of growth." He goes on to express his belief that cultural continuity between contemporary Native peoples and "earlier people on the Plateau" is highly likely, although in need of additional research. "At the beginning of this section," he states, "I wrote that the empirical record precludes establishing

---

How Did the Missoula Floods Change the Landscape?

During the last 2,000 years of the Pleistocene (ca. 15,000 to 13,000 years ago), the Cordilleran Ice Sheet advanced and retreated multiple times from British Columbia into northern Washington State, northern Idaho, and western Montana.[13] Of particular interest here was the blockage caused to the drainage of the Clark Fork River near the present Idaho-Montana border associated with each advance. As described by Bjornstad, the blockage of the Clark Fork River formed "hugh, ice-dammed lakes...creating an inland sea of fresh glacial meltwater...twice the size of Rhode Island." Over time the ice dam broke such that "the entire lake [Lake Missoula] would suddenly let loose, resulting in an earth-shaking glacial outburst flood...consisting of up to 500 cubic miles of bashing, grinding, roaring water that raced through Idaho, across the channeled scablands of eastern Washington and down the Columbia River all the way to the Pacific Ocean." The rate of flow for the largest of these floods has been estimated at "17 million cubic meters per second, or about 10 times the flow of all the rivers in the world combined!" Speeds reached have been estimated at "80 miles per hour." Current research has postulated as many as 100 independent flood events over the 2,000-year period.[14]

All the water exiting Lake Missoula stalled and collected in the mid-Columbia Basin as the floodwaters

cultural continuities or discontinuities across increasingly remote periods. However, if the available evidence cannot be used to show continuity, it is equally refractory for demonstrating discontinuity."[11]

While persuasive as a viable archaeological argument for cultural continuity worth additional study, Ames' investigation was less compelling as a legal argument for affiliation. On August 30, 2002, following six years of litigation and absent a demonstrable direct cultural link to modern Plateau people, U.S. Magistrate John Jelderks ruled that the Ancient One was not affiliated with a current "tribe, people, or culture that is indigenous to the United State" and therefore "not Native American" under the Native American Graves Protection and Repatriation Act (NAGPRA). Based on this judicial finding, the Ancient One would remain in a box on the shelves of the Burke Museum in Seattle; no repatriation to or reburial by the Tribes would be allowed.[12]

---

reached Wallula Gap—the only exit out of the basin. Because of this dynamic, floodwaters behind the Gap "backed up and created a hugh temporary lake called Lake Lewis. In the Tri-Cities, only the crests of the higher ridges poked out above the lake that was up to 900 feet deep." This translates to floodwaters reaching an elevation of up to 1,200 to 1,250 feet within the Pasco Basin. It would take from seven to ten days for this transient lake to drain through Wallula Gap after each flood event.[15]

As succinctly stated by Bjornstad: "the devastation the floodwaters wreaked on the landscape is almost unbelievable. That much water... was bound to change the shape of things." Indeed, elsewhere in his book he notes: "The Ice Age floods permanently altered portions of the several major rivers in the Columbia Basin." As an example, he explains that at various times during this period, the Columbia River flowed first through Gable Gap, then south through Moses Lake and Lower Crab Creek, and eventually north of Gable Mountain in its current path.[16]

The source of the floodwaters (i.e., the Cordilleran Ice Sheet) "had all but melted" by 10,000 years ago, "except for ice packs in the upper mountain ranges of British Columbia." This residual ice would contribute to periods of extensive flooding within the Columbia River system throughout the early Holocene.[17]

The Hanford Site

Does the archaeological record for the Hanford Site better demonstrate cultural continuity over time? Archaeological evidence indicates that the stretch of the Columbia River passing through the Hanford Site (that is, the Hanford Reach) was used extensively by Native Americans prior to the non-Native settlement of the region. Recent archaeological evidence has suggested a time depth of at least 11,000 years.[18] Thousands of years of prehistoric human activity have left extensive archaeological deposits marking winter villages, temporary camps, hunting sites, plant gathering sites, fishing sites, and other activity areas along the river shorelines; well-watered areas inland from the river also show evidence of concentrated human activity. Graves are common in various settings, and spirit quest monuments (rock cairns) are still found on high, rocky summits of the adjacent mountains and basin buttes. The full description and geographic distribution of these archaeological and ethnographic resources are recorded in the files of the Hanford Cultural and Historic Resources Program (CHRP) managed by the U.S. Department of Energy, Richland Operations Office (DOE-RL).

Throughout most of the region, hydroelectric development, agricultural activities, and domestic or industrial construction have covered up or destroyed the majority of archaeological sites. In stark contrast, by virtue of their inclusion on the Hanford Site, from which the public has been restricted, archaeological materials found on the Hanford Reach and on adjacent buttes and mountains have been largely spared. Additionally, the Hanford Reach is the only section of the Columbia River within the United States not impounded by a dam such that all the Holocene terraces and shorelines (dating from ca. 13,000 years ago to the present) are available for inspection. The Hanford Site, then, is a reserve of archaeological information of a kind and quality that has been lost elsewhere in the region. As described by Rex Buck Jr.: "You look around the Pacific Northwest here and you look around the area here, and what place is the most richest in having the things—the way things were for hundreds if not thousands of years. And this is probably one of the prime, or one of the prime places, if not the prime place that has everything here."[19]

But archeological resources are more than just artifacts. Within Indigenous communities, archaeological resources are the tangible remains of prior peoples; they are the irreplaceable links between past and present generations. Archeological sites and artifacts are the possessions of the ancestors extended to the living generation; they are the history that tells Native Americans about themselves; they are the heritage that binds past generations to generations yet unborn; they are the living places and burial grounds of temporally distant but knowable people. Indigenous expertise regarding these resources is an irreplaceable source of educational and interpretive value. For example, the identification and explanation of sacred, ceremonial, and traditional use areas cannot be accomplished without the assistance of the Elders and spiritual leaders. Their involvement is needed to recognize those areas for which no on-the-ground evidence exists as to historical or continuing use. Consequently, archeologists, independently and as a discipline, are working more closely with descendant communities to better understand tribal histories and the area in which they live. Rex Buck Jr. has summarized this collaborative effort on the Hanford Site in these words:

> ...by being a part of the [archaeological data recovery] process it brought things back that might have not been brought back because some of that knowledge, oral knowledge, was generations upon generations so what we could see on the surface, we couldn't identify with what was underneath...it helped understanding what those oral things we're talking about, that they were real, you know. I'm not saying we doubted them or I doubted them, but I'm saying you could parallel it then with geological events that were recorded, you know or could be looked at so—you know, that's ok.

In his view, archaeology has value both in confirming traditional knowledge and extending oral histories back in time.[20]

A total of 140 radiocarbon dates have been obtained from the Hanford Site; 108 of these date cultural materials (such as charcoal, bone, shell) from archaeological sites.[21] The chronological sequence noted by Ames for the Columbia Plateau is reflected in the dates obtained for the Hanford Site, particularly with respect to the concentration of dates within specific time ranges. In this sense, settlement and use of the Hanford Site, when partitioned vis-à-vis Ames, reflects the pattern observed for the greater Columbia Plateau.

The occupational history of the Hanford Site, as currently documented by radiocarbon dates, is shown in Figure 1.1.[22] As illustrated, no dates have been obtained yet for cultural materials prior to 9000 BP. It is not known if Native Americans were present on the Hanford Site during the terminal Pleistocene or witnessed any of the Missoula Floods; however, the Ice Age Floods Institute recently reported that Nez Perce, Umatilla, and Warm Springs Elders have referenced legends of "massive floods going back to 14,000 years ago" among their oral histories. It is important to note that smaller-scale floods "no less catastrophic with regard to human occupation and archaeological preservation" continued within the main-stem Columbia River system through ca. 11,000 years ago. Whether these Indigenous flood stories document the Late Pleistocene Missoula floods or extensive Early Holocene floods is unascertained. In either event, the net effect of these floods was likely the removal of evidence relating to Paleo-Indian occupation, if any had existed.[23]

The earliest archaeological evidence of Indigenous people on the Hanford Site consists of Windust projectile points, dated elsewhere between 11,000 to 8000 BP; unfortunately, none of the Hanford Site points was obtained from a dateable context—only one was not a surface find.[24] Also noticeable in the Hanford Site chronology is the fact that the period from 9000 to 6000 BP is underrepresented in terms of the number of dates, with observable gaps bridged primarily by the plus and minus error factor associated with each date. The fact that identified and dated ancestral channels and terraces of the Columbia River that may contain evidence of Early- to Mid-Holocene use, including the shoreline along which the Ancient One may have walked, have not been surveyed may be a contributing factor to the lack of early dates.[25] That is, because of the emphasis on cleanup, the modern channel of the Columbia River alone has been the focus of archaeological work on the site. Additional surveys broadening the area of interest beyond the current channel could go far in addressing this apparent data deficiency.

Two other notable gaps in the record occur; one between 6000 and 5000 BP, and another between 3500 and 3000 BP. The thousand-year gap is problematic in light of Ames' finding that "the available evidence suggests that what little there was in this area [the mid-Columbia Basin] prior to c. 4000 BC [c. 6000 B.P.] occurred within about a mile of the

Columbia River."[26] One would expect that shoreline sites on the mainstem Columbia River would not have been abandoned, particularly given the climatic warming occurring at this time at the height of the Holocene Optimum. This gap in the record may be due to a then on-going erosional

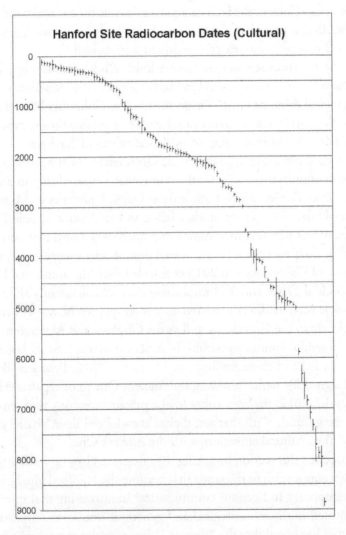

Figure 1.1 Hanford Site radiocarbon dates. Courtesy of Thomas Marceau.

event accompanying creation of a new, lower river terrace such that occupational information may have been removed. In contrast, the 500-year gap between 3500 and 3000 BP occurs during a period of aggradation, and the reason(s) for this gap is as yet unexplained. Settlement and use of the Hanford Site after 3000 BP appears to be fairly continuous. As with the Columbia Plateau, the archaeological evidence for cultural continuity over a 9000-year period on the Hanford Site is highly suggestive; however, additional gap-related research is required here as well.[27]

So, the question remains, is there a link? While establishing a linear connection between the Ancient One and modern Native Americans, using archaeological evidence either within the broader Columbia Plateau or on the Hanford Site itself, remains problematic, it is nonetheless evocative. Fortunately, an additional line of evidence exists. In furtherance of the objective to show a direct, genetic link, DNA testing of the Ancient One had been conducted in 2000 by three universities specializing in ancient DNA analysis (University of California at Davis, University of Michigan, and Yale University). These studies failed to extract any useable DNA; however, recent advances in ancient DNA analysis changed that outcome. Publishing their results in *Nature*, a coalition of scientists gathered at the University of Copenhagen in 2015 concluded that "the autosomal DNA, mitochondrial DNA and Y chromosome data all consistently show that Kennewick Man is directly related to contemporary Native Americans [most closely to the Colville, as well as the Objibwa and Algonquin], and thus show genetic continuity within the Americas over at least the last 8,000 years."[28] In light of these findings, in December 2016, President Barack Obama signed legislation allowing the Ancient One to be repatriated. On February 17, 2017, the area Tribes held a private ceremony that returned him to the ground. With that act, they acknowledged their "shared group identity" (i.e., cultural affiliation) with the Ancient One.

We opened this section by asking the question: How far back into the past can a connection to the lands that became the Hanford Site be made by contemporary Indigenous communities? In answering that question, we examined both archaeological and genetic information. Archeologically, Ames has noted that the "Plateau Pattern" or the annual subsistence round as described by Frank Buck and other modern informants (see below), has an ancient origin: "The evidence is overwhelming that many aspects of the 'Plateau Pattern' were present between 1000 BC and AD 1, and that the Pattern itself…was probably fully in place by AD 1."[29] Based on these observations, at a minimum, the ancestral Wanapum and other Indigenous people may have been living on and around the landforms of the Hanford Site and the greater Columbia Basin, with their attendant ceremonies, legends, songs, and teachings pertaining to proper use, for over 2,000 to 3,000 years. This time depth may extend much further into the past if connections between modern peoples and archaeological cultures older than 3,000 years could be substantiated through additional research focused on illuminating current gaps in the record. As a starting point, the genes of the Ancient One have been observed in modern Columbia Plateau populations, and could, in theory, extend physical, spiritual, and mythological connections to the Basin's landforms back some 9,000 years.

THE TRANSFORMATION OF GEOGRAPHY THROUGH CULTURE

On more than one occasion, Native Americans with ancestral ties to the Hanford Site reminded the author that cultural resources are more than just "stones and bones." For Native American communities, cultural resources consist of air, water, land, rocks, animals, and plants, all of which must be protected and used with care. But it is not only the resources themselves; in their view it is also the interrelationships between these resources and man that need to be acknowledged and maintained. As expressed in ceremonies, the mutual dependence of the "two-legged [people], the four-legged [animals], the rooted [plants], the winged [birds], and the finned [fish]" is central to the worldview and survival of native peoples on the Plateau.

How deep-rooted is this cultural tie to the land? How is it formed? In Columbia Plateau Indian Country, it is both proper and often expected that an individual speaker will introduce himself/herself by first giving their "borrowed language" name (English), then their Indian name (Sahaptin), followed by a short recitation of their lineage (their ancestry), as well as where they are from (their "country"). So closely linked is personal identity with history and place, that knowledge of one's genealogy and geographic ties is actively maintained and strengthened through recitation at ceremonial and secular events. Additionally, the landscape within which one lives is permeated with meaning through religious and social rituals, stories and songs, legends and myths, histories and events, all of which reinforce one's connection to a specific people and place. In his oral interview in 2003, Gabe Bohnee, at the time a staff member of the Nez Perce Environmental Restoration and Waste Management (ERWM) Program, offered the following insight into the longevity of life-directing legends and stories tied to the Columbia Plateau "Written history, the laws—they're always either broken or they're lost, but our oral traditions and our coyote [the law giver/trickster] stories have lived for a time immemorial. Who knows who made these stories. It was our ancestors and it goes word of mouth on to the next generation…Our laws are not written. We learn from our elders. If we do things wrong, the elders are there to correct us, and lead us in that manner, and that's how our culture functions."[30] In Indigenous Plateau societies, where knowledge, collectively referred to as "the teachings," has passed orally from generation to generation for millennia, unvarnished, faithful recitation of rituals, legends, and histories relating to the land, its resources, and proper behavior is of existential importance to continuing group identification and long-term survival.

Cultural Landscapes/Landmarks

Man's relationship to or use of the natural landscape renders it cultural. For Native Americans this relationship is explicit and lies at the heart of their belief system. All biological, botanical, and geological resources are culturally defined. Within Indigenous communities, all resources possess a complete and distinct cultural system and cosmology; each is a living resource; each is approached and utilized by traditional people with respect and proper ceremony befitting their status as "people," and only after their consent has been obtained. For example, in addressing something as foundational as stones to be used in making tools, the American Indian Writers Subgroup (AIWS), a consortium representing seventeen Southwest Tribes and organizations, have opined: "Rocks have power. It is recognized that some rocks have more or different power than others. Breaking a rock or removing it from its place without fully explaining these actions not only releases the power inherent in the rock, but also angers the rock. This can result in the creation of a source for cultural anomalies, which upsets the balance of the cultural ecosystem and affects Indian people."[31] Traditional prayers or ceremonies offered prior to using a resource are meant to minimize or avoid any imbalance.

Furthermore, human dependence on these resources for survival establishes the role of traditional people as caretakers; they must speak for those who cannot speak for themselves. Rex Buck Jr. explains this relationship for the Wanapum: "And all of these resources we take care of were put here to provide for us. We don't have to do things to go out and disturb something that we shouldn't disturb so that we can have our subsistence. It's all provided for us right here. But we have responsibilities to those things… [these resources] don't belong to me. It belongs to our children and it belongs to our grandchildren and those who aren't born. Belongs to them. We just here to take care of it. And pass it on to them."[32]

The linkage between traditional people, natural resources, and geographic places is immutable and has existed "since time immemorial." For example, the identification, selection, and preparation of food and medicinal plants are clearly rooted in cultural norms and mythologies. Given hundreds of potentially usable resources, one's culture will limit both the number and location of those plants which are actually utilized. That is, only "this plant" from "this place" will suffice; no others are acceptable, because this is where the connection between the people, the land, and the plant exists; this is where the responsibility for mutual protection lies. Place makes a difference. "Indian people are of the opinion that while areas may appear to be similar [with respect to plant and animal resources], they may in fact, be viewed as vastly different" based on the site-specific nature of resource use.[33] With respect to Hanford Site botanical resources, Nez Perce Elder Veronica Taylor (known to friends as Mae) stated in her 2003 oral interview that "we're having a hard time trying to replace some of the stuff that we had here. We don't have access to them anymore…So it's not the same…even though we used to have it from here, it's not the same that we get over there, in another area, it's not the same. They might grow the same things but all plants are—have a special meaning."[34] In this statement, Taylor joins with other Native Americans in pointing out that plants, **and particularly the areas from which they are gathered**, are vital to both the cultural identification and continued economic survival of Indigenous peoples.

An examination of landmarks also is instructive in furthering the concept of physical landscapes as cultural repositories. Richard W. Stoffle, David B. Halmo, and Diane E. Austin define a landmark as "a small part of the local geography that is topographically and culturally unique."[35] With respect to Native American communities, Nieves Zedeño and co-authors note that the significance of landmarks lies in the fact that "they have been transformed, through human activity, into reminders of the history of land and resource use by a particular people. Landmarks are historic places of great significance for societies lacking formal writing systems, for they are **used in transferring knowledge about past events, everyday activities, social and ritual conduct, and moral lessons.**" In concluding this discussion, they remark: "Landmarks, therefore, are essential for shaping the future of generations in accordance with traditional lifeways."[36] Specific landmarks within the landscape, then, are the embodiment of tribal memory and history—a cultural mnemonic device literally hiding in plain sight. In this way, individuals and communities establish "their place" on the ground.

Cultural landscapes, then, are symbolic, social constructs. That is, the physical landscape becomes a cultural landscape that reflects the aesthetic, religious, and cultural values of the people whose activities or occupancy shape it.[37] Moreover, a single landscape can have more than one cultural interpretation. As Stoffle, Halmo, and Austin point out: "When more than one social group occupies or otherwise has some reason to establish a cultural perception of a landscape, then competing views emerge."[38] It is entirely possible, however, that these landscapes may be mutually exclusive since "a landscape valued by one group may be simply invisible, or even offensive, to another."[39] Landscapes, simply stated, are comprised of elements, both natural and cultural, which characterize or define specific populations. It is critical to note that within traditional communities damage to the landscape damages the social group(s) that uses it.[40]

Sacred Sites

Sacred sites are an especially vital component of cultural landscapes. "Sacred sites often occur within a larger landform or are connected through features or ceremonies to other sites or a larger sacred landscape."[41] In common with all Native American homelands, the Hanford Site contains numerous ceremonial resources and power places that are crucial for the continuation of Indigenous culture, religion, and society.[42] In speaking of sacred places on the Hanford Site, Rex Buck Jr. has said:

> And there's a lot of things out here that are still very sacred and very important to us and we never want to give those up to—for no reason, because we can't. We don't have the authority to do that. Because everything, how it was interpreted and how it was put here, that's how it has to remain. I can't change it and interpret it in another way. I have to interpret it the way it was from generation upon generation, orally and traditionally, so that it can perpetuate and live that way. So that's how it is.[43]

Native American religion, as Rex notes, is inherently conservative in that it seeks to maintain the status quo as expressed in times long passed. Native American religions also are intricately tied to specific places on the earth. In his dissenting opinion in *Lyng v. Northwest Indian Cemetery Protective Association*, U.S. Supreme Court Justice William Brennan captured the site-specific nature of Native American religion in a concise, yet powerful statement. "Native American faith," he wrote, "is inextricably bound to the use of land. The site-specific nature of Indian religious practice derives from the Native American perception that land itself is a sacred, living being…Rituals are performed in prescribed locations not merely as a matter of traditional orthodoxy, but because land, like all other living things, is unique, and specific sites possess different spiritual properties and significance."[44]

Vision quest sites are an example of this phenomenon. Vision questing, and the locations in which they take place, are critical in maintaining the cultural identity of some Native American communities. The acquisition of spiritual guidance and assistance through direct, personal contact with spirits by means of a vision quest is deeply rooted in the religious practices of the Indigenous people of the Columbia Plateau. High spots are selected for vision quests because they afford both extensive views of the natural landscape and seclusion for quiet meditation. The view, however, is not the objective. Rather, height and view are meant to remind the quest-seeker of how inconsequential he/she is relative to the land and all of creation. Areas of high relief with known religious significance on the Hanford Site include the tectonic "folds" known as Rattlesnake Mountain (*Laliik* [Standing Above the Water]), Saddle Mountain (*Wasatos* [Spirit Power Place]), Gable Mountain (*Nooksiah* [the Otter]), and Gable Butte (*Etoilaseeka* [the Scorpion]).[45] This listing is not exhaustive since "experience has shown that in many instances, Indian people will intentionally omit or 'not remember' resources which may be threatened or considered sacred."[46] For instance, in addressing additional sacred locations extant on the Hanford Site, Rex Buck Jr. offered only that "some of the areas that are very sensitive to us **that we don't talk about** are within the protected areas and the boundaries of the area here."[47] No other information was provided or solicited with respect to these specific sites, and what or where they might be. Clearly, sacred and ceremonial places exist across the Hanford Site that will never be revealed to non-Native peoples, but their central importance in maintaining traditional culture is unquestionable.

In addition to vision quests, many other ceremonial events require privacy and seclusion when being conducted, since noise "may disrupt important ceremonies that help the plants, animals, and other important cultural resources flourish, or may negatively impact the solitude that is needed for healing or praying."[48] In discussing noise, specifically noise attributable to children when ceremonies are being conducted, Mae Taylor explained that "when we were children, they would tell us, 'Don't play here because this is where the adults are doing their things.' They don't want children here to be making noise and to get into—getting mischievous and doing things you're not supposed to do. You know, because sometimes they're going through sacred services and they don't want anybody making noises or talking or scolding children there, so the children were kept at bay and kept quiet."[49]

Disruption of the natural environment also diminishes or destroys the purity and power of sacred areas. Religious ceremonies, particularly those centered on the development of personal medicine or tribal welfare "entail intense meditation and require the practitioner to achieve a profound awareness of the natural environment...the practitioner must be surrounded by undisturbed naturalness."[50] Radiation, in particular, holds a unique place among Native Americans with respect to its inherent environmental dangers. For example, in protesting the placement of a high-level radioactive waste and spent nuclear fuel repository at Yucca Mountain in southern Nevada, the American Indian Writers Subgroup (AIWS) expressed their concern that "air can be destroyed by radiation…thus causing pockets of dead air. There is only so much alive air which surrounds the world. If you kill the living air, it is gone forever and cannot be restored. **Dead air lacks the spirituality and life necessary to support life forms.**"[51] The Indigenous peoples of the Southwest and the Pacific Northwest, at a minimum, share this trepidation with respect to the dangers of radiation to the air, the land, the environment, and all its resources (see below).

ENFORCED EVACUATION: WARS HAVE CONSEQUENCES

In early 1943, the U.S. government took possession of 670 square miles of land adjacent to the Columbia River for construction of the Hanford Engineer Works. "Declarations of Taking" were issued to the residents of the Priest Rapids Valley living in the agricultural communities of White Bluffs, Hanford, and Richland, as well as their hinterlands. "The government provided from 90 days to as little as 48 hours" for residents to gather their belongings and leave.[52] The Wanapum also were evicted from their winter village near Vernita Bridge; an event they knew nothing of until they tried to return home: "This village [Tɛksa] was suddenly

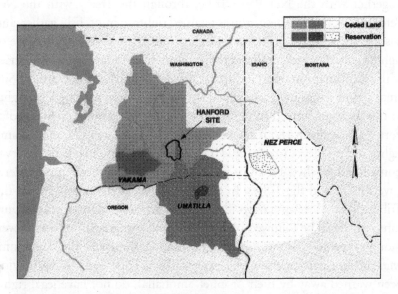

Figure 1.2. Map of traditional Native lands. Courtesy of the Confederated Tribes of the Umatilla Indian Reservation, Mission, Oregon.

abandoned at the beginning of World War II when the Federal government took over the area in order to establish a military reservation. As the Indians were not present at the time [due to seasonal activities away from the river during the summer of 1943], all of their houses and belongings remained just as the inhabitants had left them; the Indians were not allowed to return for their belongings. However, the houses were soon broken into by irresponsible whites and the belongings of the Indians taken or strewn about the area."[53] This was not the first time the Wanapum had seen their possessions go away—nearly a century earlier they had lost legal rights to a critical portion of their homeland; these rights would be claimed by others.

Treaty Rights

The Hanford Site is located on lands ceded to the United States by the Confederated Tribes of the Umatilla Indian Reservation through the Treaty with the Walla Walla, Cayuse, etc., 1855, and by the Confederated Tribes and Bands of the Yakama Nation through the Treaty with the Yakima, 1855.[54] Indeed, the boundary between the Yakama and Umatilla ceded lands cuts longitudinally through the Hanford Site (see figure 1.2). Together with the Nez Perce Tribe, through the Treaty with the Nez Perce, 1855, each of these groups retained rights to hunt, fish, gather, and pasture their horses in "usual and accustomed" territories.[55] Because of rights granted to each of these groups through intermarriage and alliances with the Wanapum, each group included the lands of the Hanford Site among their usual and accustomed territories, thereby gaining legal rights to this area guaranteed in perpetuity. That is, the treaties established at Fort Walla Walla in 1855 secured to the Nez Perce, Umatilla, and Yakama rights and privileges to continue traditional activities outside the reservation and established a trust or fiduciary relationship between the federal government and the Tribes. In effect, the U.S. government assured the Tribes that their resources would be protected such that traditional pursuits still could be followed on lands that were important to them, even though they no longer resided on those lands. Ironically, the Wanapum, who did not participate in the treaty talks at Fort Walla Walla (having been warned away by their prophet Smohalla), do not have legal rights to their traditional homeland—now acknowledged by treaty to others.

The desire to retain ancient lifeways lay at the heart of Indigenous negotiations during the treaty talks; money or other payments were of no consequence. In his oral interview in 2003, Russell Jim, a Yakama Elder and former director of the Yakama Nation Environmental Restoration and Waste Management (ERWM) Program, noted that "the Yakama Nation refused any compensation eventually, **because the words of the treaty meant more to them, to be able to utilize the land as it was intended in the beginning**" was of utmost importance. "The treaty is alive and well," he proclaimed. "There are many people who truly misunderstand what the treaty means to us. To us it is as long as a mountain stands, the river flows, the grass shall grow, the sun shall shine, etc. For good reason is that we do not wish to assimilate to the mainstream of society. We can live side by side by side."[56]

Outside a treaty context, the identification of usual and accustomed territories is expressed in the "annual round" associated with a specific group, that is, the path taken throughout the year to obtain the organic and inorganic resources necessary for group survival. According to Russell Jim, the "Hanford area was our wintering ground, the Palm Springs of the area. And the winters were milder here, and so therefore we moved here and disbursed to all other parts of the country when the spring came. We lived in harmony with the area, with the river, with all of the environment. All the natural foods and medicines were quite abundant here."[57] It is important to note that the Yakama sometimes consider the Wanapum to be a band within their nation, so discussion of "Yakama" use of the Hanford area can be problematic—just who is being referenced here, Yakama or Wanapum? As Bobby Tomanawash made plain to this author early in his career on the Hanford Site: "No one speaks for the Wanapum; only the Wanapum speak for the Wanapum."[58]

Given this latter statement, Frank Buck, a former Wanapum Elder and community leader, described their annual round this way in the mid-1980s: "We used to live [by the Columbia River] in the tules (reed huts) until spring, then we take them apart, put them away and we move. First, we move after the root feasts, clear up to Soap Lake and Waterville. Then down to Ellensburg. Horn Rapids for fishing. Naches Pass for berries and more fishing for several weeks. After this we come back to Priest Rapids, where our home was for winter. We just went over this year after year. We just circle the same way every time."[59] More recently, his nephew Rex Buck Jr. delimited their homeland this way: "Wanapum aboriginal traditional land was all the way from present-day Wenatchee over to present-day Moses Lake, Washington, over to the Naches area and down to the mouth of the Snake River and Columbia River."[60]

Eviction

None of their prior occupation or use of the Hanford area mattered to the U.S. Army regardless of how many generations may have passed. In 1943, all residents of the Priest Rapids Valley, Native and non-Native alike, were evicted; an eviction that was enforced by the military. "It was kind of a shock. It was a disbelief…These military people will be here and we couldn't get through them and they had guns and things and they blocked the door…These were hard things for us because I have never been approached by a military police person that had a gun in his hand and said, 'You can't go this way. You go back. Turn around and go back because you can't go on this road.'"[61] This first-person recollection was shared by Mae Taylor, a young Nez Perce girl at the time, in describing her encounter with a chained Hanford Site entrance in 1943.

Figure 1.3. Johnny Tomanawash (left) and Johnny Buck AKA Puck Hyah Toot (right) at the Yakima Barricade, circa 1943. Courtesy of the Wanapum Heritage Center.

A generation removed, Rex Buck Jr. shared his thoughts on the enforced removal of the Wanapum from the area in his oral interview: "When they closed the site, they took away—just like you would say, they took away a part of you, that's how our people felt, they took something away from us that was a part of us. And when they took that away, we didn't know how to feel about it because we never had that done to us. Our people never had that done to us and when they took that away it was really not good, you know… And they just felt like they were losing something that they didn't know what they did or why they were going to not be able to continue to go to places they always had gone to." Rex went on to explain that his Elders had been told "when the war was over, that they would be able to come back and that they would be able to return and do some of the things that they had always done. So, they felt good about that, but that never did happen that way as time went on."[62] Instead, the Wanapum and others with ancestral ties to the Hanford Site saw their culture and lifeways impacted in several ways following their removal and closure of the area.

Sociocultural Impacts

Sociocultural impacts, defined as any change that leads to the impairment or loss of the societal, cultural, or religious use of a resource as a result of actual risk(s) or the perception of risk, often are not accounted for by Western society and scientists in assessing either risk or loss. With respect to former nuclear sites, such as Hanford, the assessment of risk is intricately tied to "exposure pathways" that might bring people in contact with harmful radionuclides or toxic chemicals, accompanied by calculations designed to quantify that risk as acceptable or not. As a result, scientific and quantitatively based risk assessments are departmentalized into discrete units of analysis. This fits Western norms, but "Indian people desire to reassemble the artificially disassociated components of their culture so that the fullest native cultural meanings associated with things and places are recognized and protected." In identifying sociocultural impacts, one must employ an alternative approach, one that uses a "holistic analytical perspective" in an "attempt to seek to understand culturally different cognitions of environment, history, and place." Zedeño and co-authors have called holistic analysis a "contextual" model "that incorporates historical, ecological, and geographic variables with knowledge about how social groups interact with the landscape." Critical to this current discussion is the finding that the **perception of risk alone** is sufficient to cause sociocultural impacts. In very simple terms, "a perceived danger or hazard associated with something can be very real to Indian peoples." The general response to danger (i.e., risk) or perceived danger is to avoid the area or resource. This is detrimental to Indigenous lifeways when traditional foods and medicines are not consumed because of a fear of contamination, for example.[63]

An analysis of sociocultural impacts on Native Americans attributable to the closure of the Hanford Site has yet to be conducted as an alternative to risk assessments meant for the general population. As a beginning, the following paragraphs identify a few areas where such an analysis would be fruitful in documenting damages specific to the Native American community.

Loss Due to Denial of Access

Common to both accounts of eviction given above is the affront on being denied access to land; this is something neither the Wanapum nor Nez Perce had experienced before. Their assessment of the threat(s) that removal posed is not unique, though. Responding to similar circumstances regarding their removal from traditional lands in the Southwest because of pending government actions to store high-level nuclear waste underground near Yucca Mountain, the American Indian Writers Subgroup (AIWS) also asserts that the inability to gain access to areas "where ceremonies have or need to occur, where plants need to be gathered, and where animals need to be hunted in a traditional way" dramatically affects traditional life. This consortium of seventeen Tribes and organizations goes on to explain: "One of the most detrimental consequences to the survival of American Indian culture, religion, and society has been the denial of free access to their traditional lands and resources. **Loss of access to traditional foodstuffs and medicine has greatly contributed to undermining the cultural well-being of Indian people.**" Their most important testimony on this point, though, is expressed in their summary statements that conclude with a nod to social justice: "Indian people have experienced, and will continue to experience, breakdowns in the process of cultural transmission due to lack of free access to government controlled lands and resources...**No other people have experienced similar cultural survival impacts.**"[64] While these words do not come from a Hanford-related group, their clarity and passion make obvious that loss of access to traditional lands negatively impacts individual and community well-being, spirituality, transfer of knowledge, and the long-term sustainability of the culture itself. These are quality of life impacts of the highest order, regardless of where they occur or to whom.

Loss of Critical Resources and Places

Mae Taylor, in common with other people with ancestral ties to the Hanford Site, has experienced resource loss directly associated with lack of access: "I was just a young girl when that [i.e., eviction] happened," she said, "and we had to not come over this way for a long time. And that has affected our lives from that time on because they took over this area and we couldn't come to this area anymore. We couldn't come do our things because of the changes...All I know it affected our lives, our fishing and our gathering of food." Expanding her concerns to non-subsistence resources, she continued: "**Lot of the places where the elders would go and hold ceremonial services was being affected because we couldn't go there anymore.** And so, I know that, to us, this hasn't—it has hindered our lives quite a bit, changed our lives and our lives to this day is changed and it has affected us."[65]

More important than just the loss of access to resources and places, Taylor also noted a fundamental loss of confidence or trust in the Hanford area and its resources: "Nobody said that that was going to be a problem, that it's going to affect our water and our lands and our animals. They used to go hunting over here all the time for elk and deer and things, and now you talk to a lot of the Indian people to this day they don't want any animals from here. They won't come here and dig roots here anymore; they don't come here and get things that had happened in the past. It's no longer available to them because **people are scared to come over and get anything here anymore.**" The level of anxiety over resources lost from Hanford might be generationally linked, since she qualified her discussion by noting further: "But I'm talking about my elder's elder—that these are the ones that are in the eighties and ninety years old. I'm in my seventies, so I'm talking about the ones that are in the eighties and nineties years old, 100 years old, and talking to them and they—those are the ones that won't eat the stuff from here."[66]

Hunting continues to be restricted on the Hanford Site so these biological resources currently remain unavailable to Native communities. However, in looking to the future, when asked the subjunctive question—Would you hunt or fish on the Hanford Site were you to be allowed?—Gabe Bohnee, in his early thirties at the time of his oral interview, offered this thought-provoking answer:

> That's been a question that's been posed before. I guess looking at it, to not hunt or fish this area would be the non-use of my treaty right, my right to go and get the game that is on the Hanford Site, if we were allowed to come out and hunt the Hanford Site. When you don't practice or utilize your rights, there's going to be somebody there to try to take that right away from you…So I would come over and hunt for the elk and deer on the Hanford Site to practice that treaty right that was preserved for, not only myself, but for the generations that are coming after me, so that I can teach them and that right would live on in perpetuity… Then we're getting back to where we were when Lewis and Clark came over the pass to our traditional ways that we live…**The repatriation of the Hanford Site is the beginning of our younger generations going back to the older ways.**[67]

Taken together, these statements corroborate the importance of Hanford's natural resources (such as plants, animals, minerals) to the Indigenous communities living nearby. Indeed, as expressed by Gabe Bohnee, these resources not only remain integral to living a traditional life, but also offer hope for the resurgence of traditional lifeways in the future. The loss of these resources becomes even more critical as the area around Hanford continues to develop, resulting in additional habitat loss.

Loss of Long-Term Social Relationships
The Hanford area was important in initiating and sustaining social relationships among the Indigenous people of the Columbia Plateau. "The Hanford Site," we are told, "was the traditional spot for the Nez Perce to come trade and visit with our sister Tribes, the Umatillas, the Yakamas, the Colvilles. The Columbia River was a mecca for Northwest tribes. It

supplied the fish and the resources that brought the people together."[68] This message is echoed in a statement made by Russell Jim, who noted categorically in his interview that the "Columbia River is the lifeline of the Pacific Northwest. It has been such since the beginning of time."[69] Trade and exchange among people has always been a way to establish and maintain both personal and societal relationships. In times of shortage or an outright resource failure, good trade relationships can mean the difference between survival and starvation. Mae Taylor summarized the importance and centrality of trade among the Columbia Plateau Tribes this way:

> And the fisher people that lived along the Columbia River used to have fish, dried fish, and they would trade that for dried meat and game from other tribes that lived out in the plateau areas that had that kind of food. And they would have—it was kind of like a—probably like a farmer's market…and because of the roots grow in different areas not all of us have the same types of roots and berries and teas, medicines. They grow different in different areas, different regions, and that was why the Indians traded so much. And they still trade…So this area has always played a very important part in all Indian lives in the northwest area.[70]

Outside of subsistence resources, exchange networks also functioned to establish a pool of eligible wives and husbands. As Taylor explained, in addition to trading, "they would also have like the—at the long houses they would have like weddings and different things and families would come in and trade materials for weddings." "Eventually," Taylor continues, "we would lose contact with some of these people. And we would lose contact with some of the food and things that we used to trade with and for in this area." That is not to say trade doesn't take place now, or that intermarriages do not occur, but the pre-existing societal "balance" has been impacted—directly because of these severed contacts, as well as indirectly through loss of access to the area in which these collective activities were traditionally conducted.[71]

Loss of In-Place Traditional Knowledge Transfer

The loss of subsistence resources attributable to lost access is significant, but even more critical is the lost opportunity to transfer secular and sacred knowledge between generations. For example, the site-specific nature of Native American religion requires that "the teachings" regarding a particular ceremony be given at the specified location. As expressed by Rex Buck Jr.: "You know, they [i.e., Elders and children] have to be able to be out there. They have to be able to stand on this land and they have to be able to look and identify things from what their mind is so they can see it and know and really get a connection with those things." That is, and had been, the natural order, yet as Mae Taylor points out: "[T]his was a sacred place for our people. It's not that way anymore. Some of our people are afraid to come over here. It's hard to get us—to get our elders to come over here…because they know what happened here and what they built here, and they're scared of it." Traditional knowledge (both secular and sacred) is being impacted, or worse lost, because Elders cannot or will not go to the locations required for proper transfer to occur. Rex Buck Jr. has direct experience with both the benefits of being on-site to receive traditional information, as well as the effects on cultural transmission when one is prohibited from being on the land. In his 2003 interview he recalled his feelings when he first set foot on the Hanford Site as a youth:

> I felt like I was walking in somewhere that was important to who I was, you know, and I wanted to know about it. I wanted to—I could feel it, but I wanted to understand it more. That's how I felt. I could feel something. I came with a bunch of elders, and they were talking in the native language. And I—my body could feel it, but I didn't really get the understanding of it because, I mean, I didn't know something… I wanted them to talk more because they were telling stories about different things, people, things that they did, where they lived, where the camp was at, you know, and it was just like a book, you know, but it was living, you know.

As an Elder himself now, Rex has gained both a greater appreciation for and deeper insight into how he had been taught first-hand and on-site, since, away from the precise location(s), he found he "couldn't transfer that knowledge because that knowledge couldn't be transferred because it was hard to transfer it, you know. I don't know how to put it, you know." His frustration in not being able to take children to the specified location(s) when teaching the next generation is palpable.[72]

As individuals learn more about Hanford, particularly those who come to work more directly with cleanup efforts, attitudes about the site's potential dangers can change. Again, Rex Buck Jr. is illustrative: "You know, I feel comfortable about being out here. I even come out here myself, with an elder or even sometimes myself that I come out here and go to places and do things that I need to do, to take care of this place." Conscious that traditional ceremonies must be held at specific locations and times, Buck is willing to take the steps necessary to maintain Wanapum ancestral ties to the land—even in the face of perceived risk. But one man alone does not a proper ceremony make; the "things" Rex Buck does are only placeholders awaiting the time when the entire community can be present to learn about and participate in these activities as well.[73]

A PARTIAL RETURN: CURRENT ACCESS

With their signatures on the Treaties of 1855, Native Americans with ancestral ties to the Hanford Site ensured the continuation of their traditional lifeways. Specifically, they reserved the rights to hunt, fish, gather, and pasture in usual and accustomed places. In accepting their ceded territories, the U.S. government assumed the long-term responsibility to protect and preserve those resources that would be hunted, fished, or gathered from those lands. The Native American communities, therefore, view any actions that impede or prevent following traditional lifeways as an abrogation of the Treaties. Access to and traditional use of animals, fish, plants, and minerals, in their view, was guaranteed, as Russell Jim said, as long as the grass grows.

In addition to seeking protection for subsistence resources (such as animals and plants), Indigenous communities, both in the Columbia Basin and across the country, also sought protection for and access to resources of traditional religious significance throughout the mid-twentieth century. Following many years of debate, in 1996, President Bill Clinton issued Executive Order 13007, Indian Sacred Sites, largely in response to the national movement of Native Americans, building on passage of the American Indian Religious Freedom Act of 1978 (AIRFA), nearly twenty years earlier. Section 1(a) of Executive Order 13007 directs Federal agencies to "**accommodate access to and ceremonial use of** Indian sacred sites by Indian religious practitioners and [to] avoid adversely affecting the physical integrity of such sacred sites." Protection of sites of traditional religious or cultural significance from adverse effects also had been required by the National Historic Preservation Act of 1969 (NHPA), but not to the specificity of Executive Order 13007. Since the identification of these sites is problematic, because little or no physical evidence of use may exist to identify them, the Archaeological Resources Protection Act of 1979 (ARPA) requires that all Tribes "having aboriginal or historic ties to the land" be contacted in order to determine "the location and nature of specific sites of religious or cultural importance." In discussing the beneficial effects of NHPA, ARPA, AIRFA, and related legislation on Native Americans, Zedeño and co-authors assert that this "legislation acknowledges the need to reproduce traditional cultural practices by granting practitioners access to traditional lands and resources located beyond the boundaries of reservations...legislation that is significant as a formal reaffirmation of traditional interactions with land and resources."[74]

To ensure compliance with these acts and the executive order, the U.S. Department of Energy (DOE) issued its own implementing regulations. In October of 2000, DOE released Order 1230.2, the American Indian and Alaska Native Tribal Government Policy, which confirmed that the U.S. government, through the Department of Energy, had a trust responsibility "to protect tribal sovereignty and self-determination, tribal lands, assets, resources, and treaty and other federally recognized and reserved rights...from Departmental actions which may potentially impact" these values, resources, and rights.[75]

Given these legislative directives, on-site visitations by tribal members became more common post after 2000, particularly after all weapons-grade plutonium had been removed from the Hanford Site. More specifically, the U.S. Department of Energy, Richland Operations Office (DOE-RL) began allowing formal tours of the site by members of the Indigenous communities that included both adults and children—a very significant accomplishment given DOE-RL's reluctance in the early 2000s to allow anyone under 18 years old on-site. This action was both positive and long overdue. As assessed by Rex Buck Jr.: "Here in the last probably, at least ten years if maybe a little bit not longer than—we've been granted a little more unrestrictive use of the areas, although it's not to where we would like it to be but it is—it's a lot better than it was, in the 40s." Expanding on this last point, Rex both explained and complained: "The tours—it's always a [controlled bus] tour, you know. It's not like going out there and sitting along the river and listening to the elements and identifying those things that are important to us. And really realizing what is there."[76]

Unrestricted, unaccompanied access to traditionally important areas is a goal as yet unmet on the Hanford Site. The importance of free movement across an area is contextualized by Stoffle and his co-authors in their discussion of storyscapes found in the American Southwest: "A story about the movements of mythic beings conveys the sense of purpose in the behavior of the mythic beings, but the story itself also is tied to places where either events occurred or the mythic being specifically established some relationship with the landscape…Were one to pass along the path of the story, the landscape would be marked with story or song points. Moving from point to point permits a living person to physically reenact and directly experience the story or song."[77] Storyscape landmarks, together with their spatial distribution and their physical settings, are character-defining elements of any Indigenous landscape. Nevertheless, on the Hanford Site, tribal people are restricted from following any "path" to access storyscapes which are located either entirely on the Hanford Site or are elements of a more complex regional storyscape. This begs the metaphorical question, how well would one understand critical religious, cultural, or historic events if the book containing this information had pages missing?

NIGH

Following their removal from the Hanford Site in 1943, the Wanapum moved upriver to Priest Rapids—a traditional winter village and "a very sacred place to the Wanapum people." Here they continue to live as traditional a life as they can in the modern era, and without access to a large portion of their homeland. Some comfort could be taken with this relocation since, as Rex relates, "we never ever lost our tie and our belief of our ways, that these ways would take care of us. And we continue to do that as—strictly as it was said that we needed to do it…We were going to stick strictly to the way things were supposed to be done and the way things had been done…to make sure that their [the ancestors] presence was unbroken… to seek whatever alternatives there were to maintain what was important to them." While acknowledging what had been lost, Rex nonetheless focuses on what was retained: "We lost a lot of people, lost a lot of personal things, a lot of people lost a lot of things. We lost because we didn't get to come here, but we were very— had an opportunity to still live in that type of an atmosphere where we were told about things and we could identify with them when we got to come here. And so that's important to us, you know. We knew about them and we were still living here, and we will still live next to the river and we never ever left so—and we always were concerned about this place. We never—broke no gap in there so—that's how things are."[78] These statements make explicit that the Wanapum, in their judgment, have never left and never will leave the area in which they were created; that their connection with their ancestors in their "holy land" has not been broken. This is particularly notable in the specific wording Rex used, that is, "to make sure that their presence was unbroken" and "no gap in there"—this latter statement in particular harking back to the investigation of the archaeological record as reported earlier in this chapter.

In his recounting of past loss, Rex also made reference to the future noting that "the time is going to come when that—**we're going to have to make sure that we're ready and we're in the place that we need to be where we were put.** That's why our people would never leave this place because we have to continue to live here, we have to continue to do our part to this land. And we have to identify with those messages that are coming and interpret that."[79] As noted, communications between the human and spiritual worlds (either sought or unsought) are not uncommon among traditional people on the Plateau. Nonetheless, per Rex's 2003 interview, to receive the "messages," one must remain attentive and be at the right place at the right time:

> And when that light changes, that message will come and you have to be there to receive that message…The words are kept in a certain place and when all the things line up just right, you have to be there. If you're late you're there at the wrong time, you didn't listen. You didn't understand. You're going to miss it. You're not going to hear when the message comes, so you have to be observant [only the sound will identify itself].[80]

In the face of continuing restrictions, the Wanapum, among others, are steadfast in their belief that the land itself remains strong, and is fully capable of supporting them—when they are allowed to come back. But, as Rex Buck Jr. points out, the people and the land must remain as one to ensure their mutual survival:

We believe that this land, through how it is interpreted—takes care of itself and takes care of us, the people who were put here. And it's not just—it's just not a thing we have control over, it's something that's bigger…

We believe that that [i.e., survival] was the sense of the land. That's how strong the things were being interpreted, and how long that those things had been and always has been interpreted…So these things are real to us and that thing—that's how we live. We live by that generation upon generation, and that's how we're going to continue to live…We have to do it the way it was supposed to be done and the way it was put here and continue to live that way. That way the land will be able to help itself. If we don't, the land can't help itself because we are part of the land.[81]

Maintaining their continued presence, then, is required for reciprocal benefits to accrue to both the people and the land. There is no incentive to leave, and every reason to stay.

This chapter briefly investigated the questions of how old the Hanford landscape is, and how deep the Indigenous tie is to this land as a way to demonstrate how consequential the separation of the people from the land has been. After thousands of years, the Hanford landscape has been infused with historic, cultural, and religious significance attributed to various places and landforms on the site. Following closure, access to personal, family, and community spaces and places of significance has been lost, resulting in the concomitant loss, among other things, of age-old subsistence resources, the ability to conduct ceremonies at traditionally designated locations, and the ability to adequately transfer knowledge about these things. This may seem negligible to the Western mind; after all other resources could be substituted and new places to hold a ceremony or teach the young found. But imagine a very traditional Christian being told, from this time forward, that they would have to celebrate Christmas in February. While the change could be accommodated, it would never feel or be right. Moreover, Indigenous communities, such as those with ancestral ties to the Hanford Site, are bound to their homelands in ways not readily comprehended by Western culture—they do not leave, their responsibility to the land is permanent, and has existed since "time immemorial." As documented in their own words, significant sociocultural impacts have occurred and continue nearly unabated. As long as enforced removal remains, these losses can never be made whole.

In Columbia Plateau Indian country, when one is finished talking, the word "*Nigh*" is spoken—a Sahaptin word taken by the author to mean "That's what I want to say" or "That's all I have to say" or something similar. It is in this sense of the word that I conclude this chapter. *Nigh*.

Notes

1. Rex Buck Jr., Interview by Cynthia C. Kelly and Thomas E. Marceau, Atomic Heritage Foundation. "Voices of the Manhattan Project." Richland, Washington, September 2003. manhattanprojectvoices.org/oral-histories/rex-bucks-interview. Accessed August 6, 2018.

2. American Indian Writers Subgroup (AIWS), "American Indian Perspectives on the Yucca Mountain Site Characterization Project and the Repository Environmental Impact Statement," Consolidated Group of Tribes and Organizations, American Indian Resource document, DOE-Nevada, 1998, 2–9.

3. Richard W. Stoffle, David B. Halmo, and Diane E. Austin, "Cultural Landscapes and Traditional Cultural Properties: A Southern Paiute View of the Grand Canyon and Colorado River," *The American Indian Quarterly*, 21:2, (1997), 231.

4. Ibid., 234. Emphasis added.

5. Stephen P. Reidel, et al., "The Columbia River Flood Basalts and the Yakima Fold Belt," in T.W. Swanson, ed., *Western Cordillera and Adjacent Areas, Boulder, Colorado, Geological Society of America, Field Guide 4*, (2003), 87.

6. Ibid.

7. Robert S. Yeats, *Living with Earthquakes in the Pacific Northwest*, (Corvallis: Oregon State University Press, 2010), 6–23.

8. Reidel, et al., 94–95.

9. James C. Chatters, "The Recovery and First Analysis of an Early Holocene Human Skeleton from Kennewick, Washington," *American Antiquity*, 65:2 (2000), 300–304.

10. Francis P. McManamon, "The Initial Scientific Examination, Description, and Analysis of the Kennewick Man Human Remains;" and, Kenneth M. Ames, "Review of the Archaeological Record: Continuities, Discontinuities and Gaps, Cultural Affiliation Report," National Park Service, U.S. Department of the Interior, Archeology Program, Washington, DC In *Report on the Non-Destructive Examination, Description, and Analysis of the Human Remains from Columbia Park, Kennewick, Washington*, edited by Francis P. McManamon, National Park Service, Department of the Interior, Washington, DC. 1999. www.nps.gov/archeology/kennewick https://www.nps.gov/archeology/kennewick/ames7.htm. Accessed May 21, 2018.

11. Ames. Emphasis added.

12. John Jelderks, *Opinion and Order (Civil No. 96-1481-JE)*, In the United States District Court for the District of Oregon, Portland, Oregon, 2002.

13. See John E. Allen, Marjorie Burns, and Scott Burns, *Cataclysmic Floods on the Columbia: The Great Missoula Floods*, revised second edition, (Portland: Portland State University, 2009); David Alt, *Glacial Lake Missoula and its Humongous Floods*, (Missoula: Mountain Press Publishing Company, 2001); Bruce Bjornstad, *On the Trail of the Ice Age Floods: A Geological Field Guide to the Mid-Columbia Basin*, (Sandpoint, Idaho: Keokee Books, 2006).

14. Quotes are from Bjornstad, 1–2.

15. See Allen, *Cataclysmic Floods*, Alt, *Glacial Lake Missoula*, Bjornstad, *On the Trail*, and J. Harlen Bretz, "The Channeled Scabland and the Spokane Flood," *Proceedings of the Academy and Affiliated Societies*, Geological Society of Washington, 43rd Meeting, Washington, DC, 1927. Quote is from Bjornstad, 4.

16. Quotes are from Bjornstad, 1 and 39, respectively.

17. Quote is from Karl R. Fecht, et al., "Late Pleistocene- and Holocene-age Columbia River Sediments and Bedforms: Hanford Reach Area, Washington, Part I," *Geological Atlas Series*, BHI-01648, Rev. 0, (Richland, WA: Bechtel Hanford, 2004), 12. See also, Gary Huckleberry, et al., "Recent Geoarchaeological Discoveries in Central Washington," in Terry W. Swanson, ed., *Western Cordillera and Adjacent Areas*, (Boulder, CO: Geological Society of America, Field Guide 4, 2003), 237–249.

18. James J. Sharpe and Thomas E. Marceau, *Archaeological Excavation Report for Extraction Well C3662 in Support of the 100-KR-4 Pump-and-Treat Project*, BHI-01556, Rev. 0, Bechtel Hanford, Inc., Richland, Washington, 2001.

19. Rex Buck Jr. Interview.

20. Ibid.

21. Karl R. Fecht and Thomas E. Marceau, "Late Pleistocene- and Holocene-Age Columbia River Sediments and Bedforms: Hanford Reach Area, Washington, Part 2," *Geological Atlas Series*, WCH-46, Rev. 0, Washington Closure Hanford, (Richland, Washington, 2006), 5–14 and Table 5-9. All dates in the Hanford Site dataset are reported as $\delta^{13}C$ corrected dates. No calibrations (either BP or BC/AD) have been applied. They are consistent, then, with the uncalibrated radiocarbon dates used by Ames for the Plateau. See, DOE-RL (U.S. Department of Energy, Richland Operations Office), *Hanford Cultural Resources Management Plan*, DOE/RL-98-10, Rev. 1, U.S. Department of Energy, Richland Operations Office, Richland, Washington, 2003.

22. DOE-RL (U.S. Department of Energy, Richland Operations Office), *Hanford Cultural Resources Management Plan*, DOE/RL-98-10, Rev. 1, U.S. Department of Energy, Richland Operations Office, Richland, Washington, 2003.

23. Quote is from, "Indigenous Flood Stories from over 14,000 Years Ago," *Ice Age Flood Institute*, http://iafi.org/indigenous-flood-stories-from-1400-years-ago. Accessed on March 23, 2018. See also, Huckleberry, et al., 242.

24. Sharpe and Marceau.

25. Fecht and Marceau.

26. Ames.

27. Fecht and Marceau; Huckleberry, et al.; and, Karl R. Fecht, et al., "Late Pleistocene- and Holocene-Age Columbia River Sediments and Bedforms: Hanford Reach Area, Washington, Part 1," *Geological Atlas Series*, BHI-01648, Rev. 0, Bechtel Hanford, Inc., Richland, Washington, 2004.

28. Morten Rasmussen, et al., "The Ancestry and Affiliations of Kennewick Man," *Nature*, (Vol. 523), 2015, p. 458; and Francis P. McManamon, et al., "Examination of the Kennewick Remains – Taphonomy, Micro-Sampling and DNA Analysis," in *Report on the DNA Testing Results of the Kennewick Remains from Columbia Park, Kennewick, Washington*, 2001.

29. Ames.

30. Gabriel Bohnee, Interview by Cynthia C. Kelly and Thomas E. Marceau, Atomic Heritage Foundation. "Voices of the Manhattan Project." Richland, Washington, September 2003. http://manhattanprojectvoices.org/oral-histories/gabriel-bohnees-interview Accessed August 6, 2018.

31. American Indian Writers Subgroup (AIWS), "American Indian Perspectives on the Yucca Mountain Site Characterization Project and the Repository Environmental Impact Statement," Consolidated Group of Tribes and Organizations, American Indian Resource Document, DOE-Nevada, 2–16, (1998).

32. Buck Jr. Interview.

33. AIWS, "American Indian Perspectives."

34. Veronica Taylor, Interview by Cynthia C. Kelly and Thomas E. Marceau, Atomic Heritage Foundation. "Voices of the Manhattan Project." Richland, Washington, September 2003. http://manhattanprojectvoices.org/oral-histories/veronica-taylors-interview Accessed August 6, 2018.

35. Stoffle, et al., 237–238.

36. Nieves Zedeño, Diane Austin, and Richard Stoffle, "Landmark and Landscape: A Contextual Approach to the Management of American Indian Resources," *Culture & Agriculture*, (Vol. 19, No. 3, 1997), 125. Emphasis added.

37. Charles A. Birnbaum, "Protecting Cultural Landscapes: Planning, Treatment and Management of Historic Landscapes," *Preservation Briefs No. 36*, Technical Preservation Services, National Park Service, Washington, DC, 1994.

38. Stoffle, et al., 233.

39. Alice E. Ingerson, "What Are Cultural Landscapes?" The Arnold Arboretum of Harvard University, Institute for Cultural Landscape Studies. 2000. www.icls.harvard.edu/language/whatare.htm.

40. Patricia L. Parker and Thomas F. King, "Guidelines for Evaluating and Documenting Traditional Cultural Properties," *National Register Bulletin 38*, National Park Service, Washington, DC, 1990.

41. Advisory Council on Historic Preservation, *Memorandum of Understanding Among the U.S. Department of Defense, U.S. Department of the Interior, U.S. Department of Agriculture,*

U.S. Department of Energy, and the Advisory Council on Historic Preservation Regarding Interagency Coordination and Collaboration for the Protection of Sacred Sites, Washington, DC, 2012.

42. AIWS, "American Indian Perspectives."

43. Buck Jr. Interview. Emphasis added.

44. William Brennan, *Lyng v. Northwest Indian Cemetery Protective Association*, 485 U.S. 439, U.S. Supreme Court, Washington, DC, 1988. Emphasis added.

45. DOE-RL (U.S. Department of Energy, Richland Operations Office), *Hanford Cultural Resources Management Plan.*

46. AIWS, "American Indian Perspectives."

47. Buck Jr. Interview. Emphasis added.

48. AIWS, "American Indian Perspectives."

49. Veronica Taylor Interview.

50. Brennan.

51. AIWS. Emphasis added.

52. Thomas E. Marceau, "Historic Overview." In Thomas E. Marceau, et al., *History of the Plutonium Production Facilities at the Hanford Site Historic District, 1943–1990*, DOR/ RL-97-1047, Hanford Cultural and Historic Resources Program, U.S. Department of Energy, Richland, Washington, 2002. For a fuller treatment of the forced evacuation of Priest Rapids Valley residents in 1943, see Robert Bauman, "'It Was Like an Invasion!' The Federal Government and the Displacement of Peoples in the Priest Rapids Valley," in Robert Bauman and Robert Franklin, eds., *Nowhere to Remember: Hanford, White Bluffs, and Richland to 1943* (Pullman: Washington State University Press, 2018).

53. F.A. Riddell, "Smohalla's Village," Department of Anthropology, Washington State University, Pullman, Washington, 1948.

54. *Treaty with the Walla Walla, Cayuse, etc., 1855*, 12 Stats. 945; *Treaty with the Yakima, 1855*, 12 Stats. 951.

55. *Treaty with the Nez Perce, 1855*, 12 Stats. 957.

56. Russell Jim. Interview by Cynthia C. Kelly and Thomas E. Marceau, Atomic Heritage Foundation. "Voices of the Manhattan Project." Richland, Washington, September 2003. http://manhattanprojectvoices.org/oral-histories/russell-jims-interview. Accessed August 6, 2018. Emphasis added.

57. Ibid.

58. Bobby Tomanawash, personal communication with the author.

59. Frank Buck, Interview by Robert W. Mull, in S. L. Sanger, *Working on the Bomb: An Oral History of WWII Hanford*, Portland State University, Portland, Oregon, 1995. http://manhattanprojectvoices.org/oral-histories/frank-bucks-interview. Accessed August 6, 2018.

60. Buck Jr. Interview.

61. Taylor Interview.

62. Buck Jr. Interview.

63. Stoffle, et al., 1997, 231; Stoffle, et al., 1991, 611–615; Zedeño, 123; AIWS, "American Indian Perspectives," 2-15.

64. AIWS, 2-19 and 2-20.

65. Taylor Interview. Emphasis added.

66. Ibid.

67. Bohnee Interview. Emphasis added.

68. Ibid.

69. Jim Interview.

70. Taylor Interview.

71. Ibid.

72. Taylor Interview and Buck Jr. Interview.

73. Buck Jr. Interview.

74. Quote is from Zedeño, et al., 127. See also, Native American Rights Fund, "'We Also Have A Religion': The American Indian Religious Freedom Act and the Religious Freedom Project of the Native American Rights Fund," *Announcements*, Vol. 5, No. 1, Boulder, Colorado, 1979; *American Indian Religious Freedom Act*, Public Law No. 95-341; 92 Stat. 469, 42 U.S.C. 1996; *National Historic Preservation Act*, Public Law 89-665, 16 U.S.C. 470 et seq., 1966; *Archaeological Resources Protection Act*, 16 U.S.C. 470aa-470mm; Public Law 96-95, 1979; *Protection of Archaeological Resources*, 43 CFR 7, 49 FR 1027, as amended at 60 FR 5260, 5261(1995).

75. DOE O 1230.2, *American Indian and Alaska Native Tribal Government Policy*, U.S. Department of Energy, Washington, DC, 2000.

76. Buck, Jr. Interview.

77. Stoffle, et al., 1995, 234–235.

78. Buck Jr. Interview.

79. Ibid. Emphasis added.

80. Ibid.

81. Ibid.

CHAPTER TWO

"What is an American?"
The Yamauchi Family, Race, and Citizenship in World War II Tri-Cities

Robert Bauman

Home on furlough from the army in December of 1943, Sergeant George Yamauchi wrote a letter to the editor of his local newspaper asking a fundamental question of citizenship, "what is an American?," since he found that his hometown community had significantly changed. Members of his family, longtime residents and successful business owners, who remained in his hometown of Pasco, Washington, now faced persistent discrimination and hostility. He noted that he was "very much disappointed in the seemingly narrow outlook on life that so many... citizens have adopted since the war began...The neighborly attitude of the people had changed to that of distrust and suspicion." Yamauchi went on to warn his fellow townspeople against "falling victim to the very thing against which Americans are giving their lives!" He then asked the readers of the local newspaper, "What is an American? Is he white, black, yellow, red, or any other certain color? It is generally conceded that he is any one of these or a mixture of them all. That is one of the principles of our Constitution, is it not?" He also noted in his letter that his older sister, Mary, had been denied the renewal of a business license to continue the café that their family had been operating for almost three decades. Since she was of Japanese descent, her application was denied. In addition, some of his family members, including his parents, were at that time imprisoned in the internment camps at Heart Mountain, Wyoming, and Minidoka, Idaho. Indeed, Yamauchi himself had been interned at Minidoka prior to

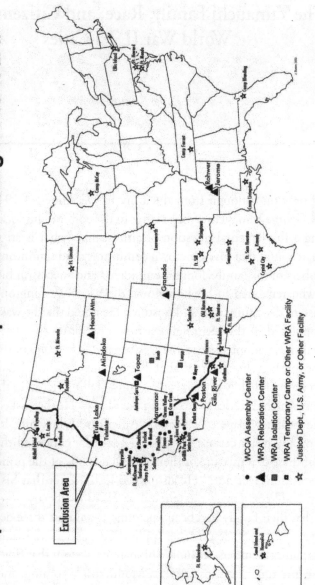

Figure 2.1. Map of Japanese American internment camps.

joining the army as one of the "yes, yes" boys of World War II. Later in the war, he was injured fighting with the 442nd Infantry Regiment in Europe. When Yamauchi penned his letter in December of 1943, his family had been torn apart by the war and the internment. This chapter uses an oral history interview with Yamauchi family members conducted in September of 2018, along with archival sources, to detail the family's story and to further explore the racial history of the Tri-Cities, Washington. George Yamauchi's letter to the editor highlights some of that racial discrimination and history.[1]

A number of scholars have written about the tragedy of Japanese American internment and the impact of that internment on the lives of Japanese Americans.[2] That scholarship, though, understandably, has focused largely on Japanese Americans in major coastal cities, such as Los Angeles, San Francisco, and Seattle. But George Yamauchi's letter to his local newspaper editor was not written to the *San Francisco Chronicle* or *Examiner,* the *Los Angeles Times,* or the *Seattle Times* or *Post-Intelligencer.* Instead, it was written to the editor of the *Pasco Herald* in the town of Pasco, Washington, a town located over 200 miles east of Seattle and nowhere near the West Coast. The War Relocation Authority had decided that the Columbia River, which separated Benton and Franklin Counties in eastern Washington, would serve as the dividing line for the internment of Japanese Americans. As a result, the Yamauchi family members who lived south of the Columbia River in Benton County were sent to internment camps. Those who lived north of the Columbia River in Franklin County, for the most part, were allowed to stay. The war, quite literally, divided the Yamauchi family.

Before writing about the Yamauchi story, though, I will provide some context to their story by exploring the history of Asian Americans in the Tri-Cities area prior to World War II. In many ways, the story of Asian Americans in the Tri-Cities region reflects the larger narrative of Asian Americans throughout the American West. As was the case in many regions in the American West, the first group of Asian Americans to arrive in the mid-Columbia region were Chinese immigrants who came for mining opportunities along the rivers of eastern Washington. Many had initially immigrated to California from China in the 1850s and when opportunities in California dried up, some moved to the Pacific Northwest. Chinese laborers mined the sandbars of the Columbia River and the Snake River to such an extent that they outnumbered white miners in the area by a two-to-one margin. Approximately seventy-five to one hundred Chinese miners stayed at Wallula, east of the Tri-Cities region, every winter in the late 1860s. The miners often lived in dugouts and, in addition to mining, raised produce that they sold to white settlers.[3]

When mining began to dry up in the 1870s, many Chinese laborers became railroad workers. They were both critical and essential in the completion of the Northern Pacific Railroad in Tacoma in 1873. By then, Chinese laborers made up two-thirds (17,000) of the railroad's work force. In 1879, Chinese laborers began working on railroads in eastern Washington, including a line of the Northern Pacific through the mid-Columbia region. As part of their construction work, railroad workers built the town of Ainsworth, located on the east side of the Snake River at the confluence of the Snake and Columbia Rivers. Ainsworth became the hub of the Northern Pacific in eastern Washington for several years while laborers built a railroad bridge across the Snake. In 1880, 50 percent of the roughly 600 railroad workers at Ainsworth in Franklin County were Chinese immigrants. From 1883 to 1887, Ainsworth served as the seat of the newly created Franklin County.[4]

When laborers completed the bridge from Ainsworth over the Snake River in 1884, the entire company of 300 Chinese laborers moved to Pasco. As a result, Pasco, which became the new county seat in 1887, became a major railroad junction and more Chinese came to work on a new railroad bridge over the Columbia River to Kennewick. Entrepreneurial Chinese immigrants quickly established a Chinatown in Pasco between the railroad tracks and Clark Street. Wong How, a Chinese labor contractor, opened a general store, "Wong How Notions," on Clark Street in the late 1880s. From the late 1880s through the early 1900s, Pasco's Chinatown included several laundries, restaurants, and general stores. In addition to Wong How's store, Pasco's Chinatown featured Shoo Lee's General Merchandise store, Hop Chong's General Merchandise store, Joe Sing Ho's Laundry, and several other businesses owned and operated by Chinese merchants. After the completion of the railroads, many Chinese residents left eastern Washington. Some of those who stayed became farmers—particularly in Walla Walla—or shopkeepers. Pasco's Chinatown lasted into the early 1920s until federal agents raided it during the era of Prohibition. As a result of the raid, agents arrested six Chinese residents on narcotics charges related to opium possession and use.[5]

Chinese residents in the mid-Columbia region faced persistent and legal restrictions in the late nineteenth and early twentieth centuries. An economic depression in the Pacific Northwest in the 1880s led to increased anti-Chinese sentiments. In 1881, white Northern Pacific workers refused to work for the standard rate of $2 per day. When the Northern Pacific tried to replace them with Chinese laborers who were getting paid $26 a month, the white workers threatened to "kill any Chinaman who went to work." Anti-Chinese violence in the Pacific Northwest occurred in Seattle and Tacoma in 1886 as well as in Walla Walla and Pasco in the late nineteenth century. In 1895, the Northern Pacific dismissed a white section crew in Pasco and replaced it solely with Chinese workers. This action led to attacks on Chinese in Walla Walla and Pasco. Masked men marched the Chinese railroad crew over the bridge to Kennewick and warned them to stay out. In addition, two masked men assaulted three Chinese railroad workers at Northern Pacific housing in Kennewick.[6]

Figure 2.2. Wong How Notions on Clark Street in Pasco, circa 1900. Courtesy of the Franklin County Historical Society.

Washington State's Chinese residents faced legal discrimination as well. In 1853, Chinese were denied voting rights in Washington, and in 1863, they were forbidden from testifying in court cases involving white citizens. In 1864, the Washington Territorial government instituted "An Act to Protect Free White Labor against Competition with Chinese Coolie Labor and to Discourage the Immigration of the Chinese in the Territory" which taxed Chinese $6 quarterly. In 1937, Washington State passed an anti-miscegenation law aimed largely at Asian Americans, including those of Chinese descent.[7]

In addition, anti-Chinese sentiment and violence in the American West led to national legislation restricting Chinese immigration. As a result of the Chinese Exclusion Act of 1882 and the downturn of mining and railroad work in the late nineteenth and early twentieth centuries, the population of Chinese in Washington declined until the repeal of the Chinese Exclusion Act in 1943.

As a result of the Chinese Exclusion Act, violence against Chinese residents, and declining employment opportunities, the Chinese community in Pasco decreased in population over the late nineteenth and early twentieth centuries. Some Chinese, particularly those with families, though, stayed permanently. Perhaps the most famous Chinese American resident of the Tri-Cities region was James Wong Howe, the son of Wong How. Born in China in 1899, James Wong Howe came to America shortly afterward with his father. He grew up in Pasco. As a child, someone in Pasco gave him camera and he took it everywhere. A curious and observant child, his fascination with photography led eventually to a long and successful career as a Hollywood cinematographer on such films as *Hud* and *Funny Lady*. He won the Academy Award for cinematography in 1955 for *Rose Tattoo*. He died in 1976.[8]

Following the implementation of the Chinese Exclusion Act in 1882, immigrants from other parts of Asia began to replace those from China. Thousands of people from Japan, Korea, and the Philippines left their homelands for either the United States mainland or the Hawaiian Islands. Asaichiro (Harry) and Chika Yamauchi were among them. Born in 1877, Harry Yamauchi had grown up as the third brother in Kibatake, a rural, rice-growing region of Japan. Chika was born five years later in 1882 in Hiroshima. The name Yamauchi means "mountain home" and Harry's family, once prominent, highly regarded and related to a Japanese emperor in their distant past, had over the generations become impoverished. Since his older brother inherited what little remained of the family possessions, Harry and Chika, who married in Japan, left their native country in search of a better life elsewhere.[9]

Initially, that search took them to the Hawaiian Islands, where their daughter, Haluye, also known as Lou, was born on Oahu in 1905. Shortly thereafter, Harry left the Hawaiian Islands, where he and Chika had spent a couple of years working on a sugar cane plantation, to work on the railroads in Washington State. After finding a job with the Great Northern Railroad, Harry sent for Chika and Lou, who arrived in San Francisco one day after the 1906 earthquake. Chika often told her grandchildren that she thought the world was coming to an end on that day. Chika and Lou left San Francisco and met Harry in Cashmere, Washington, where Harry was working as a bookkeeper for the Great Northern Railroad. In 1907, the young Yamauchi family moved to Pasco, Washington. Harry

Figure 2.3. The Wong How family, with a young James Wong Howe, circa 1906. Courtesy of the Franklin County Historical Society.

Figure 2.4. Harry and Chika Yamauchi, with their daughters, left to right, Hannah, Haluye (Lou), Chiyoko, and Mary, in their general store in Pasco, circa 1912. Photo courtesy of the Yamauchi Family. Someone in the family proudly wrote, "Rising Generation" on the bottom of the photograph.

had secured a job as a bookkeeper and recruiter with the Northern Pacific Railroad and Pasco was a hub in eastern Washington for the railroad. In addition, Harry worked as a bartender at the Cunningham Hotel in an effort to save money for his growing family and because he wanted to become a businessman. In November 1908, Harry purchased two buildings on Clark Street in downtown Pasco, transforming one into a tobacco store and pool room and the other, across the street from the Wong How store, into a rooming house for some of the Japanese railroad workers. In subsequent years, the entrepreneurial Yamauchis opened first a grocery store (NP Grocery) and fish market, a hotel, and two cafés.[10]

By the 1920s, the Yamauchis owned and operated six businesses. They were by all measures a successful and well-known family in the small town of Pasco. In 1929, the Yamauchis added to their collection of businesses by purchasing the M&M Café, which became the family's most popular business, noted especially for their home-made noodles made by Chika.

Figure 2.5. Chika Yamauchi with her oldest seven children – Lou, Chiyoko, Mary, Hannah, Charles, George, and Frances, circa 1920. Sons Jimmy and Bobby completed the family. Photo courtesy of the Franklin County Historical Society.

Notably, it was the license for the M&M Café that Mary Yamauchi was unable to get renewed during World War II. Harry and Chika's nine children worked at the family businesses. Harry regularly attended city council meetings and would bring his oldest daughter, Lou, as an interpreter. He also brought candy and gifts, often hand-made needlework or small paintings, to city councilmen, which his daughter informed him that he could no longer bring as it was considered a form of bribery.[11]

The Yamauchis' success allowed the family to buy a new home on the corner of First and Lewis in Pasco. In the basement of the home, in an effort to maintain some of their Japanese culture and heritage for his children and their friends, Harry Yamauchi built a stage and painted a mural depicting the Japanese countryside. The Yamauchis held Japanese school in that basement for their children and all of the children of Japanese descent in Pasco. Harry and Chika taught the children the Japanese language and culture and Chika taught the girls traditional Japanese dances.[12]

The success of the Yamauchis and their acceptance into the community in Pasco was more of an anomaly in eastern Washington than a pattern. The residents of the small town of White Bluffs, in nearby Benton County, made it quite clear that any Japanese Americans would not be welcome in their community. An article in the *Bellingham Herald* in September 1922, titled, "No Japanese Wanted in White Bluffs District," noted:

> Adopting stringent anti-Japanese resolutions, a well-attended meeting of farmers and business men in White Bluffs Tuesday evening went on record as favoring the employment of every peaceful and lawful means of discouraging Japanese settlement in this valley. There are no Japanese here now, and the meeting Tuesday evening is the result of a report that a colony was planning to acquire land either by lease direct or through an agent. About two years ago a Japanese invasion of this district was threatened and a mass meeting of the citizens at that time passed resolutions similar to those adopted Tuesday. Added significance to the anti-Japanese sentiment in this district was given by a meeting of ex-service men who have taken up land here in the White Bluffs-Hanford state land settlement project, at which anti-Japanese resolutions as stringent as those adopted at the mass meeting were passed.[13]

The response by the residents of White Bluffs to just the *potential* addition of people of Japanese descent to their community demonstrated the powerful anti-Japanese sentiment in eastern Washington. And, by using the term "invasion," the *Bellingham Herald* adopted a trope popular among nativists throughout American history—portray immigrants, particularly nonwhite immigrants, as an invading army, intent on destroying all that Americans hold dear. That response was not unlike the virulent, and often violent, anti-Japanese sentiment that permeated most communities in the western United States that had any sizeable Japanese American population. Anti-Japanese sentiment was perhaps strongest in California, but it had led to Alien Land Laws, which prohibited non-citizens (that is, people of Asian descent) from owning land in the Pacific Northwest as well. Indeed, in 1921, the state of Washington passed an Alien Land Law, modeled on California's law, that restricted individuals who were prohibited from becoming naturalized citizens from owning land. That new law legitimized anti-Japanese sentiment in towns like White Bluffs and in the nearby Yakima Valley, where angry white mobs targeted Japanese American residents in 1923. This strident anti-Japanese violence also was encouraged and incited by the revived Ku Klux Klan, which had targeted the Yakima Valley as a place ripe for converts. Nationally, the 1920s Klan

Figure 2.6. Japanese men playing pool at the Yamauchi pool hall, which daughter Lou often managed and frequented, undated. Photo courtesy of the Yamauchi Family.

boasted a membership of over four million, including 500,000 women, at its height and targeted all nonwhites, immigrants (particularly those who were Jewish or Catholic), and opponents of prohibition as threats to "native, white, Protestant supremacy." In eastern Washington, the Klan saw Japanese Americans as a primary threat.[14]

Japanese Americans were not the only Asian Americans targeted by whites in eastern Washington during the 1920s. In 1927, white mobs in the town of Toppenish in the Yakima Valley raided the home of a Filipino man, Ellis Peregrino, who was married to a white woman, as well as local boardinghouses that housed Filipino workers who had migrated to the valley to work as agricultural laborers. A number of Filipinos, seen by whites as both a racial and labor threat, were forcibly removed from Toppenish and the Yakima Valley.[15]

While anti-Asian violence and discrimination was often the norm in eastern Washington during the 1920s, the Yamauchis continued to thrive in Pasco. Lou Yamauchi was the first Asian American to graduate from Pasco High School in 1924. She graduated as valedictorian and became the bookkeeper for the family businesses. A regular at the family pool hall, she became "quite the pool player," according to her son, Roy Satoh.[16]

While the Yamauchis seem to have been generally accepted by most of Pasco's residents and, although there was no formal, legal segregation of Japanese Americans before the war, Japanese Americans and all nonwhites were expected to live east of the railroad tracks in Pasco. So, the small Chinese American, Japanese American, and African American populations in Pasco before the war lived in the same neighborhoods in East Pasco. As mentioned earlier, the Yamauchi boarding house was located across the street from Wong How Notions. The Yamauchis and Wong Hows knew each other well. Lou Yamauchi's best friend was Gladys Sutton, a young African American whose parents had migrated to Pasco in 1906, just one year before the Yamauchi family, for employment opportunities that included her father's job with the Northern Pacific Railroad. Lou and Gladys grew up in the same segregated neighborhood in East Pasco. Lou was the first Asian American, and Gladys the first African American, to graduate from Pasco High School in 1924. Lou and Gladys remained close friends, sending each other photographs and

Figure 2.7. Lou Yamauchi and her younger sister, Hannah, inside the Yamauchi grocery store with Lou's best friend, Gladys Sutton, circa 1915. Asian Americans and African Americans in Pasco lived in the same neighborhood in East Pasco, as they were prohibited from living west of the railroad tracks. Photo courtesy of the Yamauchi Family.

Christmas cards, in addition to spending considerable time together, for the remainder of their lives. For most of Lou's and Gladys's lives, and the lives of their children, West Pasco was off-limits to all nonwhites. Indeed, two Yamauchi grandchildren, Linda Yamauchi Adkinson and Brenda Kupfer, in a 2018 oral history interview, remembered with great detail the dangers of crossing into West Pasco through the underpass that connected the two sections of the town. Into the postwar years, West Pasco was strictly off limits.[17]

As it did for all Japanese Americans residing in the United States, the events of December 7, 1941, and President Franklin Roosevelt's signing of Executive Order 9066 which ordered the removal of all people of Japanese descent on February 19, 1942, had a profound and lasting impact on the Yamauchi family. Members of their family were among the 120,000 Japanese Americans imprisoned during the war, and the general acceptance of the Yamauchi family into the Pasco community was tested during World War II.

The boundary line for the evacuation of Japanese Americans in eastern Washington was the Columbia River. People of Japanese descent living on the Benton County side of the river were ordered to internment camps, while those on the Franklin County side were supposed to be able to

Figure 2.8. Arlene and Connie Minotoya, daughters of Chiyoko Yamauchi and Kahn Minotoya, and granddaughters of Harry and Chika Yamauchi, at Heart Mountain Internment Camp in Wyoming in 1942. Photo courtesy of the Yamauchi Family.

stay. Harry and Chika Yamauchi, despite residing in Franklin County, were sent to an internment camp in Arkansas because they were Japanese nationals and he was a prominent businessman. Their son, Charles, who was not interned because he was an American citizen and he lived in Franklin County, pursued their release and, in 1943, with the help of some prominent citizens in Pasco, was able to get them removed from the internment camp in Arkansas and relocated to Spokane, about 100 miles north of Pasco. They were not allowed to return home to Pasco as it was considered too close to the top-secret defense site at Hanford and Pasco was home to a Naval Air Station as well.[18]

The internment also disrupted the lives of many of the Yamauchi children and their families. Chiyoko Yamauchi Minotoya and her husband, Kahn, and their daughters, Arlene and Connie, were sent to the internment camp at Heart Mountain, Wyoming. George Yamauchi, who was a student at the University of Washington, and his wife, Mari, were sent to Minidoka in Idaho as mentioned earlier. George later became one of the "yes, yes" boys of the internment camps, enlisted in the Army and served in the 442nd combat unit in Italy. As a result, his wife, Mari, was allowed to return to Pasco. Two of the Yamauchi daughters, Mary and Frances, were allowed to stay in Pasco during the war. They operated the M&M Café until late 1943, when Mary was unable to renew the family's business license because of their Japanese heritage.[19]

The story of the Yamauchis' oldest daughter, Lou, her husband Henry Satoh, and their infant son, Leonard, is one of the more unique stories of the Japanese American experience during the war. They initially were held at the Justice Department Detention Center at Fort Missoula, Montana, because Henry Satoh, as a Japanese national and successful businessman, was considered a threat.[20] As Lou and Henry Satoh's son, Roy Satoh, remembered in a 2018 oral history interview:

> My dad was a businessman. He worked for an import-export company in Portland and Seattle. He had a lot of business contacts with other Japanese businessmen and companies. So when they interned him he was shipped to Montana.... The government was more concerned about him because of his business contacts.... When they eventually released him, he was given the choice of going to a regular internment camp or to go back to Japan. He was kind of disgruntled with the way he and

his family had been treated, so he chose to go back to Japan.... They ended up back in a small farming community in Japan. The people there thought enough of my dad that they eventually elected him Mayor of that small community. But my mother, being an American, she was looked down upon, kind of ostracized. She was the foreigner, she was the American, the enemy. My dad died there of cancer, but the war was still going on.... My infant brother [Leonard] had passed away from diphtheria. So, she was pretty much alone with me, an infant son... and there wasn't much help from the local community. I remember hearing stories later about the family here in the United States sending care packages to her in Japan which oftentimes she didn't receive.... She struggled for a couple of years until the war ended. When the people there realized that they were not going to win the war, then they came to my mother and asked her to teach them English.... Finally, in 1950, she brought me back to the States after the war had settled.[21]

The Satoh story highlights the variety of ways Japanese Americans, and members of the Yamauchi family in particular, experienced the war. While some family members spent the war in Pasco, others spent it imprisoned, some served in the armed forces, and the Satohs spent the war in Japan. Indeed, Roy Satoh and his mother, Lou, were not able to return to the United States until 1950, after years of family efforts. When they did return, Roy, who to that point had spent all of his six years in Japan and spoke only Japanese, had to adjust to American culture and the English language. In fact, he only knew two English words—Roy Rogers. When Roy and his mother returned to the Tri-Cities area, his family told him he had to choose an American name. They thought his school mates would not be able to pronounce his given Japanese name of Masashi. Given that ultimatum and his limited English-language knowledge, and the fact that he had a cousin named Roger, Satoh chose the name Roy.[22]

According to the Yamauchi children and grandchildren, Harry and Chika Yamauchi, like many former residents of the internment camps, rarely mentioned their imprisonment. Their daughter Mary, who lived to be 102 years old, said of her grandfather in 2005, "he didn't talk too much about the experience but he was kinda perturbed. He knew in his heart that he didn't do anything that was against the government." The Yamauchi grandchildren reiterated that sentiment, saying that neither their parents nor grandparents ever talked about their internment experience. According to grandson Roy Satoh, he learned many of the details of his family's ordeal during the war only after his grandparents had passed away, by discovering family letters and documents and by talking with family friends, decades after their internment.[23]

Other Tri-Cities' residents had similar experiences of families torn apart by the war and internment. Some Japanese Americans who migrated to the Tri-Cities during the Cold War told similar stories. Roy Ko was born in Bellingham, Washington, to Japanese immigrant parents in 1921. Ko was not the family's original last name, but it became Ko because an immigration official wrote it that way in the family's immigration documents. Roy was a sophomore at the University of Washington in 1942 when Executive Order 9066 forced him initially to Camp Harmony in Puyallup and then to the internment camp in Minidoka. Roy stayed for a year or so at the camp until his release, then left to finish his college degree at the University of Texas at Austin. Two years after the war ended, Roy, with a degree in chemistry, was hired to work at Hanford, the place that had made the plutonium used to kill tens of thousands of Japanese citizens in Nagasaki.[24]

Over sixty years later, when he was eighty-seven years old, Roy Ko, along with a number of other Japanese Americans who had been students at the University of Washington during the war, were awarded honorary degrees by the university. Roy remembered his internment experience, saying, "to me it was an adventure. To my parents it was a tragedy. Looking from a distant point of view it was a gross injustice." Ko's parents had to give up their family businesses during the war and never fully recovered. Ko's daughter Karen's thoughts reflected those of the grandchildren of Chika and Harry Yamauchi. Karen noted in 2008, "in a lot of ways I'm a little angrier [than her father.] I think there's also a lot of denial about the effects and the impacts on people. It's taken them a long time to reconcile this whole business."[25]

As it did to the Wanapum, the war fundamentally impacted Japanese Americans like the Kos and the Yamauchis. The war and the construction of the Hanford Site forced the Wanapum from their traditional lands and limited their ability to maintain some of their traditional cultural ways. For some of the Yamauchis, the war meant removal from their homes and imprisonment, and the loss of at least one of their family businesses.

In many ways, George Yamauchi's December 1943 letter was a fundamentally significant expression of the Japanese American experience. As his niece, Linda Yamauchi Adkinson expressed, the letter "was just a plea to remember who we all were"—a plea to remember who the Yamauchi family was and their significant role in the Pasco community and a plea to remember what it meant to be an American citizen. Indeed, you can argue that the African Americans whose stories Robert Franklin and Laura J. Arata explore in their chapters were defining their freedom and citizenship by migrating to the Tri-Cities and challenging the racial status quo there. The Wanapum, as described by Tom Marceau, challenged the restrictions placed on their traditional practices, like hunting and fishing. The Yamauchi family's experience of discrimination and internment reflect the continuing racial scripts for nonwhites in the Tri-Cities. George Yamauchi defined his citizenship in part by expressing his freedom of speech and using the freedom of the press in a time when he and other family members experienced restrictions on their freedom, along with imprisonment, hatred, and bigotry. His poignant plea, "what is an American?" and his answer to that plea, demonstrate ways nonwhites in Pasco and the Tri-Cities area fought racial prejudice. His eloquent words and heartfelt message remain just as relevant and important in the twenty-first century as they were in 1943.[26]

Notes

1. George Yamauchi, Letter to the Editor, *Pasco Herald*, December 16, 1943; Brenda Kupfer, Roy Satoh, Linda Yamauchi Adkinson, and Bruce Yamauchi, Interview by Robert Bauman and Robert Franklin (hereafter Yamauchi Family Interview), Hanford History Project (HHP), September 18, 2018.

2. See, for example, Gary K. Okihiro, *American History Unbound: Americans and Pacific Islanders*, (Berkeley: University of California Press, 2015); Okihiro and Joan Myers, *Whispered Silences: Japanese Americans and World War II*, (Seattle: University of Washington Press, 1996); Roger Daniels, *Concentration Camps, U.S.A.: Japanese Americans and World War II*, (New York: Holt, Rinehart and Winston, 1971); Daniels, *Prisoners Without Trial: Japanese Americans in World War II*, (New York: Hill and Wang, 1993); Alice Yang Murray, *Historical Memories of the Japanese American Internment and the Struggle for Redress*, (Stanford: Stanford University Press, 2008); Wendy L. Ng, *Japanese American Internment during World War II: A History and Reference Guide*, (Westport, CT: Greenwood Press, 2002).

3. Art Chin, *Golden Tassels: A History of the Chinese in Washington, 1857-1977*, (Seattle: Art Chin, 1977), 17–25; Lorraine Parker Hildebrand, *Straw Hats, Sandals and Steel: The Chinese in Washington State*, (Tacoma: The Washington State American Revolution Bicentennial Commission, 1977), 11–18; Gail M. Nomura, "Washington's Asian/Pacific American Communities," in Sid White and S.E. Solberg, eds., *Peoples of Washington: Perspectives on Cultural Diversity*, (Pullman: Washington State University Press, 1989), 113–155. For an excellent general work on Asian American history, see Erika Lee, *The Making of Asian America: A History*, (New York: Simon & Schuster, 2015).

4. Walter A. Oberst, *Railroads, Reclamation and the River: A History of Pasco*, (Pasco: Franklin County Historical Society, 1978); Chin, 30.

5. Oberst.

6. Ibid.; Chin, 52–73.

7. Chin, 52–53; Hildebrand, 15–16; Nomura.

8. Oberst.

9. Ted Van Arsdol, "The Yamauchis in the New World," *The Franklin Flyer*, 20:2 (July 1987), 1; Susan Davis Faulkner, "Thoroughly Modern Mary," *The Franklin Flyer*, 47:1 (March 2014), 1.

10. Ibid., 1–3; Andrew Sirocchi, "Members of Pioneering Family Celebrate Their Heritage in Pasco," *Tri-City Herald*, August 16, 2005; Linda Yamauchi in Yamauchi Family Interview.

11. Van Arsdol, "The Yamauchis," 4; Faulkner, "Thoroughly Modern Mary," 4; Sirocchi, "Members of Pioneer Family,"; Linda Yamauchi in Yamauchi Family Interview.

12. Van Arsdol, "The Yamauchis," 4.

13. "No Japanese Wanted in White Bluffs District," *Bellingham Herald*, September 23, 1922.

14. For more on the broader Japanese American experience in the American West, including the creation of Alien Land Laws, see, Ronald Takaki, *Strangers from a Different Shore: A History of Asian Americans* (Boston: Little, Brown and Company, 1998); and Gary K. Okihiro, *American History Unbound: Asian Americans and Pacific Islanders* (Berkeley: University of California Press, 2015). On the Klan in eastern Washington, see Trevor Griffey, "The Ku Klux Klan and Vigilante Culture in Yakima Valley," *The Seattle Civil Rights and Labor History Project*, University of Washington, 2007. http://depts.washington.edu/civilr/kkk_yakima.htm. Retrieved November 11, 2019.

15. Steve Ross, "The Yakima Terror," *Slate.com*, August 4, 2017. Retrieved November 11, 2019; "Mobs Drive Filipinos from Valley Town," *Yakima Morning Herald*, November 11, 1927.

16. Roy Satoh in Yamauchi Family Interview.

17. Linda Yamauchi and Brenda Kupfer in Yamauchi Family Interview; "1st Black Pasco Graduate Dies at 73," *Tri-City Herald*, November 24, 1976.

18. Linda Yamauchi in Yamauchi Family Interview. Sirocchi, "Members of Pioneering Family."

19. George Yamauchi, Letter to the Editor.

20. Sirocchi, "Members of Pioneering Family"; Roy Satoh in Yamauchi Family Interview.

21. Roy Satoh in Yamauchi Family Interview.

22. Ibid.

23. Ibid; Mary Yamauchi quoted in Andrew Sirocchi, "Members of Pioneering Family."

24. Chris Mulick, "A Degree of Satisfaction," *Tri-City Herald*, May 16, 2008; Roy Ko File, Hanford History Project.

25. Mulick, "A Degree of Satisfaction;" Roy Ko File, Hanford History Project.

26. George Yamauchi, Letter to the Editor; Linda Yamauchi in Yamauchi Family Interview.

CHAPTER THREE

"I Chose East Pasco Because I Didn't Have No Other Choice"
African American Migration, Segregation, and Civil Rights at Hanford and the Tri-Cities, 1943–1960

Robert Franklin

This chapter examines the African American contribution to Hanford and the Tri-Cities community through the themes of segregation, migration, and civil rights in the pre-1960s civil rights era, surveying the legacies of African Americans' migration to the Tri-Cities and the segregation they confronted in the "Birmingham of Washington."[1] The Tri-Cities' African American community, with help from outside organizations like the National Association for the Advancement of Colored People (NAACP) and the National Urban League, but led by local activists, fought for greater commercial, residential, educational, and economic opportunities in their communities. Local residents pushed against job segregation, confronting white supervisors and asserting their skills and competency; created local chapters of national civil rights groups like the NAACP that worked to ensure that African American workers received equal pay and treatment for government work; worked for education reform and the presence of Black teachers in the classrooms; and lobbied continuously for basic city services, such as sewer connections, street paving, and lights, in the community of East Pasco. The waves of African American migrants that came to the Hanford and Tri-Cities area faced, and sought to reform, a system of segregation usually associated with the Jim Crow South. That this exclusion and resistance happened

75

in a rural part of the Inland Northwest is a legacy of both the already established racial scripts in the region and the major changes wrought by the Manhattan Project and the resulting transformation of the scientific and social fabric of the Hanford area. Later in this study, chapter 5 examines these themes in the 1960s and early 1970s as Hanford and the Tri-Cities transitioned through the Civil Rights era.

MANHATTAN PROJECT

The Manhattan Project, the secret WWII project to build the world's first atomic weapons, transformed the United States into an atomic power and thrust it into the Cold War. The Manhattan Project was comprised of three sites: Oak Ridge, Tennessee, where uranium was separated in centrifuges for the "Little Boy" bomb dropped over Hiroshima; Hanford, Washington, where plutonium was made in first-of-their-kind facilities for the Trinity Test (the first test of an atomic weapon) and the "Fat Man" bomb dropped over Nagasaki; and Los Alamos, New Mexico, the scientists' enclave where the products were received and assembled into weapons of war.

The Manhattan Project was the costliest construction project of World War II and communities appeared almost overnight for the men and women who built and operated these new atomic factories.[2] At the Hanford Site, what had been the rural towns of Richland, Hanford, and White Bluffs, with a combined population of about 1,500, grew to a wartime force of approximately 63,000.[3] About 45,000 of the workers in the Hanford Construction Camp were tasked with building the reactors, processing and fuel fabrication facilities, utilities, security, and the care and feeding of these workers. Nearly 18,000 people in the town of Richland were charged with operating the plants and providing community services. The Manhattan Engineer District of the Army Corps of Engineers (MED) had tasked the DuPont Corporation, the sole contractor for the Hanford Site, with the recruiting of this workforce, and approximately 120,000 men and women passed through Hanford, although many left due to its remote and inhospitable conditions. As Vanis Daniels, whose father was one of those Hanford workers, noted, "They always...had a termination line and an employment line. The termination line was just as long as the employment line."[4] DuPont recruited workers mainly in the South, where it was thought that the high wages would appeal to southern laborers. Although President Franklin Roosevelt's Executive Order 8802, issued in 1941, had "banned discriminatory employment practices by Federal agencies and all unions and companies engaged in war-related work" and the Fair Employment Practice Committee (FEPC) provided oversight of this order, the MED and DuPont, with urging from local governmental officials, limited the employment of Blacks to 10 to 15 percent of the total Hanford workers—a calculated effort to avoid unwanted attention from the FEPC nor to upset white residents of Kennewick and Pasco, and white southern laborers.[5] Moreover, Pasco's city government saw the hiring of Black laborers as a temporary necessity and asked DuPont and the MED for assurance that Black workers would be transported back to the South after the Hanford work was completed.

Almost all those who arrived for work at Hanford came into the railroad depot in Pasco, about forty road miles from the site. Blacks were limited to staying east of the railroad tracks, in an area known as East Pasco, until they could move to segregated facilities on the Hanford Construction Camp. They were not allowed to stay at hotels in West Pasco or Kennewick. Pasco, the oldest of the Tri-Cities, was the rebirth of Ainsworth, a rowdy railroad town located several miles southeast of downtown Pasco at Ainsworth Junction, at the confluence of the Snake and Columbia Rivers.[6] As a railroad town, Ainsworth (and later Pasco) was built largely by immigrant labor and a small number of Chinese laborers moved to Pasco and settled east of the railroad tracks. Later African American railroad workers would be forced to settle mostly east of the tracks (or limited to Fourth Street west of the tracks) and were discouraged from living in Kennewick. Pasco's Black population was small, numbering only in the teens, and did not cause alarm among city leaders or other Tri-City residents until larger numbers of African Americans arrived during World War II. However, because of its decades-long association with nonwhite residents, East Pasco was deemed the only acceptable part of the Tri-Cities for African American workers to reside and active steps were taken to discourage Black settlement outside of East Pasco. The segregation of the Tri-Cities and its racial scripts thus became more rigid and entrenched as appreciable numbers of African Americans began to arrive seeking opportunities offered by the military-industrial complex.

AFRICAN AMERICAN MIGRATION DURING
THE MANHATTAN PROJECT

The anxiety of local leaders resulted from the immense boom of construction at Hanford and the tens of thousands of workers who converged on the Tri-Cities area, and the thousands of African Americans among them. Further concerning city leaders was the presence of African American servicemen brought to the area beginning in 1944 as part of the Naval Air Station Pasco (now the Tri-Cities Airport) and the Pasco Engineer Depot/Big Pasco, one of the largest and busiest railroad hubs of WWII. The presence of African American soldiers on the streets of Pasco "presented the community with a problem it has hitherto not had to solve" as reported in the *Pasco Herald*, causing the base commander Lieutenant Commander McKalip to state that the "colored boys prefer to be segregated" and pledged the Navy's cooperation with the local community.[7] Furthermore, the DuPont Company had consulted with Pasco city authorities about its plans to tap southern labor, and Pasco city leaders demanded that DuPont provide African American workers

Figure 3.1. Ainsworth, Washington, in 1884. Courtesy of Manuscripts, Archives, and Special Collections, Washington State University Libraries, Pullman, Washington.

with tickets and traveling expenses back to the South when their work was over.[8] This demand was agreed to by DuPont, although never formally carried out because most workers left of their own volition when Hanford construction wound down in early 1945, and clearly shows the racial anxiety of Pasco city leaders for whom "the influx of Negroes was viewed…as a temporary expedient, to be accepted as one of the sacrifices of war."[9] White Pasco residents presented a petition to restrict incoming Black workers, many bound for Hanford, from the downtown area after a small group of cabins and a church was built on property owned by Reverend Samuel Coleman, for fear that it would "depress property values and create a 'public nuisance.'"[10] The same article reported that a section of East Pasco was "set aside for a colored section and all Negroes urged to live there."[11] The railroad tracks became the unofficial barrier between the two Pascos, only connected by the Lewis Street underpass. While some Black families, like the Colemans, lived west of the tracks, they were largely confined east of Fourth Street. While no Home Owner's Loan Corporation maps exist for Pasco, several interviewees stated that in the 1940s and early 1950s, no financial institution would lend to those who lived east of Fourth Street.[12] With concerted effort, city and financial leaders were able to segregate the thousands of wartime African American workers who arrived in the Tri-Cities.

DuPont recruited workers through a variety of means—identifying skilled workers in existing DuPont facilities, newspaper ads, the radio, and many came just by word of mouth. Joe Williams and his then-wife Velma (who was also interviewed), along with two other African American workers (whose names Joe could recall as Long Coat and High Pocket) drove from California to Hanford in five days, averaging twenty-five miles an hour. Katie Barton and Vanis Daniels are just a small part of a large extended family network near Kildare, Texas, that began to migrate to the Hanford area beginning in WWII after a school principal read about the Hanford Project in the local newspaper and "told all the people in the city about it." Barton went on to say that "[t]hey started applying for those jobs. Most of those people that came to the Hanford Project, they were recruited. They came in here by the carloads, like our family—it was word of mouth."[13] When asked about how he heard of Hanford, Olden Richmond stated, "Well, I heard it on the radio. That they was

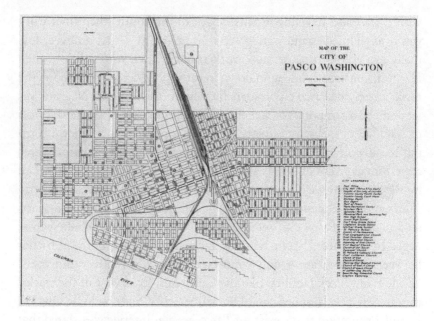

Figure 3.2. Map of the City of Pasco and Vicinity. Courtesy of
Manuscripts, Archives, and Special Collections, Washington State
University Libraries, Pullman, Washington.

going to put up a plant at Hanford, and so I check with Mr. Daniels,
my cousin [and the father of Vanis Daniels the younger], and got with
him, and we made it up to come to Pasco."[14] Lastly, many like Benny
Haney left Kansas City, Missouri, and followed friends or relatives who
visited home for the holidays and spread the word of well-paying jobs
in the Northwest.

Wages were perhaps the most persuasive pull factor—DuPont paid
relatively high wages for wartime work, and because of FEPC legislation,
had to pay equal wages for equal work, providing most African American
workers with wages unheard of in the southern communities they left.
Thomas "Tommy" Moore left Alice, Texas, with a friend to take a cook job
at Hanford advertised at $1.00 an hour. In Texas, Tommy was making $17
per week working seven, twelve-hour days, effectively making $0.20 an
hour there.[15] Luzell Johnson heard about Hanford from his sister, Velma
(Ray) and her husband Joe Williams when they came back to Finchburg,
Alabama, in February of 1944. Johnson grew up sharecropping with his

parents and by World War II was working at a creosote plant for $0.35 an hour. Luzell followed his sister and brother-in-law back to Hanford with several other in-laws and found work as a cement finisher for $1.75 an hour. After construction was completed in early 1945, Luzell returned to Alabama but, dissatisfied to find his wage would continue to be $0.35 an hour, came back to Pasco and ended up buying a home in segregated East Pasco.[16] Olden Richmond was a sharecroppeer before coming to Hanford and in addition he worked off his farm for $3.75 a week in extra income; he made $1.00 an hour at Hanford.

For those arriving to work at Hanford, they were there to perform a variety of construction tasks that, while paying above the prevailing wage, required workplace segregation. Luzell Johnson was hired in as a cement finisher in an all-Black construction group. Vanis Daniels recalled that his father, Vanis Sr., and uncle, William, helped to pour some of the first mud (African American laborers referred to concrete as "mud") at the B Reactor. By virtue of their age and supervisory experience, the Daniels brothers took on more of a supervisory role at Hanford.

> By them knowing how to read and write, and my uncle was also a college graduate...they were instrumental because there were a lot of people that didn't know how to read and write, then my dad and my uncle on Friday mornings, would help pass out the checks...help cash their checks, help write letters back home to their families and send money back to them. My dad, like he called it, would get set up, that he would be foreman over a group and they had certain jobs to do. The most they would ever tell is about digging ditches with shovels.[17]

In a later interview, Vanis Jr. and his brother Edmon talked about how labor at Hanford was fundamentally different from what their parents experienced in Texas:

> EDMON DANIELS: My father said that they went to work, and he said they was getting breaks and everything—
>
> VANIS DANIELS: Never heard of it before.
>
> EDMON: All of a sudden, wait, we can quit working, sit and talk for ten minutes...It was just different out there...the money was great, and you didn't have to do that much with it.[18]

Joe Williams recalled segregation matter-of-factly: "It was segregated. The Blacks worked with the Blacks, and the whites worked with the whites."[19] Williams worked in the 200 Area, where plutonium was separated from the irradiated uranium slugs. "I was assigned out as being chief rubberizer, spark-proof, stop and leaks that ever started. Weren't but eight peoples in the United States had that trade and I was dumb enough to be one out [of] the eight."[20] While the jobs at Hanford paid a prevailing wage for construction work, almost all African Americans were hired on as temporary laborers, living either in segregated barracks at the Hanford Construction Camp or in East Pasco and having to commute the fifty miles to work at Hanford. By contrast, the town of Richland, where the operators and support personnel for Hanford lived, was a town of approximately 18,000 inhabitants by the end of 1945 and almost exclusively white. Richland was not purposely segregated as was Pasco, but rather it was a town reserved for permanent employees of the Manhattan Project contractor DuPont (and later General Electric); the Hanford Construction Camp was from the outset a temporary camp. DuPont did not hire African Americans for permanent positions at Hanford and thus Richland was in effect a whites-only community during the war. Things began to change slowly in the early postwar period, and then by the early 1950s there were a few African American families in Richland, and the men mostly worked in blue-collar or menial labor positions, such as janitors. As Dallas Barnes explained in his interview, jobs at Hanford were still coveted by the African American community as they generally paid well for physical labor and carried a measure of stability and respect. As Barnes noted,

> [I]t was a prize for a black to work inside a building. You see, if you had a job at Hanford, you were going to be working outside, either as a laborer or something like that, but inside as a clerk or something like that...I did hear talk among the men folks about just simply having a job and getting some overtime. Even as a janitor, that was supposed to be a prize kind of a job for a black man.[21]

The inside/outside divide among racial lines at Hanford largely persisted until affirmative action legislation forcibly desegregated employment beginning in the mid-1960s.

SEGREGATION AT HANFORD CONSTRUCTION CAMP

At the Hanford Construction Camp, the barracks, mess halls, workforce, even the Christmas entertainment, were segregated by race.[22] The barracks were also segregated by gender; even married couples were separated. Women were allowed to visit men's barracks (and go into their rooms) but men could only go into the reception room at the women's barracks; they were not allowed to enter the women's rooms. Resembling something of a prison, the women's barracks featured armed guards and razor wire surrounding the buildings. Joe Williams and his wife Velma Ray both mentioned the barracks in their interviews. Velma said "he [Joe] could come into the dorm and take me to [his] barracks, but I wasn't allowed to come down."[23] Joe Williams lived in Barrack 205 and recalled "they had wired fences up like penitentiary around all the women barracks...they had a big recroom and that's as far as you could get. You didn't know what room she slept in...a man couldn't go in the women's barrack without going through the police."[24] Olden Richmond recalled the same type of experience when visiting his wife, who came to join him at Hanford and, like Velma, worked in the mess hall.

> They had separate barracks. It had wire fences around it...wire all the
> way up. They'd let you up there at certain times and certain times you
> had to get out. If you had a wife, you could go in there...about 5:30,
> 6:00, what time you got through eating, then you go and stay with your
> wife until about 8:00, 9:00. Then they had guards at the gate. If you
> stayed too long, then he's going to find you and get you out of there.[25]

What was an inconvenience for men and husbands was deemed necessary by DuPont to protect women in the overwhelmingly male construction camp. Women were free to visit their husbands in their barracks, but they then took the danger of entering male spaces unescorted. Velma Ray recalled the danger and fear she felt after being catcalled and harassed on her way to see her husband in the barracks.

> Those men was raping women so bad...I didn't know how dangerous
> [it] was. Usually you could go where he was, but this was a time, it was
> too dangerous. And I didn't know that. And I don't think he knew it.
> And I was walking down, then after a while a man comes up to me, and
> I said 'don't you see my husband?' And I just lied...if I hadn't've told

them lies, I don't know what they would have done. But they was coming up to me, 'Lady, so-and-so—.' I said, don't you see my husband? And that was not my husband; that was just a man about far from that tree [points to a tree about 20 feet away]. And they would leave me alone. But the time I get that far, I had said, don't you see my husband?—Oh, Lord, I had so many husbands! When I got to that barracks, I fell across that bed. I told my husband I was never coming down there no more. And I wouldn't either. He would come up there and get me. Because I wasn't going down there no more. I'm even nervous, now, just to think about what I would so. Girl, talk about some hard praying.[26]

For some married couples, the distance from one's spouse likely served to heighten the isolation of the dusty and bleak Hanford Construction Camp. However, several interviewees mentioned that their segregation from their spouse served to strengthen the bonds between them. Talking about their parents, Vanis and Edmon Daniels compared the visitation to the female barracks akin to a courtship ritual, and that this rekindled a romance between their parents. Velma also compared Joe's visitation to her barracks after the above incident as courtship.

Most barrack rooms slept two individuals, and if privacy was needed couples could rent a room in Pasco or Kennewick, but only if they were white. It was the same for shopping, recreation, eating out, and medical care outside the Hanford Construction Camp; African Americans were not welcome in the towns of Pasco or Kennewick, which at this time had little to no retail businesses. African Americans had to travel to Yakima to rent hotel rooms or receive basic services. Reverend Samuel Coleman recalled that before 1944, when the Black population in Pasco was small, meaning less than thirty inhabitants, African Americans were welcomed into many establishments in Pasco. The arrival of thousands of African Americans in 1944, for Big Pasco as well as to work at Hanford, changed that dynamic. Coleman recalled that Pasco as a whole closed all the cafes to Blacks, and recent Black migrants could not "get a doctor to see a colored person in Pasco, or get a tooth pulled."[27] The Colemans would gather those who needed services and transport them by car to Yakima. For others, Yakima offered a kind of refuge from the segregation of Pasco and Kennewick. For the Daniels, who could not rent a room in Pasco or Kennewick, Yakima offered some semblance of humanity. As Edmon explained:

They'd catch the bus and go to Yakima. It's so odd the way people's mind worked, but an Oriental guy in Yakima let the Blacks have rooms. They was out there building something to drop over there [on Japan], yet the Oriental guy was the one that treated them like they were people instead of just someone.[28]

The elder Daniels would also take the ferry across the Columbia River, to Franklin County, and have a picnic—a date. "It was sort of like courting all over again, only he didn't have to worry about appearances, it was just the way things were."[29] For single men, like Benny Haney, Yakima offered a different kind of experience as a place of socialization. Haney mentioned that he would go to Yakima for the weekend because "there was girls in Yakima…[we] just sat around and talked…have a little snort once in a while. That's where the company was. There wasn't no company at Hanford, just the beer hall and you get tired of going there."[30] Unaffected by the thousands of migrants and with a long history of African American settlement and farming, Yakima replaced Pasco as a place where African Americans could recreate or stay overnight without experiencing overt segregation.

In addition to the camp, segregation persisted in bussing and in the community of Pasco. Shortly after arriving at Hanford, African American workers contacted the local and national offices of the NAACP to lodge complaints primarily against segregated bussing. This action triggered the attention of Thurgood Marshall, Special Council to the NAACP, who "wrote state and federal officials demanding an end to segregated busses. Four months later, DuPont stopped the practice."[31] Here is evidence of temporary laborers, working with national organizations, taking action to end a practice of workplace segregation. Knowing that segregation was persistent and not satisfied with this singular change, the NAACP sent Rev. Emmett B. Reed to observe conditions in Pasco. There Reed found discriminatory signage reading "we reserve the right to refuse service," "no colored business solicited," and "we are open for white trade only" adorning many businesses in Pasco. Reed confronted Pasco city leaders and was offered "pathetic" explanations of the disconnect between Black workers fighting for democracy while facing retail segregation as being "not seemingly due so much to race prejudice but the right down lack of business acumen."[32] A later investigation by special assistant council

E. R. Dudley in May 1944 of conditions at the Hanford Construction Camp found persistent employment discrimination with Black men being largely assigned menial or construction jobs and women, recruited under the promise of clerical work, being relegated to domestic labor. These inequalities persisted throughout the life of the wartime project.

SEGREGATION IN PASCO

Many Hanford workers had more free time than they were used to—eight-hour days (with breaks) were standard with a six-day work week. Baseball was extremely popular among the Hanford Construction Camp workers who had a baseball league, and unlike other aspects of life at Hanford, the baseball league was not segregated. Vanis and Edmon Daniels both recalled that their father Vanis Sr. was well known for his skills on the diamond. Thomas Moore remembered playing baseball most Sundays with the other men. Moore also mentioned that when he arrived at Hanford there were few single women there, and that at one game a wife of one of the players showed up to watch, and the men broke up the game to go look at her.[33] Vice was a fact of life on the Hanford Project, and in the surrounding community of Yakima (as Benny Haney mentioned in his interview), several arrests for prostitution occurred within the Hanford Camp itself. Workers could go to the beer halls, but as Olden Richmond explained, gambling was a common occurrence along with bootleg liquor.[34] Perhaps the most common, and talked about, activity outside work was church. Reverend Samuel Coleman started the first church for Black workers in the summer of 1944 on property he owned on Shoshone Street in Pasco, west of the train tracks. Samuel and his wife Gladys (Sutton) were transitional figures in the Pasco community, both having resided in Pasco before World War II, and Gladys was the first African American graduate of Pasco High School in 1924. Before the surge of new residents beginning in 1942, the Colemans were members of the very small and thus mostly non-threatening Black population of Pasco. As city leaders worked to constrain the new Black arrivals, the previous freedoms enjoyed by the Colemans—to own property west of the tracks and build on that land—came under severe limitations. The Colemans and others reached out to national groups like the Urban League and the NAACP to help fight racial covenants and institutional racism in Pasco.

City of Pasco records show that in March 1944, Reverend Coleman petitioned the city to build cabins on land he owned west of the tracks to house some of the influx of Black workers.[35] A week later a local petition came before the city, "A Petition to Halt and Remove the Construction of A Colored Settlement on Shoshone Between Tacoma and First" brought by fifty property owners, who brought forth concerns about sanitary conditions, building code violations, and "having goats and chickens running at large."[36] Coleman eventually withdrew his effort to construct cabins for African Americans to focus on his efforts to construct the first African American church in Pasco.

The trouble started when seven ministers came to Reverend Coleman, concerned that so many whites were coming in there would "be no room for colored" and "we think you should build them, your people, a place to worship."[37] The Colemans, who had been travelling ministers for over a decade by 1944, did not wish to build a church because they did not have the funds on hand and did not want to cede their property to another

Figure 3.3. Entertainment schedule for the 1944 Christmas season at the Hanford Construction Camp. From E.I. DuPont De Nemours and Company, Inc. "Construction, Hanford Engineer Works, U.S. Contract No. W-7412-ENG-1, DuPont Project 9536, History of the Project" (Wilmington, Delaware: 1945), 171.

Figure 3.4. In 1944 Wilson "Ducktail" Alexander Sr. was the 24-year-old player and manager of the Hanford Eagles, the lone African American team in the eight-team Hanford Baseball League. Courtesy of the National Archives and Records Administration.[38]

organization. In addition, some unscrupulous workers at the Hanford Camp began collecting donations for the "church" but the money did not make its way to the Colemans. However, the lack of services for Blacks in Pasco and the appearance of "we cater to white trade only" signs convinced Reverend Coleman to begin construction of the city's first Black church in the summer of 1944.[39] The city of Pasco desired that all nonwhites live on the east side of the tracks, and the city council offered to Reverend Coleman that if he gave up his property in exchange for property on the east side then the city would extend water and lights to the property. This offer happened as a group of east side residents were petitioning the city council for sewer connections for their community, ultimately to no avail.[40] The east side did not have full sewer service until sometime in the mid to late 1950s. Coleman refused "out of principle" and thus began a tug of war between Coleman and the City Council to construct, or obstruct, the building of the church. Coleman hired a plumber to put toilets in

Season's Greetings and Good Wishes
for the New Year

Figure 3.5. Reverend Samuel and Gladys Coleman, undated. The Colemans gave this holiday card to the Yamauchi family. Courtesy of the Hanford History Project.

the church, and the city changed the regulations requiring Coleman to connect his building to the city sewer before the toilets could be installed, and placed pressure on the plumber to drop the project. At a later meeting, the City Council changed regulations on new construction from one toilet per sixty people, to one toilet per fifteen people. Coleman then travelled to the Urban League office in Portland, Oregon, and hired a white plumber who was licensed and paid the county to dig the required trench to the new sewage system.[41]

The next battle with the city would be over the required piping for the church. Despite a wartime shortage of essential materials like cast iron, the city insisted that Coleman procure the material, which he did from a supplier in Portland. The piping never arrived, as Coleman stated, "I told the city about it and the truck was stopped in Pendleton and made to unload there." Eventually, Coleman (along with other plumbers) received a variance authorizing materials other than cast iron piping to comply with city ordinance for the duration of the war.[42] Later Reverend Coleman opened a café in West Pasco, but had to appeal to the state to force the city to grant him a license to operate the café. In these small battles with the city, Reverend Coleman attempted to carve out a space for the Black community on land that he owned—to entrenched resistance.

THE COSTS OF SECRECY

With its high pay and relatively good food and entertainment, Hanford asked much of its workers in terms of secrecy and security. Almost all workers had no idea of the specifics of what they worked on, and most did not ask for fear of losing their jobs. DuPont and the Army Corps both employed security agents and "spies" to monitor workers both on and off the job. In addition, the issuing of clearances to Hanford operators required many background investigations and interviewing of family, former employers, and even neighbors. When asked if he had any idea of what he was making, Olden Richmond replied "No. No. Because we had FBIs, they'd come on through there, they walked all day long through there, asking questions…[we] don't know what we were supposed to do, we were just there working, there to make a living."[43] Joe Williams, who was one of eight men who spark-proofed concrete in the processing plants, concurred with Olden—"we never knew what each other was doing…they never would let but two of us work side by side… it always be somebody else that you didn't know and they didn't know you when you was in those cells."[44] Williams' then-wife Velma Ray, who worked in the mess halls, also remembers the secrecy imposed on the job. "When he [Williams] was working at Hanford job, we wasn't allowed to talk. They had a sign up, talk with nobody about your work…and we couldn't about our work…we [didn't] even know what was going on, because it was a secret job. But I do know they was building ammunitions to fight."[45] Thomas Moore also made the connection to ammunitions, saying, "we all knew he [E. I. DuPont] made shotgun shells, but we didn't know—nobody knew he was making an atomic bomb."[46] Reflecting on the character of the African American workforce, Katie Barton praised that first generation of workers—"they were loyal, these men that worked out there, they really were loyal. They didn't come home and tell anything about what was going on."[47] Manhattan Project construction was finished by early 1945 and thousands of construction workers left the site for other wartime work. Large factories in Seattle and the Kaiser Shipyards and the town of Vanport on the Columbia River were major attractions for those former Hanford workers. The Hanford Construction Camp became a ghost town as the (at that time) white operators of the Hanford Site lived in the transformed community of Richland.[48]

POSTWAR HANFORD—COLD WAR BUILDUP
AND MIGRATION

In many ways, the Manhattan Project was just the beginning of the intertwined histories of atomic weapons and race relations at the Hanford Site. The original three reactors built in World War II had expanded to eight by 1955, and advancements in irradiated fuel processing required the construction of two more "canyons," long concrete buildings where the highly radioactive fuel was broken down and the prized radioactive material separated (and the bulk of the unwanted and highly radioactive byproduct placed in underground waste tanks). In addition, the postwar period saw the construction of many new dams on the Columbia and Snake rivers for hydropower and irrigation. These large concrete structures, specifically the McNary, Priest Rapids, and Wanapum Dams on the Columbia and the Ice Harbor Dam on the Snake, drew a large number of African American workers back to the Tri-Cities area and the Black communities in Pasco and for a time, Hermiston, Oregon. These new facilities required thousands of construction workers and a new construction camp sprung up in North Richland.

For African American workers arriving to the area who could not find space in North Richland, or who were drawn to the area by the variety of construction jobs, the only area available to live in was the Black community in East Pasco. Some of the construction workers, who had in 1945 left for other war jobs on the West Coast, began to filter back into the local area and over time, sent for family and friends to join them. A small but significant number interviewed had gone to the Kaiser Shipyards in Vanport (near the Vancouver/Portland metro area) which was subsequently destroyed by flooding in 1948. This flooding and the massive construction efforts in the Tri-Cities area convinced several Vanport residents to return to the area. The large-scale development of the Pacific Northwest that began in World War II continued through the Cold War, as defense contracting and agriculture were major drivers of migration to the area. What this second migration of African Americans to the Tri-Cities found was the legacy of the Manhattan Project here—good paying jobs in construction and a segregated community that desired their labor but, in many ways, resisted their presence.[49]

The post-WWII migration to the Hanford area was more complex than the migration to the Hanford Construction Camp during the war. Both shared the same pull factor—available labor jobs that paid good wages—but the early Cold War buildup had several different factors that influenced Black residents to stay in the Pasco area. While not a well-known metropolitan area, many African Americans had heard about the Hanford jobs and the good pay, and that there was a Black community in East Pasco. Richland, which in 1948 billed itself as the "Atom-Bustin' Village of the West" was now the home of permanent Hanford employees, with the aforementioned North Richland Construction Camp housing the temporary workers.[50] More services were available to newcomers than had existed during World War II and a general sense of postwar optimism and opportunity pervaded old and new residents.[51] If Tri-Cities residents felt anxiety about growing Cold War tensions it does not appear in most reports, newspaper coverage, or oral histories. Most, if not all, were concerned with finding opportunity, and especially for Black residents,

Figure 3.6. The Hanford Site in the early 1960s when it operated at peak production. The steam plumes are two of the nine operating reactors. African Americans drawn to work at the Hanford Site.

resisting segregation and discrimination while seeking to provide for their community and families.

Of those interviewed, most arrived in the Tri-Cities area from 1947 to 1950, lured to the area by a sense of greater opportunity in construction jobs and to create businesses that could serve the Black community. Many who migrated to Hanford in the early Cold War lived in the North Richland Construction Camp, which like the WWII-era Hanford Construction Camp was segregated by race. Sometime in the late 1940s, Emmitt Jackson's parents moved to the North Richland Construction Camp. As Jackson put it, "I actually lived in a segregated community. Because North Richland, the trailer courts were divided. You had your Black section and your white section as well."[52] After the camp closed down in 1954, the Jackson family moved to Richland where they were one of the few African American families to have permanent employment at Hanford and thus were able to live in Richland. Jackson's father worked as a janitor for General Electric. Another Black Richland family

primarily worked in construction, helping to build the reactors seen here, or in menial or general labor. Courtesy of the Department of Energy's Hanford Collection.

was the Mitchells who migrated to the Pacific Northwest in late 1951. CJ, the patriarch, first came to the Hanford area in 1947 when he was sixteen years old as he followed some of his relatives looking for work. Initially he stayed in East Pasco until he could move into the barracks in north Richland. CJ Mitchell worked for three months until he got homesick and went back to Texas. Later, he brought his growing family back to the Tri-Cities, initially working construction at McNary Dam and on the Pioneer Bridge that connects Pasco and Kennewick. At Hanford, Mitchell helped construct the two K Reactors, East and West, as well as the PUREX facility in the 200 Area. In the spring of 1955, he went to work for General Electric in the fuel preparation department in the 300 Area, becoming a regular Hanford employee and thus able to get housing in the town of Richland. Mitchell's efforts to buy a house in Richland, though, took years as most realtors refused to sell him a home there. Eventually, though, he was able to purchase a house in Richland sometime in the 1970s.[53]

CJ Mitchell was one of several residents of the small town of Kildare, Texas, who migrated to Hanford after the war, joining extended family such as the Daniels, Bartons, Davises, and Sparkses. Bobby Sparks, a descendent of WWII and early Cold War Hanford workers, noted that his grandfather, Connie Davis, moved to the area to work construction during World War II as migrant labor and then went back to Kildare. Bobby's uncles Dave Smith, and James and Alford Sparks, moved to the Hanford area in the early 1950s on the advice of Connie. In 1965, Bobby's father Bill, moved Bobby and his thirteen siblings to Pasco, Washington, on the dual advice of Vanis Daniels Sr., who had been Bill's teacher back in Kildare, and Connie Davis, the father of Bill's wife Annie May.[54] Vanis Sr. and his wife Ida Lee, who had come to Hanford in 1943, along with their oldest daughter Lily Mae, migrated back to the Hanford area in 1947 to join the Cold War buildup. In 1951, they sent for the remaining seven children to come up from Kildare to join the family in segregated East Pasco, where the family lived in a trailer on a lot, surrounded by "nothing but tumbleweeds and fields." This extended family migration was typical of the Great Migration out of the South.[55]

In late 1947, Marion "Crack" Barton, related to the Daniels family, came to Hanford to work at the Hanford Site. In 1948, his wife Katie followed and found employment in the Hisman Cafeteria at the North Richland Construction Camp. In a 2002 interview, Barton detailed her work life and how the contributions of Black Hanford workers went unacknowledged:

> I worked the morning shift, from 6 to 2. At that time you would get $1 an hour...that was really good pay because I used to work for $1 per day in [Houston]. People don't believe that kind of stuff, but I have even worked for less than that...growing up in the south. When we moved out here, you got paid $1 an hour, you make $40 per week—that was really good money. My husband worked at the Hanford Site until the 1970s [as] a laborer. So for the Black people getting any kind of notice, they didn't. Most of the Black people built Hanford, but we didn't get recognized. In so many ways, we just got left out. We were unknown, as far as the project getting built.[56]

The Bartons' original plan was to come to Hanford, make money, and then return to Texas. However, the Bartons ended up staying in Pasco and Katie specifically worked to better her adopted town, which she considered to be in many ways more discriminatory than the South. "They [Kennewick] had signs up that 'we reserve the right to refuse service to anyone.' [At] the cafeteria, you could sit down and eat with people, they didn't have no signs, cause it was a government project. But in the towns, like Kennewick, that was just horrible, they didn't even want no Black people in Kennewick. You couldn't buy a house there; you couldn't go to the movies there; they wouldn't put you in jail there. [The] Tri-Cities was worse than the south ever was, because you knew where you stood there. But you didn't know where you stood here."[57] Like other Black migrants to the Tri-Cities, Katie Barton faced hostile and racist attitudes from many residents and was forced to reside in segregated East Pasco, a part of town where the city did not provide many basic services.

As many interviewees noted, the availability of construction work at Hanford attracted African Americans to the area. One of these migrants was Edward Ash, who traveled to Hanford in 1947 with Forrest Lee White, a friend who had worked at Hanford for DuPont during the war. Ash was a general laborer and worked in just about every area of the site. He noted, "I worked first over in 300 Area (where the fuel was fabricated)...then I worked at 234-5 (the plutonium finishing plant)...I worked at 100-H, B, C, D, DR, K East, K West, all of the N (all of the production reactors on site), and I worked at all the other Hanford buildings."[58] Ash was proud that he was able to raise and provide for his family from his work, but he did note that it was the laborers' job to decontaminate radiation zones for other crafts, and that they were not always informed of the danger of the zones to their long term health. These kinds of disparities were common for Black employees at Hanford—while pay was regulated to be the same, white employees often held better and more secure jobs while Black workers were "last hired, first fired" making it hard for them to build seniority among contractors or within the labor union. In addition, treatment on the job depended on the supervisor. Ash described an account where a supervisor tried to segregate restrooms at a J.A. Jones (a Hanford contractor) worksite. Other interviewees described efforts in the 1940s and 1950s to keep African Americans out of skilled trades, and not until the late 1960s were Black workers permitted to make gains in those fields at Hanford.

Joe C. Guice came to Hanford in the late 1940s from Longview, Texas, (near Kildare) as a laborer who specialized in cement finishing, and later worked on Lower Monumental, Little Goose, and Ice Harbor dams, as a foreman for an all-Black labor crew.[59] He impressed on his son, Gordon, the importance of regular work and the high wages that Hanford provided to the men of his generation. For James Pruitt, it took two trips to the Tri-Cities area to decide to stay permanently in 1948. While Pruitt recognized the economic opportunity present in the Tri-Cities, he was shocked to find entrenched systems of racism and segregation in the Inland Northwest, as he noted in his interview:

> INTERVIEWER: [In] 1948, what was the relationship between the African American and the white community or the majority community at that time?
>
> PRUITT: Bad. Very, very prejudiced. Very racist. I was surprised when I came here to find a place that I had left a few years back from Mississippi and came here and found the same thing that I found in Mississippi.
>
> INTERVIEWER: Was it on the job?
>
> PRUITT: It was on the job, it was in housing, it was in foods, restaurants, it was in the bars, in the lounges, and wherever you went, there was a

sign—[LAUGHTER] If it wasn't a sign, it was, no, we don't serve you here. We don't serve your kind.[60]

Pruitt quickly became involved in civil rights efforts in Pasco, joining the East Pasco Improvement Association in 1949, and then the Tri-Cities Human Rights Commission. In the 1960s, he became one of the first African American employees of the city of Pasco, serving as a liaison between the all-white Pasco police department and the majority Black community in East Pasco.

Other Black migrants came to the area to open businesses that would serve the segregated Black community in East Pasco. Rickie Robinson's parents moved to Pasco in 1947 from Seattle to open up a dining establishment that became known as the Queen Street Diner. Robinson's parents were originally planning to move to San Diego but "they told me they heard about this place in southeastern Washington where you could go and make a lot of money...so they drove over here and liked what they saw and decided to stay."[61]

Chain migration was also common to the Hanford area. Virginia Robinson, mother to Rickie, sent for her cousin Rose Allen to come to

Figure 3.7. An example of signage typical outside of East Pasco refusing service to African Americans. James T. Wiley Jr., "Race Conflict as Exemplified in a Washington Town," 1949.

work at the Queen Street Diner in 1953. Rose, living in rural Arkansas at the time, was happy to leave the South for opportunities in Pasco. In 1943, Thomas Moore came out to the Hanford Site as a DuPont employee to do surveying work. "My job was I drove a jeep, and we had concrete on a sled. When the surveyors would put a stake down, I'd have to come along and take it back, dig it up, put a little concrete in there, and put the stake back. Because when the wind blows so bad, the stake would blow all the way around."[62] Moore left Hanford in 1945 when construction was over to travel to Seattle for more war work, but migrated back to Pasco sometime in December 1949, to purchase the "Poulet Palace"—a restaurant and cocktail lounge located on Lewis Street in East Pasco.[63] A multitude of Black-owned businesses served the growing Black community of East Pasco, including "The Montana" or as it was better known, "Virginia's" or the "Chicken Shack." Virginia Crippen started the business in 1948 when she migrated from Portland, Oregon, because she heard "there was work here and no place for Blacks to eat."[64] Crippen set up her business on Eighth Street in East Pasco due to the concerted effort to keep the Black community in East Pasco, as she said—"[I chose East Pasco] because I didn't have no other choice, they didn't allow the Blacks to have business no place else…we had it tough here. The bank wouldn't lend you no money."[65]

The lack of financial institutions available to Black residents of the Tri-Cities was mentioned by several interviewees, as was the general lack of acceptable facilities in East Pasco. Vanis and Edmon Daniels explained that their father tried for years to get financing from the bank to buy a house in East Pasco. Joe Williams left Hanford in the late 1940s and tried, with several other Black residents, to start a mortgage company in East Pasco. As the Daniels brothers noted, East Pasco was without paved streets, streetlights, and a sewer system for most of the 1950s. Aubrey Johnson, who arrived in Pasco in 1948 with his parents, lived in a shotgun house with an outhouse and the only source of running water was a cold-water faucet at the corner of the property.[66] CJ Mitchell lived in East Pasco until 1955, when he hired on with General Electric and was able to qualify for a house in Richland. He recalled that in East Pasco there were few homes with indoor plumbing, the streets were not lit, and, in many ways, it was like rural East Texas, where he and other recent migrants had lived as sharecroppers.[67]

REPORTS ON THE "NEGRO PROBLEM"

These firsthand accounts are supported by two 1948 surveys of the Black community in East Pasco. Both were connected to Washington State College (WSC; now University); one was completed under contract to the Pasco City Council by the Community College Service, the Department of Sociology, and the Business Office at WSC, and the other was a master's thesis by James T. Wiley. Both used anonymous interviews with sample populations to get at the feelings of whites and Blacks in Pasco. The first, "A Community Survey: Pasco-Kennewick, Washington" found that almost 80 percent of Blacks in Pasco were employed at Hanford, and 0 percent in Kennewick, and that white residents of Pasco and Kennewick listed "negroes" as the number one problem which their communities would face in the next five years. The survey authors noted that the Pasco "situation" was different because northern cities with large influxes of Blacks are usually relatively industrial cities.[68] The survey also engaged with the misconception that white Southerners brought discrimination with them to the Inland Northwest. Instead, surveyors found that only 16 percent of the new white residents came from the South, but that a majority of Blacks seemed to blame discrimination on the belief that new white residents were southern. Clearly, existing residents expected the segregation of the new Black arrivals, and the new Black arrivals were not surprised by the prevailing segregation. Instead, Black migrants expected segregation to come from Southerners rather than Northerners.

To white residents polled, segregation was most important in housing; about 75 percent polled said that grocery stores and restaurants did not need to be segregated.[69] However, to whites the phrase segregation meant housing whereas Black residents saw segregation as extending beyond housing into jobs, retail establishments, and restaurants. Lastly, the survey quizzed residents about whether segregation could solve the "negro problem" in Pasco and Kennewick. Not surprisingly, 85 percent of Black residents felt segregation would not ease tensions, but it would only make them worse. On the other hand, 70 percent of whites felt that segregation would ease tensions. This divergence and inattention to the problems facing the Black community of Pasco would come to a head in the 1960s as the Black community in Pasco joined the national civil rights movement.[70]

The second survey, James T. Wiley's *Race Conflict as Exemplified in a Washington Town*, was conducted in 1948 and was not a product for Pasco city leaders, but rather served as an outsider perspective into a changing community, one filled with surprising insights. Of the approximately 10,000 residents of Pasco in 1948, about 2,000 were Black, up from 27 in the 1940 census. Thus, while the white population of Pasco increased twofold in eight years, the Black population of Pasco saw a seventy-four-fold increase in the same time. Wiley documented an almost complete segregation adopted by the white majority in Pasco, and frequently heard that Blacks should build their own town east of the railroad tracks (the area known as East Pasco), and some even "wistfully" suggested that they should have kept Pasco "lily-white."[71] Pasco was not a strictly segregated town, however. As noted earlier the Colemans lived and owned property west of the railroad tracks and some white families did live in the area of East Pasco. Present in the thesis are photos and documentation of the shockingly substandard and squalid living conditions in East Pasco. Many Blacks lived in "ancient" automobile trailers on cinderblocks; many residences were nothing more than shacks made of tarpaper, salvaged wood, and sheet metal, and on average were no more than eight-by-ten feet in size. In addition, most dwellings lacked electricity or plumbing as water was supplied on outside taps; toilets were outhouses, and only a few communal showers served the bathing needs of the community. Cooking was done on wood, coal, or kerosene stoves that doubled as the only source of heat in the winter. Wiley observed that most of these dwellings housed five or more residents, and that rents were $15 to $20 a week.[72]

Here a comparison must be made to the community of Richland, where permanent Hanford workers lived and recreated in a brand new suburban community, replete with a brand new shopping mall (the Uptown, a precursor to the large shopping centers of the 1960s), a library, grocery stores, paved and lighted streets, and most importantly: the Alphabet Houses. Designed by Spokane architect G. Albin Pehrson, these houses, first constructed in World War II, had by the late 1940s

expanded to twenty-two different styles, each given a corresponding letter of the alphabet. Pehrson was heavily influenced by precepts of New
Deal communitarian planning and sought to build a model utopia for
those involved in the production of plutonium—a Plutopia.[73] The houses
Pearson designed and built ranged from duplex units, the "A" and "B"
designations, meant for blue-collar workers, to "G", "L", and "Q" types
for middle to upper management. All were built with solid lumber, mostly
Douglas fir extracted from the Tillamook National Forest, cedar shingles,
asphalt roofs, windows on each elevation for airflow, and all placed on
comfortable lots with grass seed supplied by the government. In addition,
about 2,000 one-, two-, and three-bedroom prefabricated units were
constructed to meet Richland's housing shortage. These "prefabs" were
New Deal-era units originally designed by the Tennessee Valley Authority
and built by the Prefabricated Housing Company in Portland, Oregon.
These units were assigned to a variety of Richland residents, although
they tended to be blue-collar in their occupation. Although somewhat
flimsy with two-by-eight construction, plywood walls, and flat canvas
roofs, they were new and a welcome respite to those living in tents or in
barracks while awaiting housing in Richland.[74]

The disparity of the housing situation and discrimination between
Richland and East Pasco is clear—while approximately 80 percent of the
Black population of Pasco in 1948 is recorded as working at Hanford
in some capacity, these were exclusively segregated and low-skilled labor
jobs, and they lived in squalid and unhealthy conditions compared to
the modern community of Richland. More egregious is what each community paid for housing. A Richland resident could rent a 600 square
foot two-bedroom prefabricated unit for $30 a month, or a 1,200 square
foot three-bedroom "A" duplex for $37 a month, both unfurnished.
Even the smallest 300 square foot one-bedroom prefabricated unit cost
only $27.50 a month. Compared to the rents in the East Pasco housing
of between $15 to $20 a week, or $60 to $80 a month, the disparity
between the then all-white community of Richland and the mostly Black
community of East Pasco becomes clear.

Wiley recorded that many of the white interviewees hoped that Black
residents would leave and saw little or no need to improve conditions in
East Pasco. Blacks, on the other hand, hoped to stay and many began

Figure 3.8. A 1948 picture of East Pasco as part of a survey by then-
Washington State College into the conditions of African American residents.
James T. Wiley Jr., "Race Conflict as Exemplified in a Washington Town,"
1949.

erecting their own houses, using whatever materials were available. The
lack of water mains and fire hydrants, both not provided by the city to
their community, made insurance rates prohibitive; the weeds, trash, and
flimsy nature of the construction created a fire hazard in the hot and dry
summers. In addition, there were no accommodations for recent Black
arrivals in downtown hotels and rooming houses. Recent arrivals were
forced to walk the streets, lie down in doorways, or sleep in cars. Only
Reverend Coleman offered rooms to Blacks in the aforementioned church,
which by 1948 was converted into a series of sleeping rooms.[75] In short,
Wiley found that Black residents of East Pasco were frustrated by the
lack of water and sewage systems, fire lines, and fire hydrants in their

community, and that little was being done, officially or unofficially, "to remedy the conditions under which Negroes live in Pasco, or to improve relationships between the races."[76] While the two reports mentioned are excellent documentary sources of a postwar community undergoing rapid change, they did little to change the minds of city leaders and residents who encouraged and supported racial segregation.

CONCLUSION

Studies of the "Great Migration," or the mass exodus of African Americans from the South between World War II and the Civil Rights era, have illuminated the "vast and leaderless" movement of six million in six decades. In *The Warmth of Other Suns*, Isabel Wilkerson frames the migration as a "turning point in history [that] transformed Urban America and recast the social and political order of every city that it touched."[77] However, fewer studies have focused on the effect of the migration on the American West and especially the Pacific Northwest. In the urban areas of the American West and Pacific Northwest there were sometimes small Black communities that simply could not absorb the newcomers. In Los Angeles, Josh Sides in *L.A. City Limits* explores the tension between the pre-existing small African American community and those that came during the Second World War, the latter of whom were enticed by well-advertised jobs and cautiously optimistic about the potential for racial equality.[78] In the Pacific Northwest and its urban areas of Portland, Seattle, and to a lesser extent Vancouver, much of the history is written by Quintard Taylor. The Northwest was especially transformed by the WWII boom in industrial work, as that conflict "radically transformed small Black communities, allowing Blacks to move into industrial work, increase political influence, strengthened civil rights organizations, and encouraged anti-discrimination legislation."[79] Like in Los Angeles, the movement of Blacks into the Northwest highlighted tensions between old and new residents while creating overcrowded urban areas. In the urban northwest then there was an improvement in wages and accommodations, but a decline in other aspects—primarily housing.

Where then does Hanford fit into the larger story of the Great Migration and African American history? The migration of thousands of Blacks to Hanford and Pasco is similar to others as a part of the large migration to defense contracting. However, unlike other scholarship on race in the American West, Pasco was different in two aspects—it had almost no existing Black population before World War II, and it was rural. From 1940 to 1948, Pasco saw its Black population increase from 27 to 980, a 3,529 percent increase. That Pasco was rural and had a miniscule Black population meant that the new migrants found no real existing Black infrastructure—cultural institutions, shops, stores, and other elements of a functioning community. Here at Hanford they created these largely from scratch and for a time they endured, as by 1950 almost 20 percent of Pasco's population was Black, the highest per capita in the entire Pacific Northwest. Here at Hanford and Pasco the new migrants found a system similar to Jim Crow—harassment, segregation that was quickly institutionalized, and substandard housing conditions. Yet unlike the Jim Crow South there was no systematic racial violence (although police harassment was alarmingly common) and there were opportunities for more and higher-paying jobs and desegregated education. Nevertheless, African American migrants found that even in the Pacific Northwest, they may have escaped the worst abuses of Jim Crow, but they were still second-class citizens in communities that resisted their presence.

The aspect of race in the Atomic West is largely underserved in that literature, and the experience at Hanford shows that race is indeed an important part of nuclear historiography. Thousands of African American workers left the South as part of the second Great Migration, following well-advertised defense contracting positions. At Hanford, they found both higher wages and a system of segregation, the latter hurriedly imposed by the surrounding Tri-Cities community as local leaders "scrambled" to deal with the "negro problem." Many of these migrants did not intend to return to the South, and at Hanford and in Pasco, they created a Black community replete with cultural, social, and retail institutions. Local civil rights leaders worked with national associations like the NAACP and the Urban League to put pressure on city governments and federal government contractors, but more often, they worked within the community to push for equal housing, jobs, and educational accommodations. This attitude reflected both the desire of

African Americans for equal opportunities and treatment and the isolated environment of southeast Washington state. The Manhattan Project at Hanford did more than transform the vast, rural area into a plutonium production facility; it also changed the racial landscape of the Inland Northwest, bringing thousands of African American workers to the Hanford Construction Camp and East Pasco. Good wages and their economic transformation were accompanied by segregationist attitudes and a Jim Crow system, as concerted efforts were made to disenfranchise the sizeable Black minority. The postwar migration, largely to East Pasco, would help build Hanford during the Cold War buildup, thereby contributing again to the national defense while continuing to live and work in a segregated system. In the telling of Manhattan Project stories at Hanford, the achievements of Black workers in the construction of Hanford have been overlooked in official narratives for decades. In addition, the recognition of segregation and Jim Crow in northern communities is sometimes missing in civil rights narratives. Black workers at Hanford made essential and important contributions to intertwining stories in Hanford and the Tri-Cities. Their contributions can no longer be overlooked.

Notes

1. Robert Bauman, "Jim Crow in the Tri-Cities, 1943–1950," *Pacific Northwest Quarterly*, Vol. 96, No. 3 (Summer 2005), 124.

2. Those interested in an overview of the Manhattan Project should examine Richard Rhodes, *Making of the Atomic Bomb*. A thorough history of the built environment history of the project's three key sites is *Atomic Spaces: Living on the Manhattan Project* by Peter Hales. Several key figures dominate the historical scholarship of the Manhattan Project; two of the most important are General Leslie R. Groves, the Army Corps engineer who oversaw the entire project, and Robert Oppenheimer, the head physicist at Los Alamos. Robert S. Norris, in *Racing for the Bomb: General Leslie R. Groves, the Manhattan Project's Indispensable Man*, gives an in-depth treatment of Groves. Groves himself wrote his version of events, *Now It Can Be Told: The Story of the Manhattan Project* in 1962, with significant attention given to his relationship with Oppenheimer, and while an interesting read it should be read with a grain of salt towards the large personality at the center. Those interested in the viewpoint of the chief physicist would be served by *American Prometheus: The Triumph and Tragedy of J. Robert Oppenheimer* by Kai Bird and Martin J. Sherwin.

3. For more on these pre-1943 communities, see the first volume in this series, *Nowhere to Remember: Hanford, White Bluffs, and Richland to 1943*, Robert Bauman and Robert Franklin eds., Pullman: Washington State University Press, 2018.

4. Katie Barton, Vanis Daniels, and Velma Ray, interview by Ellen Prendergast, October 4, 2001, Richland, tape, African American Contributions to the Manhattan Project Oral History Project, Accession number ELPVD100401, Hanford Cultural Resources Laboratory (HCRL) Oral History Program, Richland, Washington.

5. Robert Bauman, "Jim Crow in the Tri-Cities, 1943–1950," *Pacific Northwest Quarterly*, Vol. 96, No. 3 (Summer 2005), 124–125.

6. Jim Kershner, "Pasco—Thumbnail History," *Historylink.org*, accessed March 29, 2019. https://www.historylink.org/File/8604. For more on Ainsworth, see chapter two of this volume.

7. "Advent of Colored Sailors Presents Problem to Town" *Pasco Herald*, June 14, 1943.

8. James T. Wiley, *Race Conflict as Exemplified in a Washington Town* (State College of Washington, 1949), 13–14.

9. Wiley, *Race Conflict as Exemplified in a Washington Town*, 14.

10. "Council Gets Kick On Negro District," *Pasco Herald*, August 3, 1944; Mr. and Mrs. Samuel Coleman, interview by Quintard Taylor, Dec. 8, 1972, Pasco, tape, Black Oral History Interviews, 1972–1974 (acc. 78-3), Manuscripts, Archives, and Special Collections, Washington State University Libraries, Pullman.

11. "Council Gets Kick on Negro District."

12. A number of AACCES interviewees mention the restriction on lending east of 4th street including Joe Williams, interview by Vanis Daniels, The Dalles, AACCES Oral History Project, RG2D-4D, Hanford History Project at Washington State University Tri-Cities, Richland.

13. Barton, Daniels, and Ray interview.

14. Olden Richmond, interview by Vanis Daniels, June, 21, 2001, Pasco, AACCES Oral History Project, RG2D-4D, Hanford History Project at Washington State University Tri-Cities, Richland.

15. Thomas Moore, interview by Vanessa Moore, June 23, 2001, Pasco, AACCES Oral History Project, RG2D-4D, Hanford History Project at Washington State University Tri-Cities, Richland.

16. Luzell Johnson, interview by Vanis Daniels, Vanessa Moore, and Leonard Moore, Feb. 18, 2002, Pasco, AACCES Oral History Project RG2D-4D, D8-16, Hanford History Project at Washington State University Tri-Cities, Richland.

17. Barton, Daniels, and Ray interview.

18. Edmon and Vanis Daniels, interview by Robert Franklin, May 7, 2018, Richland, Hanford Oral History Project, Washington State University Tri-Cities.

19. Williams interview.

20. Williams interview.

21. Dallas Barnes, interview by Robert Franklin, March 22, 2018, Richland, Hanford Oral History Project, Washington State University Tri-Cities.

22. E.I. DuPont De Nemours & Company, Inc. "Construction, Hanford Engineer Works, U.S. Contract No. W-7412-ENG-1, DuPont Project 9536, History of the Project," (Wilmington, Delaware: 1945), 171.

23. Barton, Daniels, and Ray interview.

24. Joe Williams interview.

25. Olden Richmond interview.

26. Velma Ray, interview by Vanessa Moore, Pasco, October 6, 2014, AACCES Oral History Project RG2D-4D, D8-10, Hanford History Project at Washington State University Tri-Cities, Richland.

27. Coleman interview.

28. Vanis and Edmon Daniels interview.

29. Vanis and Edmon Daniels interview.

30. Benny Haney, interview by Vanis Daniels, Pasco.

31. Bauman, "Jim Crow in the Tri-Cities", 125. Those interested in a more detailed account of NAACP activity at Hanford should consult this article.

32. Emmett B. Reed, reel 19, pt. 15, NAACP papers .

33. Thomas Moore interview.

34. Olden Richmond interview.

35. Ty Phelan, Wilson 'Ducktail' Alexander, Sr. (1919–1950), February 20, 2019. Blackpast.org. Accessed 7/26/2019.

36. Coleman interview; City of Pasco, City Council Meeting, March 21, 1944. https://egov-pasco.com/weblink/DocView.aspx?id=543715&dbid=0.

37. Council Meeting minutes, April 4, 1944, City of Pasco. https://egov-pasco.com/weblink/DocView.aspx?id=543717&dbid=0.

38. Coleman interview.

39. *Pasco Herald,* June 14, 1944.

40. *Pasco Herald,* July 3, 1944.

41. Bauman, "Jim Crow in the Tri-Cities," 127–128.

42. City of Pasco, Resolution 248 "Authorizing Materials Other Than Cast Iron…" February 11, 1945.

43. Olden Richmond interview.

44. Joe Williams interview.

45. Velma Ray interview.

46. Thomas Moore interview.

47. Barton, Daniels, and Ray interview.

48. The Hanford Construction Camp was so thoroughly deserted that a February 24, 1946, edition of the *Sunday Oregonian* was titled "Hanford: Back to Ghosts and Goats."

49. Taylor, Quintard. *A History of Blacks in the Pacific Northwest, 1788–1970*, University of Minnesota, 1977; Melissa E. E. Williams, "Those Who Desire Very Much to Stay: African Americans and Housing in Vancouver, Washington, 1940 to 1960," MA Thesis, Washington State University, 2007.

50. This phrase was used by the Richland Junior Chamber of Commerce to describe the town in 1947 and 1948 for community celebrations such as "Richland Day" and "Atomic Frontier Days."

51. Washington State University, General Extension Service, "A Community Survey of the Pasco-Kennewick Area, November 1949," (Pullman, Wash., 1949), 31.

52. Emmitt Jackson, interview by Robert Franklin, March 23, 2018, Richland, Hanford Oral History Project, Washington State University Tri-Cities.

53. CJ Mitchell, interview by Robert Bauman, October 30, 2013, Richland, Hanford Oral History Project, Washington State University Tri-Cities.

54. Bobby Sparks, interview by Robert Franklin, May 8, 2018, Richland, Hanford Oral History Project, Washington State University Tri-Cities.

55. Edmon and Vanis Daniels interview. For more on the Great Migration, see, Annelise Orleck, *Storming Caesars Palace: How Black Mothers Fought Their Own War on Poverty*, Boston: Beacon Press, 2005; and Isabel Wilkerson, *The Warmth of Other Suns: The Epic Story of America's Great Migration*, New York: Random House, 2010.

56. Barton, Daniels, and Ray interview.

57. Barton, Daniels, and Ray interview.

58. Edward Ash, interview by Vanessa Moore, August 25, 2001, Pasco, AACCES Oral History Project RG2D-4D, D8-14, Hanford History Project at Washington State University Tri-Cities, Richland.

59. Gordon Guice, interview by Robert Franklin, January 23, 2018, Richland, Hanford Oral History Project, Washington State University Tri-Cities.

60. James Pruitt, interview by John Skinner, October 18, 2001, Pasco, AACCES Oral History Project RG2D-4D, D8-18; D8-19, held by Hanford History Project at Washington State University Tri-Cities, Richland.

61. Rickie Robinson, interview by Robert Franklin, February 16, 2018, Richland, Hanford Oral History Project, Washington State University Tri-Cities.

62. Thomas Moore, interview by Vanessa Moore, June 23, 2001, Pasco, AACCES Oral History Project RG2D-4D, D8-12, held by Hanford History Project at Washington State University Tri-Cities, Richland.

63. Thomas Moore interview.

64. Virginia Crippen, interview by Vanessa Moore, Pasco, AACCES Oral History Project RG2D-4D, D8-13, held by Hanford History Project at Washington State University Tri-Cities, Richland.

65. Virginia Crippen interview.

66. Aubrey Johnson, interview by Robert Franklin, April 9, 2018, Richland, Hanford Oral History Project, Washington State University Tri-Cities.

67. Duke Mitchell interview.

68. "A Community Survey," 55.

69. Ibid, 66.

70. Ibid.

71. James T. Wiley, *Race Conflict as Exemplified in a Washington Town* (State College of Washington, 1949), 53.

72. Ibid.

73. For more information on the social and cultural fabric of the town of Richland, see Kate Brown, *Plutopia: Nuclear Families, Atomic Cities, and the Great Soviet and American Plutonium Disasters*. Oxford: Oxford University Press, 2013.

74. For more information on the Alphabet Houses see Robert Franklin, "Alphabet Houses" [Richland, Washington], *SAH Archipedia*, eds. Gabrielle Esperdy and Karen Kingsley, Charlottesville: UVA Press, 2012– , http://sah-archipedia.org/buildings/WA-01-005-0019. Accessed 2019-05-30.

75. Wiley, 61.

76. Wiley, 138.

77. Isabel Wilkerson, *The Warmth of Other Suns: The Epic Story of America's Great Migration* (New York: Random House, 2010), 2

78. Josh Sides, *L.A. City Limits: African American Los Angeles from the Great Depression to the Present* (Berkeley: University of California Press, 2003), 2.

79. Quintard Taylor, *The Forging of the Black Community: Seattle's Central District from 1870 through the Civil Rights Era* (Seattle: University of Washington Press, 1994), 5.

CHAPTER FOUR

"To Better My Condition"
African American Women in the Tri-Cities, 1940–1970

Laura J. Arata

They arrived with hope, determination, and sometimes the benefit of a network. A few had family and friends already living in the arid Washington desert. Lured by the promise of wartime industrial work, higher wages, and an escape from the oppressive social and economic conditions of the South, most African American migrants felt the stinging disappointment of finding that racism limited their opportunities even in this atomic Western promised land. Caught in the interstices of oppression and necessity that shaped race relations in a country at war with enemies abroad and domestic alike, the African American population of the Tri-Cities represented just one small part of a much larger movement. Millions had already joined a human flood out of the South, a flow that was so vast and so leaderless and "crept along so many thousands of currents over so long a stretch of time as to be difficult for the press to truly capture while it was under way."[1] Eventually known as the Great Migration, it reshaped the entire country, carrying millions of Black Americans from southern cotton fields to cities like New York, Chicago, Las Vegas, Los Angeles, Portland, and Seattle. While those larger communities blossomed and became more visible in the second half of the twentieth century, in the Tri-Cities, growth by numbers was far less significant than the agency of smaller movements: from the segregated east side of Pasco to the formerly whites-only neighborhoods of the rest of that city, as well as neighboring Richland and Kennewick.

As with other parts of the country, many were drawn by a potent combination—the sometimes tenuous promise of opportunity, and the relative security of kinship bonds. The safe arrival and success of family members and friends encouraged others to set out on similar journeys. Those who managed to secure employment and housing often returned or sent for spouses, siblings, relatives, and friends left behind. Thus, within the expansive scope of the Great Migration, smaller patterns emerged depicting the movement of individuals from specific areas of the South to equally specific locations outside of it. In Las Vegas, for instance, a substantial portion of migrants came from the Louisiana Delta. The Tri-Cities, too, represented one of these channels of migration, with a firm anchor point in Kildare, Cass County, Texas, leading in a direct line to East Pasco, one of the Tri-Cities, in Washington.[2] "We had uncles that were up this way," Emma Mitchell Peoples recalled, and their experiences encouraged her older brother, CJ, to set off in search of work. In an oft-repeated pattern, once he was established, CJ sent for Emma and other family members later followed.[3] They became part of a rapidly growing, segregated but vibrant community.

Figure 4.1 Emma Peoples.
Courtesy of Hanford
History Project.

The Tri-Cities' population expanded with uncomfortable speed at the onset of construction for the Hanford Engineer Works in 1943—everyone felt the pressure, but perhaps none as acutely as those who congregated in East Pasco. To keep pace with wartime exigencies and desperate need for labor, the DuPont Corporation, the primary contractor charged with constructing the Hanford Engineering Works as quickly as possible, "aggressively recruited black laborers from the South."[4] An influx of arrivals swelled the African American population from just twenty-seven individuals in 1940 to many thousands—an exact number is hard to come by—during the war years. "The war-induced labor shortage coupled with President Franklin Roosevelt's Executive Order 8802, which prohibited employment discrimination in firms with government contracts," hypothetically created significant space for African Americans in a growing industrial workforce, an appealing option for ambitious men and women in search of a way out of the South's vicious, poverty-bound agricultural systems.[5]

But of course, they were not the only ones on the move in search of opportunity. Along with Black job seekers came white ones committed to maintaining the familiar color lines and unequal treatment that existed in the South. They found both open and tacit support for their positions with local and federal officials, and perhaps nowhere in Washington was this more clearly on display than in the dichotomy that came to exist in the Tri-Cities. African Americans hired to work on the construction of the Hanford Site found themselves confined to living in segregated barracks or in an already dilapidated section of East Pasco, and excluded from the cities of Richland and Kennewick. DuPont, seeking to quell initial dissent to even this limited space, forged an agreement with the city of Pasco "that the company would pay to transport blacks back to the South after their work was completed."[6] Thus Jim Crow segregation took hold and grew along with the Tri-Cities as a result of both local and transplanted prejudice. While cities in other parts of the state, most notably Seattle, also sought to cope with rapidly shifting demographics as a result of wartime demand and population migration, because the Tri-Cities were not particularly multiracial before the war, African Americans bore the full brunt of discrimination there.[7] The impacts were felt in working, living, and social contexts. Black men found themselves performing the most physically demanding manual labor, from pouring concrete and spreading mud to unloading bricks, regardless of qualifications. Facing discriminatory treatment was a disappointment, but not a surprise.

Few, if any, African American women were shocked to discover that they faced similar inequities, lured by the promise of war-related or clerical jobs, then shunted into tedious menial positions with little opportunity for advancement. In a situation that played out again and again during these years, "black women nationally continued to face gender and racial discrimination and thus remained an underutilized workforce," even when labor shortages were acute.[8] Many found themselves resigned to domestic service work, but even this paid better than anything available in Texas. The women interviewed for the Hanford History Project made clear an acute, ingrained awareness that sometimes opportunity was in the eye of the beholder. Even with challenges and limitations posed by de facto segregation, the Tri-Cities presented opportunities nearly unimaginable in the South. Drawing on the handful of oral histories from African American women the collection reveals nuanced layers of optimism, disappointment and determination that shaped their experiences in equal measure.[9]

Some of the African American women who arrived in the Tri-Cities during and after the war years were following husbands or joining family members already in the area. Others came alone, of their own volition, in search of the means to build a better life. For most, no matter how challenging either the social or physical conditions, the Tri-Cities represented a means of escape from the brutal cycle of poverty that accompanied entrapment in the remnants of the South's sharecropping economy. Wartime aside, a crucial push factor had already arrived in the form of mechanized harvesting equipment in the 1940s. The sharecropping system, already in its death throes, convulsed a final time as the labor of African Americans who tended and picked cotton was further devalued. Women bore the brunt of economic and social degradation.

African American women caught up in this system faced the dire prospects of being stuck in a seemingly endless cycle of poverty, pregnancy, and the strain of raising children with severely limited resources on top of often brutal physical labor. Some risked early marriage in hopes of escaping, only to find themselves facing the additional hardships of abusive partners or abandonment.[10] For some it created a nearly hopeless system that threatened to crush any chance of escape for themselves or their children. As a result, tens of thousands had already begun to leave the South in the early twentieth century. By the 1940s, "the fate of entire black communities, no longer needed for their labor, became uncertain. Social flux sparked outbreaks of violence that were fueled by racism, class antagonism, sexual tension, and meanness."[11]

Threats of violence, lynching, and rape oppressed and cast long shadows over most aspects of life in the South, and these threats were not entirely absent in the Tri-Cities. As mentioned in the previous chapter, only Velma Ray noted the overt danger that women faced there, but no doubt she was not the only woman who experienced such fear. For women instilled with the sense of apprehension that came from having to be constantly on guard against sexual aggression, it could only have seemed an all too familiar situation. For Ray, the threat occurred when both she and her husband lived in separate company barracks. After several close calls, Velma refused to undertake the walk between their barracks, judging it "too dangerous." Fearful that "men was raping women so bad," seemingly without consequences, Ray recalled one close call when a man approached her threateningly. In order to escape his advances, she indicated another man in the distance to be her husband. Afterward she pronounced to her husband "that I wasn't NEVER coming down there no more." Seventy years later, just thinking about it still made her visibly nervous.[12]

Figure 4.2 Velma Ray. Courtesy of the Hanford History Project.

Women who already had children sometimes made the heartbreaking decision to leave them behind with relatives as they sought a way out. "I married much too young," Rose Allen admitted. Born in rural Arkansas in 1931, already a mother to several children, and abandoned by her husband, Allen was tired of "living in the woods" and jumped at the chance to come to the city when a cousin sent for her—even if that city was, at the time, little but "sandstorms and tumbleweeds."[13] Forced to leave her children behind with her mother, Allen went to work at the Queen Street Diner the day she arrived. She met her second husband there, married him several years later, and eventually sent for her children. She was still not yet thirty years old. Similarly, Velma Ray left three children with her parents in Alabama in order to follow her husband west in search of war work, first in a California Navy shipyard, and then at the Hanford Site. When she could not find welding work at Hanford, Velma went to work in Mess Hall #2—the segregated eating space for Black workers.[14]

Figure 4.3 Rose Allen. Courtesy of the Hanford History Project.

Emma Peoples, born in Kildare in 1940, came to the Tri-Cities at the age of sixteen to join a relative who sent for her. "I don't know why he asked me to come," she recalled, "but there was nothing else for me to do...it was a blessing. Not a good move. A blessing." Peoples further noted that the situation in Texas was much like that which Allen left behind in Arkansas: those who were able to leave "went to where the jobs were," relying on the capacity of "strong women" to hold families together in the interim, and to rebuild them in new places.[15] Indeed, while men physically built the Hanford Engineering Works, it fell largely to women to engineer an important sense of domestic normalcy in the midst of sparse living conditions in a place that Velma Ray described aptly as "just almost a desert." Many, like Ray, could recall routine challenges like doing laundry with limited water supply and in the midst of dust storms; more than a few likely had Ray's experience of doing laundry and hanging it to dry, only to have a dust storm come up and snap the line, undoing all her hard work in an instant.[16]

The need to search for options that extended beyond sharecropping or working for the railroad lines extended into the postwar decades, as exemplified in the recollections of Rhonda Rambo, whose parents followed word-of-mouth information about Hanford to the Tri- Cities in the early 1950s. Rambo's family had roots in Bivens, Texas, little more than six miles from Kildare. Her grandfather had been a sharecropper; her father worked as a brakeman for the Great Northern Railroad. Encouraged by the promise of better conditions, and particularly better educational opportunities for his children, he moved the family initially to East Pasco. By then the area had developed a "bad reputation" as a segregated and depressed part of the city, but it also maintained an important sense of community. After her father fell ill with lung cancer and emphysema, Rambo's mother "really had to step up," working night shifts to keep the family afloat. The family made the sacrifices willingly, in Rambo's recollection, because the Tri-Cities still allowed for more opportunities than in Texas. There, "if you didn't get out, you were gonna be a farmer."[17] The forces driving migrants out of the South, in other words, extended far beyond the war years, and education always ranked high as a factor in the decision to leave. Most knew it would create opportunity long after the burst of economic energy created by wartime leveled off, and considered the long-term benefits, for both themselves and their children.

Some did come, of course, in search of immediate economic benefits. Not all of the African American women who migrated to the Tri-Cities came to join an established network of friends and family. "I came alone," Virginia Crippen explained. Born in Texas, Crippen had already braved the change of moving West, first to Portland, Oregon, where she worked briefly in a Navy shipyard. Then, "I heard there was work here, and wasn't no place for Blacks to eat, so I come to better my condition."[18] Crippen's recollections get at the heart of the situation confronting African American migrants in the 1940s. Relegated to residing on the east side of the railroad tracks in Pasco, often without water, sewer, garbage, or electricity services, many were forced to live in "cardboard houses" and other "makeshift residences, including trailers, shacks, tents, and chicken houses."[19] Pasco was not unique in this regard. Similar scenarios unfolded throughout the American West and Southwest, where Black migrants arrived to find themselves able to secure reasonably well-paying jobs, but "restricted to ghettos on the outskirts of town, with unpaved streets, outhouses, and

Figure 4.4 Virginia Crippen. Photo courtesy of Afro-American Community, Cultural, and Educational Project and the Hanford History Project.

shacks made of packing crates, tin, and tar paper."[20] Such conditions described not only Pasco but Los Angeles, Oakland, Las Vegas, and a host of other places. This dual sacrifice on the part of African Americans—of their labor during the war and their living conditions, to indifference on the part of white city authorities, which continued long after it—characterized an important part of their experience. But as Crippen's account of life in the Tri-Cities makes clear, African American women played a central role in building a sense of community through amenities where Black residents could spend some of their hard-earned money.

Initially, there were no restaurants and few stores willing to serve African Americans in the Tri-Cities. And while such overt discrimination was a painful daily reminder of battles for inclusion that had yet to be won, for those with the resources to get started, this created opportunity to establish thriving businesses in Pasco. With limited competition, and the added benefit of willingness to serve customers of all ethnicities and races, the Black-owned businesses managed to thrive. The Queen Street Diner, Hugh's Women's Apparel, Tate's Restaurant, Jack's Tavern, Johnny Reed's Dance Club, Tommy Moore's Hotel, and Mrs. Wright's Trailer Court all did brisk business. Often named for their owners, some restaurants reflected the presence of African American women in these ventures, including Sally's Restaurant, where Sally had "good food…very good food, like lunches, and had pies and everything," and Haney's Place, operated by Mrs. Haney.

Virginia Crippen opened a restaurant soon after her arrival in 1948. "Well it was really the Montana," Crippen recalled when asked about its name, "but they called it 'the Chicken Shack, let's go to Virginia's.'" Over time it came to be popularly known simply as "Virginia's Chicken Shack."[21] Crippen prepared fried chicken and barbeque—which wasn't any particularly special recipe, although some customers believed it was—and sold both take-out and sit-down orders. "You talk about that woman could make some biscuits," Jeanette Sparks remembered—served with preserves, even.[22] Virginia's did not serve liquor, but did allow local teenagers to hold sock hops. Notably, Emma Peoples met her husband there.

Acutely aware that African American residents "couldn't eat no place" else in town, Crippen did not discriminate, "didn't refuse nobody," and maintained an open-door policy for customers of all races.[23] According to Crippen, so did Johnny Reed's Dance Club, which had "lots of white customers" after hours. Crippen's recollection that customers of all races sat down and ate together without issue offers a glimpse at moments of shared community that emerged within the larger structures of segregation.[24] Crippen's experience living in Pasco captures vividly the situation that confronted African American residents there beginning in the 1940s. Determined to enforce segregation, many banks would not loan money to Black customers for starting businesses.[25] Crippen used savings to open her restaurant, while others drew upon the support of friends and family. For many, this network proved a definitive factor in the choice to remain after the war, despite an acute awareness that segregation existed even if most businesses didn't bother with putting up "whites only" signs. "That was out of the question," Crippen noted of entering white-owned restaurants.[26] Other residents recalled still being refused service well into the 1960s.

In reality, no matter how stubbornly segregation persisted in the Tri-Cities, it still presented a better chance at opportunities than what existed in Texas. "In the first place, there were no other jobs in Texas," Emma Peoples noted; Kildare, where she was born, was both rural and segregated; the closest restaurant was fourteen miles away, and Blacks who wished to eat there had to sit upstairs in a balcony.[27] At grocery stores, while light-skinned Blacks could sometimes shop without incident, dark-skinned customers had to enter through the back door. Insisting that he "wasn't born in no back door, and he wasn't gonna go in no back door to shop," Jeanette Sparks' father, who was "Black as the ace of spades" and also born in Kildare, came to the Tri-Cities for employment opportunities, having worked on dams and bridges in Oregon.[28] He eventually helped build the Blue Bridge (officially named the Pioneer Memorial Bridge), which carries US Highway 395 across the Columbia River. For many years, the nearby Pasco-Kennewick Bridge, which connected 10th Avenue in Pasco to North Gum and East Columbia Drive in Kennewick, displayed a sign stating "No Blacks in Kennewick after Dark," a stark, physical, and symbolic representation of the dividing line between the demand for the skilled labor of African Americans on the one hand, and derision toward them in any other capacity. The sign eventually came down, but Kennewick remained a "sundown town" where police harassment of Black residents was routine.[29]

The women interviewed for the Hanford History Project reflect the complicated nature of de facto segregation existing in a place where it was technically against the law, but routinely enforced by rule of suggestion. By 1970 African American residents could enter most businesses without fear or intimidation in Pasco and Richland, but Kennewick remained obstinate about changing. As late as the 1960s no African Americans lived in Kennewick, despite its population increasing to more than 14,000, and only six were employed there during the day—one as a cook, the others as auto mechanics.[30] "We didn't have no problem over here [in Pasco] whatsoever," Jeanette Sparks insisted; Kennewick was different. "They didn't want any Blacks in Kennewick...you couldn't be caught after dark, even if you worked there," Sparks recalled.[31] Rose Allen's boyfriend was once detained, threatened with jail time, and fined for being there after dark.[32] The situation improved in that Rhonda Rambo noted that by the late 1960s it was okay to go shop and spend money in Kennewick, but still it was necessary to be out by nightfall. "I never saw crosses burning," her brother Bryan added, but he did not have to: he knew instinctively "to be afraid of it."[33] This bridge would take longer to cross.

There remained, across the board, a notable lack of businesses in Pasco catering to Black women, who perhaps faced the most distinctive deprivations of all. Some of these are surprising—for instance, while there were two Black-owned barber shops that served African American customers, there were no beauty shops catering to Black women until years after the war, when Mrs. Newborn opened up "a nice beauty shop on Oregon Street."[34] Over time, more businesses opened up to African Americans, and as Virginia Crippen noted, "you could go into all the grocery stores and dress shops and all, spend your money, and they'd treat you nice, you know, you spending your money. But you better not go to the bank and ask to borrow some money. You could put money in the bank, but you sure couldn't borrow any money from the bank."[35] The businesses that did open found eager customers—"opportunities galore," as Rhonda Rambo's parents described it.[36] That, in and of itself, was not nothing.

That there was a demand for such services is clear in the recollections of Willie Daniels. Part of the contingent of early arrivals from Kildare, Daniels noted to an interviewer that in addition to working 12-hour days in construction at the Hanford Site, "I was selling stuff, like toilet goods and I was working at that for Lucky Heart, cosmetics, perfume, hair dressing powders. I was doing that on the side, some weeks I made as much at that as I did on the job...I was selling...ladies dresses, those Fashion Frocks. At night, when we come in for dinner, I'd get my little bag and go to the mess hall and recreation rooms and get some sales."[37] Traveling salesmen and mail order catalogues no doubt supplied many of the basic necessities for African American women, from toiletries and home goods to clothing and shoes.

Daniels also noted the presence of his wife at Hanford. Like Velma Ray and her husband, Daniels and his wife frequented the segregated mess hall. While by all accounts "the food was good, and plenty of it," Daniels' recollection that fights frequently broke out hints at certain challenges.[38] The occurrence of one such altercation stood out in Daniels' mind decades later, because another man jumped up on a table "and threw a cup at the wall and almost hit my wife," an act for which Daniels took offense and threatened retaliation with a jack knife before security guards arrived to put an end to it.[39] That other kinds of violence were a threat remained on Velma Ray's mind. When Daniels noted that "long as you raise your hand up, they'd bring you more," he referred specifically to women like Velma Ray, who worked as servers.

Figure 4.5 Waitresses serving drinks to customers of a segregated beer
hall at Camp Hanford. Courtesy of the Department of Energy's Hanford
Collection.

To deal with these and other challenges, Ray relied on her faith. All
of the women interviewed expressed in some form or another the strong
presence that religion and faith had in their lives. The church, in particular, became a significant site of community ties and belonging for
African American residents, as well as an important staging ground for
protesting inequalities. Viewed in context of the very real segregation
and discrimination that existed in the Tri-Cities, the church also provides a lens through which to view the conflicted experiences of African
Americans who, on the one hand, detested unequal treatment and dis-
parate conditions, but on the other, valued the opportunities available
for employment and education. It left many struggling to reconcile the
tension between having faced overt discrimination, and resenting it, but
having also found valuable opportunities, for which they were grateful.
If none articulated clearly a sense of complicity in having participated
in such structures without personally challenging them, all expressed an
acute awareness of the much larger structures of racial discrimination that
had to be dismantled on a broad scale in order to finally effect meaning-

ful change. At least implicitly, most understood that to do so required education—something that, whatever poor housing conditions and lack of certain amenities persisted in the Tri-Cities, was vastly more available there than in the South.

Many found solace and guidance in the church, which became an important site of both communities, and later, organized resistance to persistent discrimination in the Tri-Cities. Many African American residents maintained close ties to churches in Pasco, at least one of which—Morning Star Baptist Church—was a "sister church" to a congregation that residents had belonged to in Texas. Many traditions, including food traditions, came west with residents, as did Juneteenth celebrations, which Vanessa Moore aptly described as "a tradition and celebration of what your ancestors did and went through so you could be who you are." Moore also recalled that "church became an event in itself," beginning in Texas, where people "came into town from the fields to visit all afternoon"—a tradition that was imitated to a large degree in Pasco, where African American residents of the Tri-Cities came together for services each Sunday afternoon.[40]

Figure 4.6 Vanessa Moore. Courtesy of the Hanford History Project.

Church networks, in fact, may have played a central role in drawing some residents to the area in the first place. Rhonda Rambo noted that her parents came to the Tri-Cities because "they heard the good news" about not only jobs and a "big opportunity for Black families to come raise families in a safe environment and make a decent living," but there was a support network that included church fellowship; her mother "had her children in church 3 to 4 times a week and twice on Sunday."[41] Jeanette Sparks, who became a reverend herself, recalled church being a central part of life growing up; Emma Peoples noted that "in my life it was always the center."[42]

Acknowledgement that the racial configuration of the Tri-Cities was problematic but still in many respects preferable to other places provides insight into the complications of race and memory. Not all of those who came to the Tri-Cities during and after the war chose to stay, but few ever went back to the South. If they did leave, they moved on to cities in the American West, like Seattle or Portland. Taken by her parents to visit Texas in the 1960s, Vanessa Moore recalled that "it's not like Richland." The experience felt dangerous; it came with strict rules: get off the sidewalk; don't look people in the eye; speak only to certain people. Warned by her parents that "you can't act the way you do in Richland because it would not be accepted," Moore "saw why people wanted to leave."[43] Segregation and discrimination in the Tri-Cities, while it did happen, was more subtle and covert, such as a time when Moore recalled being refused service at a local restaurant. Such passive-aggressive acts of rejection were in and of themselves problematic and should not be discounted. The fact that one form of discrimination came with less overt threats of violence does not excuse the racism that did exist, but it did give the women interviewed a nuanced perspective of their conditions in the Tri-Cities in relation to what might have been possible in other places.

Even if they had not grown up in the Jim Crow South, the women interviewed were acutely aware of the dire conditions—poverty, threats of physical harm, fear—that characterized life for African Americans there. If they had not witnessed it first-hand, they had certainly been made aware of it by parents and grandparents. These legacies, like others, ran deep and left indelible traces on the people that lived through them. This instilled knowledge may explain some of the ambivalent reactions of interviewees for the Hanford History Project to the discrimination that existed in the Tri-Cities. The world migrants chose to leave behind, and the decision to migrate at all, had indeed "shaped the lives of their descendants" in significant ways.[44] The danger and violence that accompanied life in the South left emotional scars so deep they imprinted that perspective on the generations of children and grandchildren who were born in the American West. The decision to leave, in and of itself a potentially dangerous act, shaped "the life chances of children," who came of age instilled with the knowledge that parents and grandparents had sacrificed ties to their birthplaces to give them options beyond the cotton fields. In a system built on slavery, which by definition severed social and familial connections at the whims of those in control, it was not a small act of agency to choose uprooting from a place—often the only sense of connection to distant ancestors a family had—in order to better one's condition.

Thus, Rose Allen could speak openly of her resentment toward discrimination that existed in Kennewick, recalling that "I was told not to go there after dark, so I wouldn't go there in the daylight neither," while simultaneously speaking positively of her overall experience in the Tri-Cities.[45] Having the freedom to *choose* not to go to Kennewick, after all, was also an act of agency. As a 12-year-old traveling on a bus from Michigan to Little Rock, Arkansas, Allen had seen how racial treatment fluctuated based on location. The bus leaving Michigan was not segregated, "but when it hit the Mason-Dixon Line," Allen recalled, "the driver said 'y'all niggers get to the back of the bus.'" Segregated bussing, at least, had been defeated in the Tri-Cities in 1943. Of course, "there were problems" that persisted, as Allen readily admitted, "but there were more opportunities also." As a result, "most of 'em that came here stayed," and few ever returned to the South.[46] As millions discovered during the Great Migration, certain forms of racism and discrimination persisted at a national level and would require more than just recognition of wartime sacrifice and service to dismantle; they would require that African Americans actively demand the right to be regarded as equal, and it would be a fitful road to travel.

The women who migrated to Hanford during the 1940s and 1950s may not have known the scope of the movement in which they were involved. The Great Migration of more than six million Black southerners in the mid-twentieth century left "its imprint everywhere in urban life," reconfiguring cities, giving rise to a Black middle class, and propelling what eventually developed into the "civil rights revolutions of the 1960s."[47] Whether they knew it or not, the women interviewed for the Hanford History Project who came of age in the 1960s and 1970s had their experiences profoundly shaped by these processes in important ways. They represented a much larger pattern of migration, demands for equality that proceeded unevenly and sometimes with delayed results, and hard-fought victories for the right to advancement in educational, housing, and workplace opportunities. At the core of these victories was education, and most recognized its centrality to a "better condition," in any form.

Most of the women interviewed for the Hanford History Project acknowledged a deeply engrained sense of understanding that the availability of education in the Tri-Cities was a significant factor for African American families. Many of the residents who came to the Tri-Cities as adults had no opportunity to complete even grade school in Texas, because of the harsh necessities of farm work. Even well after World War II, education remained "a rare luxury for Blacks in the rural South," caught in an economy that cycled around sharecropping. Those children lucky enough to attend school could do so "only after the cotton crop was picked," which effectively limited educational opportunities to the winter months. Thus, few could hope to get beyond an elementary or middle school education.[48] In the Tri-Cities, for all its imperfections, the possibility existed of breaking the cycle that kept Blacks intentionally uneducated.

It was not insignificant that Vanessa Moore's uncle, Willie Daniels, who was literate and had been a teacher in Texas, was in a position to help illiterate friends and family members when they arrived. Moore's father used his own education to eventually obtain better jobs, but she also recalled him stating that "I want to stay ahead of all you kids so I can help you with your school work."[49] Emma Peoples had finished high school in Texas before coming to the Tri-Cities, and recalled that "there was a rule in our house that you didn't miss school."[50] Peoples also noted that all the schools she attended in Texas were segregated. Tri-Cities schools were integrated, which afforded opportunities but also posed challenges. Even if one acknowledged the intrinsic value of an education, there was no opportunity to let down defenses on any side. Rhonda Rambo recalled that during junior high school she was teased for spending time with white friends, and felt immense social pressure to make Black friends; she thus "fit in" well with her peers on one hand, but on the other had to endure being referred to as "Oreo," "privileged," "whitewashed," and told "you think you're better because you live on the 'white' side" of town.[51] There was no space where reminders of race did not intrude on her experience.

Acceptance was far more complicated than mere inclusion or rejection; it could create profoundly uncomfortable situations. While Vanessa Moore recalled that interracial dating was "not openly discouraged" by the time she reached high school age in the 1970s, it was "understood it was not done." Moore learned a challenging lesson in such expectations after innocently attending her senior prom with a white male friend, with whom she wanted nothing more than friendship. His response to her insistence on maintaining that boundary was to ask, upset, "do you know how many friends I lost because of you?" Moore recalled on the one hand that "people looked at me as an individual, not a Black person," but also noted that some acquaintances were prone to make comments about Blacks followed by qualifiers like "not *you*, you're Vanessa."[52] Still, education proved an ongoing process for many African American residents, and some took the chance at continuing education after their children had grown up. Legacies of using education to attain a better condition were visibly on display in the achievements of Rose Allen, who was forty-five years old when she earned her college degree and a teaching certificate. She used the opportunity to go to work as a home visitor for local school children, of all races—a profound step forward in the chain of education and advancement in several respects.

Vanessa Moore recalled that the divide between Richland and Pasco, even well into the 1960s and 1970s, was noticeable. Moore remembered that even as late as the 1960s and 1970s in Richland, "you knew you were going to be the only Black face in the class photo," and as far as racial prejudice was concerned, "it was there." When she was a child, Moore's parents lived first in Pasco while her father, CJ Mitchell, took night classes to become a chem-tech. When he was denied the right to purchase a home in Richland, he became a realtor, and thus became acquainted firsthand with the prejudice, "redlining," and systematic efforts to prevent African Americans from moving out of East Pasco.[53] Determined that his children would have a "different experience" and better educational opportunities, Mitchell persisted, and took advantage of an open housing ordinance passed by the Richland Human Rights Commission in 1968.[54]

CJ Mitchell's concerns with the educational opportunities afforded to his children were based on more than principle. By 1965, with segregated facilities persistent in Pasco (and no Blacks enrolled in Kennewick schools), reportedly "only 30 percent of Blacks completed high school while over 80 percent of whites had a high school diploma," at least part of this discrepancy a result of severely unequal facilities.[55] Moore's prospects of obtaining a decent education thus increased exponentially with her move to Richland; her father's insistence on securing these opportunities ultimately paid off. At the same time, she recalled discomfort and a distinctive tension among African American peers from Pasco, with whom she maintained relationships. There was an attitude of "you live in Richland, you think you're white," Moore recalled, and the feeling of being an outsider among those she had grown up with was "very hurtful."[56] There was no place to turn where someone did not feel emboldened to observe and comment on her identity, in other words; later, as an adult, Moore moved back to Pasco with her husband.

The matter of employment opportunities also existed uncomfortably side by side with the reality of persistent discrimination. Several of the women interviewed about their work at Hanford simultaneously acknowledged that racism created barriers while discounting its overall impact on their experiences. Racial discrimination existed, Vanessa Moore believed, at least in practice if not in formal rules, "because it's human nature to gravitate toward people who are like you."[57] Rose Allen similarly recalled that when she began working at Hanford, she experienced discrimination at first, "but eventually people were nice," and things tended to improve over time.[58] Emma Peoples went to work at the Hanford Site in order to be home when her teenaged children were out of school. While Peoples recalled having "good relations" with managers and insisted that she was treated "I thought, quite well," she also observed that there was very little socializing outside of work. "Business is one thing, friendships another," she noted, and while she did not know personally of other African Americans working at the site at the time, she considered being exposed to many different kinds of people one benefit of the job. "I can't think of anything I would trade," she concluded.[59] Reading between the lines, most of the women interviewed for the Hanford History Project acknowledged their deep understanding that it was not merely a matter of changing the opinions of their immediate peers, but much larger systemic processes of race and belonging; one could not immediately resolve the other, but both improved little by little over time, and with much patience on the part of those who acted to change them, in individual and collective ways.

In some ways, perhaps, the secrecy expected from those who worked at Hanford spilled over into discussions regarding matters of race, which were similarly uncomfortable—an extension of time and place. "He didn't talk much about it," Rhonda Rambo recalled of her father, who came from East Texas to work at Hanford in the early 1950s, and soon became the first Black patrolman at the site.[60] "It was just in my opinion part of the job," Emma Peoples noted, adding that she never discussed her job with her husband, or visited him at work, even though their offices were in relatively close proximity.[61] Both these instances might have referred to the work itself or the environment that existed for African Americans.

As a result of all these collected experiences and conflicted emotions regarding the opportunities and challenges that characterized life in the Tri-Cities during these decades, most of the women interviewed expressed reticence to engage with the civil rights movement. Rose Allen "tried not to be involved," having heard of stories like the murder of Emmett Till and considering involvement "dangerous."[62] Vanessa Moore recalled viewing much of the legislation resulting from the civil rights movement as beneficial, and watching some parts of it on television, but noted that her parents declined active participation. "Mom and Dad were not the type to fill our heads with a lot of things that's gonna get you agitated" and would encourage their children to "consider the source and move on; it's not worth your energy" to get upset.[63] As with their decision to leave the South and in doing so becoming part of the Great Migration, Moore's parents' choice to shield her was also part of a larger pattern, sometimes unspoken, but never invisible and always deeply present.

Perhaps some of the reticence of these women to speak about engagement with the formal civil rights movement stemmed from their complicated legacies of their heritage, and to parents who "wanted to keep their children safe, but they didn't want to cripple them emotionally, or leave them paralyzed by fear."[64] Raised in a climate steeped with the racial violence of Southern race relations earlier in the century, many knew instinctively to fear the potential repercussions that might accompany crossing boundaries to demand better treatment. In a testament to how much this pervaded the lives of some, none of the women interviewed for the Hanford History Project had participated in formal civil rights demonstrations, though most admitted to having "heard about" demonstrations or watching them on the news.[65] The tension between wanting fair treatment and equal rights and fearing the process of demanding them ran deep.

Though its population declined, the Tri-Cities maintained a Black community in the decades following World War II. Nearly all Black residents remained relegated to a section of East Pasco, still lacking some basic amenities, until well into the 1960s. The first formal protest of the Civil Rights era in the Tri-Cities took place on a picket line in Kennewick in 1963.[66] In the wake of the Civil Rights Act of 1964 and a growing swell of protest across the country, African American residents working through their local chapter of the NAACP and Congress of Racial Equality (CORE) engaged local, state, and federal officials and demanded an end to Jim Crow conditions. Housing remained similarly substandard, with one survey noting that "the housing discrimination that occurred during the rapid growth in the area...remained in effect" long after.[67] Seeking better services and schools, an end to housing restrictions and police harassment, and improved employment opportunities, Black residents marched again in 1970, this time in Pasco. While not all African Americans who arrived in the Tri-Cities during the World War II years stayed, those who did eventually witnessed a decrease in systematic discrimination.[68]

In a footnote of rather poetic justice for African American migrants, the loss of Black residents emptied business districts and shuttered entire towns across the South. Kildare, Texas, became a casualty that never recovered from the mass exodus that occurred in the twentieth century. "Kildare doesn't exist anymore, really," a resident noted in 2017, admitting that even many Texans had no idea it was even on the map.[69] Kildare had always been small, but without the presence and labor of Black residents, it virtually vanished.

Many of the women interviewed for the Hanford History Project could probably relate to the summation Velma Ray gave of her experience adjusting to the area: "I thought I was fed up with Pasco, but you know it's a funny thing there is something about Pasco...when you come out here you may want to leave, but when you leave, you wants to come back."[70] The Tri-Cities were not a perfect Eden, but for many African American women who came to call the area home, the benefits of the decision to come to Washington far outweighed the hardships. Like Virginia Crippen, all came motivated by the desire to better their condition—and many did. Most could probably relate to the words of Rose Allen who concluded, "I was so glad to get out of Arkansas, every challenge I had I enjoyed it."[71]

Notes

1. Isabel Wilkinson, *The Warmth of Other Suns: The Epic Story of America's Great Migration* (New York: Random House, 2010), 9.

2. For more on migrants from the Louisiana Delta to Las Vegas, see Annelise Orleck, *Storming Caesar's Palace: How Black Mothers Fought Their Own War on Poverty*. Strikingly, nearly all of those interviewed for the Hanford History Project trace their roots to or near Kildare. Many noted family networks as a significant factor in their decision to move. Of the seven African American women interviewed for the Hanford History Project, three—Vanessa Moore, Emma Peoples, and Jeanette Sparks—either came directly from Kildare or had parents who did; Rhonda Rambo's parents came from Bivens, Texas, just six miles from Kildare. Virginia Crippen was born in Texas (exact location unknown). Rose Allen came from Little Rock, Arkansas, just 180 miles from Kildare.

3. Emma Peoples, Interview by Robert Franklin, Hanford History Project (HHP), May 2, 2018.

4. Robert Bauman, "Jim Crow in the Tri-Cities, 1943–1950," *Pacific Northwest Quarterly*, 96:3 (Summer 2005), 124.

5. Quintard Taylor, *In Search of the Racial Frontier: African Americans in the American West, 1528–1990* (New York: W. W. Norton & Company, 1998), 159.

6. Bauman, "Jim Crow in the Tri-Cities," 124–125.

7. Bauman, "'The Birmingham of Washington': Civil Rights and Black Power in the Tri-Cities," unpublished paper, n.d.

8. Quintard Taylor, *The Forging of a Black Community: Seattle's Central District from 1870 through the Civil Rights Era* (Seattle: University of Washington Press, 1994), 164–165.

9. Bauman, "Jim Crow in the Tri-Cities," 124–125.

10. Orleck, *Storming Caesar's Palace*, 27.

11. Ibid., 19.

12. Velma Ray, Interview by Vanessa Moore, Afro-American Community, Cultural and Educational Society (AACCES), October 6, 2014.

13. Rose Allen, Interview by Robert Franklin, HHP, January 12, 2018; Rhonda Rambo, Interview by Robert Franklin, HHP, March 23, 2018.

14. Ray Interview.

15. Peoples Interview.

16. Ray Interview.

17. Rhonda Rambo Interview.

18. Virginia Crippen, Interview by Vanessa Moore, AACCES, May 13, 2015.

19. Crippen Interview; Bauman, "Jim Crow in the Tri-Cities," 126.

20. Orleck, *Storming Caesar's Palace*, 41.

21. Crippen Interview.

22. Jeanette Sparks, Interview by Vanessa Moore, AACCES, May 5, 2015.

23. Crippen Interview.

24. Bauman, "Jim Crow in the Tri-Cities," 125–126.

25. Crippen Interview.

26. Ibid.

27. Peoples Interview.

28. Sparks Interview.

29. Bauman, "Jim Crow in the Tri-Cities," 126.

30. Bauman, "Birmingham of Washington."

31. Sparks Interview.

32. Allen Interview.

33. Bryan Rambo, Interview by Robert Franklin, HHP, March 23, 2018.

34. Bauman, "Jim Crow in the Tri-Cities," 129; Virginia Crippen Interview. Crippen noted the presence of one other beauty shop, owned by an unnamed woman and her husband, but the couple left for California before it was completed.

35. Crippen Interview.

36. Rambo Interview.

37. Willie Daniels, interview quoted in S. L. Sanger, ed., *Working on the Bomb: An Oral History of WWII Hanford* (Portland: Portland State University Continuing Education Press, 1995), 116–117.

38. Daniels, in *Working on the Bomb*, 116.

39. Ibid.

40. Vanessa Moore, Interview by Robert Franklin, HHP.

41. Rhonda Rambo Interview.

42. Peoples Interview.

43. Moore Interview.

44. Wilkerson, *Warmth of Other Suns*, 13.

45. Allen Interview.

46. Ibid.

47. Wilkerson, *Warmth of Other Suns*, 9–10.

48. Orleck, *Storming Caesar's Palace*, 17.

49. Moore Interview.

50. Peoples Interview.

51. Rhonda Rambo Interview.

52. Moore Interview.

53. Ibid.

54. Bauman, "Birmingham of Washington." See also, CJ Mitchell, Interview by Robert Bauman, Hanford History Project, October 31; 2013.

55. David Arthur Sever, "Comparison of Negro and White Attitudes in a Washington Community," Unpublished Master's Thesis, Washington State University, 1967, cited in Bauman, "The Birmingham of Washington."

56. Moore Interview.

57. Ibid.

58. Allen Interview.

59. Peoples Interview.

60. Rhonda Rambo Interview.

61. Peoples Interview.

62. Allen Interview.

63. Moore Interview.

64. Orleck, *Storming Caesar's Palace*, 20.

65. Rhonda Rambo Interview; Moore Interview.

66. Bauman, "Birmingham of Washington."

67. Ibid.

68. Ibid. Also see Chapter 6 in this volume.

69. Neil Abeles, "Woman Aims to Put Kildare on the Map," *Texarkana* (Arkansas) *Gazette*, December 6, 2017.

70. Ray Interview.

71. Allen Interview.

CHAPTER FIVE

"The Birmingham of Washington"
Civil Rights and Black Power in the Tri-Cities

Robert Bauman and Robert Franklin

On an unusually hot spring day in 1963, three months before the March on Washington, a line of demonstrators, picket signs in hand, sweat glistening on their brows, marched through the heat in the streets of a downtown area demanding an end to racial segregation. Several years later in July of 1970, on another hot day, again, a line of protestors marched through a downtown carrying picket signs, vocalizing their concerns. This time their signs demanded racial justice, a call for an economic boycott, and Black Power. Likely assumptions would be that the first scene happened in a city in the American South—Birmingham or Selma, perhaps Memphis—and that the second scene happened in a major city in the American North—Detroit, New York, Chicago, or on the coast, perhaps in Los Angeles. Those assumptions would be incorrect. These scenes took place not in the Deep South, but in the Pacific Northwest. And they did not take place in the major urban centers of Seattle or Portland, but in Kennewick and Pasco, Washington. How was it that Kennewick was experiencing a civil rights movement of its own, prior to the March on Washington and at the same time events in Birmingham were making national headlines? And how was it that Pasco experienced events that many would associate with Black Power at the same time the Black Panther Party was making national headlines? This chapter demonstrates that from the early Cold War years through the 1960s, Black residents of the Tri-Cities and in the Pacific Northwest consistently challenged the system of segregation that had been instilled during the war. These challenges culminated in marches and demonstrations that

135

eventually led to the breakdown of Jim Crow and the social, cultural, and economic empowerment of African Americans in the Tri-Cities.

As noted in the previous chapter, in the early 1950s, the Tri-Cities region was highly segregated in all aspects of life. That began to change in 1954 and 1955. Inspired by the *Brown v. Board of Education of Topeka* decision by the United States Supreme Court and the Montgomery Bus Boycott, Black Tri-Citians revived their chapter of the NAACP. This time it was here to stay.

The local chapter of the NAACP and other civil rights organizations grew slowly over time yet accomplished little in terms of civil rights until 1963.

Figure 5.1 Downtown Kennewick protest. Courtesy of the Franklin County Historical Society and Museum.

According to Dallas Barnes, a long-time Tri-Cities resident and civil rights activist, "Kennewick was known as an all-white town where Blacks were not welcome."[1]

Figure 5.2 Dallas Barnes. Courtesy of the Hanford History Project.

While segregation was not codified at the Hanford Site, and in fact prohibited due to hiring provisions connected to federal defense contracts, segregation was de jure in Kennewick. Katie Barton experienced this firsthand. Barton moved to the North Richland Construction Camp in 1948 to work at the Hisman Cafeteria. Reflecting on her impressions of the Tri-Cities when she arrived, Barton drew an immediate contrast between the government project and Kennewick.

> The cafeteria, you could sit down and eat with people, they didn't have no signs, cause it was a government project. But in the towns, like Kennewick, that was just horrible; they didn't even want no Black people in Kennewick. You couldn't buy a house there; you couldn't go to the movies there; they wouldn't put you in jail there...I had one friend, his name was Jimely Green. He got drunk in Kennewick and they tied him to a post on the corner of Washington and Kennewick Avenue and called the Pasco police and said 'come get your nigger because we don't put them in jail in Kennewick.'[2]

Thus, twenty years after the initial construction of Hanford and its concomitant system of segregation, Jim Crow remained a vital reality for African Americans in the Tri-Cities.

What became the largest civil rights march in the history of the city of Kennewick began simply enough. Reverend H.P. Hawkins, the president of the Tri-Cities branch of the NAACP, planned a march to celebrate the anniversary of the *Brown v. Board of Education* U.S. Supreme Court decision that had declared segregated schools unconstitutional. He specifically told a local newspaper reporter that the demonstrators "would not stress the Kennewick racial situation."[3]

Hawkins received angry calls from NAACP membership when the headline of *Tri-City Herald* article on May 9, 1963, said "NAACP Leader Finds Kennewick Treatment Fine." Disappointed at what he believed was a misrepresentation of his comments, Hawkins objected to that headline and the tone of the article and fired off a missive to the newspaper's editor. In his letter, he noted that he had gone "to great lengths to enumerate to the reporter some of the charges of police brutality, discrimination in housing, and other unfair and unChristian treatment of Negroes…[by] the people of Kennewick." He told the editor, that while "Negroes get along very well in Kennewick as workers (when they get a job) and as shoppers (except when they are shopping for a home)…People are saying that Kennewick is worse than Birmingham, for Negroes CAN LIVE in Birmingham."[4]

One of these people was Wallace (Wally) Webster, an Alabama native who moved to Pasco in 1962 and later became the president of the Tri-Cities chapter of the Congress of Racial Equality (CORE). Webster knew segregation, growing up just outside of Mobile and marching with Dr. Martin Luther King Jr. in Alabama before moving to Pasco. Webster said that Kennewick was locally referred to "as the sundown town. You could be there during the day, but by sundown you had to be out. It was for all

Figure 5.3 Wally Webster.
Courtesy of the Hanford
History Project.

practical purposes, segregated. Just like Birmingham. It didn't even have an East Pasco. It was white almost 100 percent all over."[5]

Hawkins was partially correct in his statement that Blacks were welcome to shop in Kennewick, but it was their money that white merchants wanted, not their presence. Some merchants prohibited Black shoppers from trying on clothes, claiming that they may not be able to sell the item to a white buyer if it was known the garment had previously been tried on by a Black shopper. Dallas Barnes noted the tension between mostly-Black East Pasco and all-white Kennewick: "There's a difference between being invited somewhere and feeling welcomed. Well, in the Black community, you are actually welcome; in the white community you might have been invited to spend your money, but just don't stay too long. And don't seek to be a part of that community."[6] On May 16, the Washington State Board Against Discrimination (WSBAD) held an all-day hearing in Kennewick. The chair of the board, Ken Macdonald, stated that the board members "heard again and again there is something in the air in Kennewick and…Negroes know they can't come and live here."[7] Among the charges brought to the board's attention that day was one that the Kennewick police department effectively carried out a "sundown ordinance" asking any Blacks who were in Kennewick after dark to leave. A Kennewick city councilman reported that in 1961 a policeman confided in him that the police chief had ordered his officers to apprehend any Blacks in Kennewick after dark. The day following the councilman's testimony to WSBAD the Kennewick City Council held a secret meeting at which the councilman was reprimanded and told to stop making such statements to WSBAD.[8]

Poor treatment of Blacks by the Kennewick police department and the existence of a "sundown ordinance" are constant and persuasive themes told by Black residents of the Tri-Cities. James Pruitt, who moved to Pasco in 1948 and later became a civil rights liaison between the Pasco Police Department and East Pasco recalled the hostility that African Americans faced in Kennewick.

PRUITT: There was no freedom to move in Kennewick. There was only one grocery store in the Tri-Cities at that time [that] stayed open after midnight. And if you go across the river to that store, the police were sitting out there somewhere. If you went anywhere like you was going downtown, they would stop you and tell you you was on the wrong side of the river. And you had to come back on this [Pasco] side.

INTERVIEWER: It was just that pervasive?

PRUITT: Yes, it was. No eating, no messing around in Kennewick. Period.[9]

As the railroad tracks that divided East Pasco from West Pasco served as a physical barrier that reinforced the residential opportunities of Black residents, the bridges over the Columbia River from Pasco to Kennewick were monitored corridors that separated "lily-white" Kennewick from Pasco. The existence of a "sundown" notice on the Pioneer Memorial Bridge (or Green Bridge as it was known locally due to its bright green paint) is something of local lore and mentioned by almost all interviewees. There is no definitive proof of the physical sign; no photographs or newspaper articles about the sign exist. But this is of little real importance—interviewees almost unanimously mention the sign's existence and the accompanying feelings of hostility on the part of Kennewick police and city leaders. Kennewick police routinely stopped Black motorists, especially young Black males, driving over the Green Bridge to question their presence in Kennewick. In the early 1970s, Rickie Robinson recalled, "I was driving in Kennewick in my car in the middle of the afternoon, and I was pulled over by the police. He wanted to know what I was doing in Kennewick…I was never on the police radar as somebody that they needed to keep an eye on. So I thought [it] was weird, that he would pull me over and ask me what I was doing in Kennewick at 3:00 in the [afternoon]."[10] The investigation that Robinson was subject to was a systemic practice designed to reinforce the sense that Black residents of the Tri-Cities did not belong in Kennewick.

Early Black residents who tried to circumvent the housing covenants were met with property violence and restrictions. In 1961, the daughter and son-in-law of Cornelius Walker inherited a house in Kennewick from friends of the family. While visiting Cornelius in Pasco, shortly after taking possession of the home, it burned to the ground. Arson was suspected but never proven. In 1964, the Slaughter family became the first Black family to rent a home in Kennewick as part of a targeted civil rights action by the Tri-Cities chapter of CORE. Earlier in 1963,

Figure 5.4 Pasco-Kennewick bridge. Courtesy of the Hanford History Project.

the Slaughter family had faced repeated refusals to rent after landlords learned that the family was Black. CORE member Nyla Brouns "went with Mary Slaughter to look at homes. She would pretend she was the one renting the house and get the landlord to say this would be fine. And then she would turn to Mary and say, 'okay, Mary, will this work for you?' And then the landlord would be trapped."[11] Later in 1965, Herb and Rendetta Jones moved to Kennewick. Within the first week of their residency, Herb's new Ford suffered cut tires and broken windows. The Joneses received threats by phone, mail, by notes left on their car, and even rocks hurled at their house doors. Rendetta worked for the telephone company in Pasco and at night Wally Webster and other CORE members took turns driving immediately behind her, escorting her from work in order to protect her against any attempts of physical violence. Interviewees mentioned these incidents specifically as reasons they felt unwelcome to live in Kennewick and why they felt it was important to march and demonstrate for civil rights.[12]

With "frustrations on the part of the…black community…high," two days after the WSBAD hearing, on May 18, 1963, a group of seventy-four demonstrators (an additional fifty marchers from Portland failed to show after their bus broke down en route to Kennewick) from various parts of the Pacific Northwest marched peacefully down Kennewick's hot, dusty streets. The marchers, led by Tacoma attorney and president of the NAACP state chapter Jack Tanner (it was Tanner who had labeled Kennewick the "Birmingham of Washington"—Tanner would later become a federal judge), paraded in the sunshine and oppressive heat carrying signs which read: "Why is Kennewick All White?," "Jim Crow is Dead, Bury Him in Kennewick," "End Segregated Housing—North and South," "I Can Scrub Your Floor, But Not Live Next Door," "I'm Just Looking for a Home," "Kennewick Racism Must Go," "Kennewick, Miss.???," and "Where are the Dogs?," in reference to what had happened earlier that month in Birmingham, Alabama. One local journalist described the scene: "crowds of several hundred persons watched from the shady side of Kennewick Avenue...At one point, young white men began making loud comments to marchers and plainclothesmen moved in and led them away." The march, which began at noon at the Kennewick Unitarian Church, lasted a few hours.[13]

Figure 5.5 Kennewick Protest. Courtesy of the Franklin County Historical Society and Museum.

Tanner led the march, with an unhappy Reverend Hawkins brooding behind him. While Hawkins was unhappy with segregation in Kennewick, he had planned the march to focus on honoring the *Brown* decision. He did not plan on it being a direct challenge to Jim Crow. In addition, as he saw it, Tanner had usurped his leadership role and authority. One reporter described the scene this way:

> This pair personified the division of sentiment among northwest Negroes over segregation and what to do about it. The placative Hawkins was mad at nobody, sought no demonstration, regarded Tanner as a brilliant colored man trying to push too far, too fast. It was no secret that the demonstration was bulled through by Tanner, who applied to the Rev. Hawkins that label so meaningful to the American Negro—Uncle Tom.[14]

Tanner's presence was the direct result of requests made by others in the NAACP's Pasco branch who were dissatisfied with Hawkins' leadership and approach to segregation and racial discrimination. Beth Hennings, education chair for the Pasco branch of the NAACP, had written to Tanner about the planned march and noted that Roy Thompson, president of the Unitarian Church in Kennewick, had volunteered to hold a meeting after the march. Hennings had declined the offer, noting that "they'd have to invite Mr. Hawkins and he would pray 'em to death."[15]

While she questioned Hawkins's leadership abilities, she was concerned about a lack of experienced leadership among the NAACP branch membership in general. She pleaded for Tanner's participation:

> I wish you could definitely be here on the 18th... Everyone here wants to help but no one wants to lead, because this will be the first time most have taken part in any demonstration. I realize that it would have a good effect on the branch if we COULD carry off a demonstration completely on our own, but there is also the possibility we will flub up somehow, and never be able to get another one going. We can do the sign-painting, and round up some people, but we need a general.[16]

Hennings, ever modest, downplayed her own leadership. The same day that she wrote to Tanner, she also penned a letter to Kennewick's political leadership directly challenging its omnipresent system of segregation.

> In tacitly accepting this as they are, you not only help to continue segregation in our country, but the city of Kennewick and its residents

thus shirk their share of a burden the city of Pasco should not have to bear alone. (The token number of Negroes employed and/or living in Richland barely affords it the claim that it is an integrated city.) Whatever the racial climate in the past, Kennewick now has the chance to prove to the entire country that it is being unjustly accused, that it actually welcomes Negroes as responsible employees, both of the city and of private firms, and as residents of the community. Until this takes place, suspicion and rumor will continue. Unfair as it may possibly seem, the burden of proof has to be on you. You alone can give the lie to 'you can scrub my floor, BUT NOT LIVE NEXT DOOR.'[17]

In 1963, few women embraced, or were allowed to accept, leadership roles in civil rights organizations that required them to be the public face of the organization. Instead, they tended to the behind-the-scenes planning and organizing, serving as bridge leaders connecting organizational leadership to the membership. Hennings seems to have been one of those "bridge leaders."[18]

Nyla Brouns was one also; an active CORE member, her daughter Kathy described her as one of "the working bees...[and] you don't have to be the leader; you just have to say 'I'll be the person to stuff the envelopes, or I'll be the person to get the poster board and paints the signs.'"[19] Kathy Brouns recalled a childhood with frequent CORE meetings at her house and that it was a family affair, "there was picketing, there would be rallies, and the kids would be making the signs. We'd have, in our basement there'd be all these posters hanging out, and us kids would be down there painting the signs that would say whatever they were." Nyla Brouns worked tirelessly to push the organizations she was involved in, the local Democratic Party, CORE, and Christ the King (a Catholic church in Richland) to embrace civil rights, sometimes fighting with the church priest over what she perceived as a non-committal stance towards civil rights (including women's liberation)—to the point where the Brounses were labeled as troublemakers. Arrest, conflict, and controversy did not deter Nyla Brouns—she was picked up for unauthorized protest for picketing a white supremacist event in Richland—and at one point she tried, unsuccessfully, to join the Black Panther Party.[20] Overall, Nyla and other women like Shirley Miller, a fellow CORE member who worked to desegregate the Tri-Cities, played crucial roles as fierce and loyal "worker bees" as well as bridge leaders.

Beth Hennings served as one of the key women bridge leaders for civil rights organizations in the Tri-Cities. She did not need to try too hard to convince Tanner about the importance of challenging segregation in Kennewick or of the need for his leadership. The following day at the NAACP Northwest Region conference in Pasco, Tanner, who was residing as president of the conference, told the delegates about the racial situation in the Tri-Cities. "All the results of segregation and discrimination exist in the area," Tanner informed the delegates. "This is especially true concerning housing, employment, and educational facilities. Although perhaps minor gains have been made in the Tri-Cities, we in the NAACP believe there must be continuing and aggressive demands made upon public officials as well as private individuals to improve conditions of Negro people in the area." Tri-Cities representatives to the conference reported that improvements toward integration were being made in Pasco, particularly in the area of school desegregation, but those developments were limited. In answering a delegate's questions about why more had not been accomplished in the Tri-Cities, Tanner argued that the area lacked strong Black leadership "because of a lack of professional Negro people such as doctors, lawyers, and educators."[21] Tanner's answer seemed to support Henning's letter to him that suggested a lack of seasoned, tested, and middle-class leadership among African Americans in the Tri-Cities.

Indeed, Tanner had backed up his conference speech by writing a letter to Governor Albert Rosellini asking for an investigation into Kennewick's segregation practices. Rosellini contacted the WSBAD, the same group that had visited Kennewick in 1950. The board quickly decided that their next meeting would be in Kennewick on May 16. Tanner's persistence had led to WSBAD's investigation.[22]

Tanner determined to pursue civil rights from the federal government as well as the state. He asked Carl Maxey, representative of the U.S. Civil Rights Commission from Spokane, to have the commission investigate segregation in Kennewick. Maxey followed through on Tanner's request and convinced the Washington Advisory Committee of the U.S. Civil Rights Commission to investigate Tanner's claims. It was in

Tanner's request to Maxey that he labeled Kennewick the "Birmingham of Washington."[23]

While the sobriquet undoubtedly exaggerated the situation in order to gain more publicity for the march, segregation remained entrenched in Kennewick in most aspects of life. The WSBAD's report confirmed that. Two months after the civil rights march in Kennewick, the WSBAD issued an eleven-page report documenting incidents of segregation and discrimination in Kennewick and making fifteen recommendations to provide equal opportunity for African Americans in the areas of employment, housing, and public accommodations. Among the evidence of discrimination investigated by the board was the fact that no African Americans lived in Kennewick (population 14,244) yet approximately 2,000 African Americans resided in East Pasco, only three miles across the river. Nor were any African Americans employed in any government jobs in Kennewick. In fact, only six African Americans were employed in Kennewick at all—one as a cook and the others as auto mechanics. All of them lived across the river in East Pasco.[24]

In addition, the board discovered de facto segregation in Kennewick schools and housing. The Sunnyslope Homes project, administered by the Kennewick Housing Authority, only allowed residents who lived in Benton County within a five-mile radius of Kennewick for three months or were employed by a company doing business in Kennewick, thus effectively excluding African Americans. An earlier survey by the *Tri-City Herald* presented this situation to E.C. Smith, executive director of Sunnyslope Homes, who noted there were some nonwhites living in the project but he was not "smart enough to tell if they are Negroes or Mexicans."[25] When WSBAD investigators asked the vice chairman of the Kennewick Housing Authority to appear before the WSBAD board to answer questions about the agency's policies and practices he refused. Instead, he told the investigator, "'I'm not going to get mixed up in any damned nigger problem.'"[26]

The fifteen WSBAD recommendations attempted to remedy these inequities. The board recommended that the city of Kennewick form an interracial Human Relations Commission to ensure equal opportunity in employment, housing, and public services; that the Kennewick Housing Authority allow African Americans to live in its developments; that the city create fair employment policies to promote job opportunities for Black residents; that the state attorney general investigate the existence of gentleman's agreements between realtors, lenders, and builders that restricted housing available to African Americans; and that the director of the state licenses department should investigate to determine if discrimination was being practiced by real estate brokers or salesmen.[27]

By 1965, the executive secretary of WSBAD, Randolph W. Carter, believed that some progress had been made in the racial climate in the Tri-Cities. Carter pointed to the employment of African Americans at retail stores in Pasco—none had been employed in Pasco stores prior to 1963. Discrimination in the retail sector had been pervasive in the white-owned businesses of majority-Black East Pasco. Both East Side Market and Slip's Firestone were located in East Pasco and both had refused to hire Black workers until pressure by the East Pasco community forced both owners to sell their stores to new owners amenable to hiring Black workers.[28] In 1965 the Pasco Safeway hired its first two African American checkout clerks. Ellenor Moore was the second clerk hired and while she was treated well by management, it was the Safeway patrons who took time to accept the situation: "I would say the first two weeks I was in there, they would line up in the other check stand...[and] it took people about two weeks to realize that, okay, it doesn't make sense for me to stand over here in this line when I can go on through [my] check stand." WSBAD staff believed the changes were due in part to the efforts of African American ministers who contacted store owners to hire young Blacks, and because of national developments in the civil rights movement.[29] Importantly, activism by African Americans had led to the WSBAD report and continued action was ensuring the implementation of some of its recommendations.

Developments later that summer in Kennewick seemed to support Carter's statements. On August 3, three days before President Lyndon B. Johnson signed the Voting Rights Act, at the urging of local CORE members and the Kennewick Democratic Women's Club, the Kennewick City Council passed a resolution creating a Human Relations Commission. The resolution declared, "As public policy for Kennewick the equal rights for all citizens and peoples to housing, public education, employment and advancement, community services and facilities, participation

in public affairs and government, and all other aspects of community life."
WSBAD's chairman, Kenneth McDonald, declared that the resolution
was "the most complete and affirmative declaration of this kind I have
ever heard." McDonald planned to take the resolution to show President
Johnson as "an outstanding example of community cooperation."[30]

Despite those improvements, the Tri-Cities remained a difficult place
for Blacks to live. In 1966, the Executive Secretary of WSBAD, Alfred E.
Cowles, argued that the living conditions for African Americans in East
Pasco were among the worst in the country. Indeed, East Pasco residents
suffered neglect through a lack of paved streets and streetlights, and a
persistent refusal by the city from the 1940s through the mid-1960s to
extend city sewer lines to the community. Aubrey Johnson lived in East
Pasco with an outhouse until 1956, and his family had to dig their own
waterline from the street, which "was just a faucet and you go and turn it
on, and it was cold water and then you boil your water."[31] Another East
Pasco resident, Vanis Daniels, remembered "we had no streets, we had
no street lights, you had no sewer. The only thing we had was running
water. You had enough electricity, 100 amps to have lights in the house.
We had oil heat, we had a woodstove…[and] my dad would buy wood
and of course my mom was accustomed to cooking on a woodstove
anyways because in Texas that's what she had."[32] In the 1960s, Pasco
had the fourth largest Black community in Washington behind Seattle,
Tacoma, and Spokane, and its Black residents were barred from using
essential city services. James Pruitt recalled that when the city of Pasco
was faced with the prospect of integrating the Memorial Swimming Pool,
they chose to fill the pool with concrete rather than let Black children
into the pool.[33] Explaining that he did not "want to see another Watts
area here," Cowles argued that the situation in Pasco was "acute" and
East Pasco was "a blighted area" due to substandard buildings, a lack of
sidewalks, and garbage in the streets. While Cowles praised Pasco city
leaders for creating a human rights commission, clearly, many of the
housing, employment, and living conditions that had plagued African
Americans in East Pasco during World War II still permeated the area.[34]

For instance, until 1965, Black children who were of elementary school
age in Pasco attended Whittier Elementary, a segregated school with
inferior facilities located in East Pasco. In response to pressure from civil

rights organizations in the Tri-Cities, notably CORE, to desegregate its schools and in further response to the school desegregation enforcement language of the Civil Rights Act of 1964, city officials closed the East Pasco elementary school in 1965. Soon after, they began bussing Black students to integrated schools.[35]

Clarence Alford moved to Pasco to take a job as a teacher after being specifically recruited by the superintendent of the Pasco School District to diversify the teaching staff, which until the late 1960s was almost exclusively white. The closure of Whittier Elementary was part of a desegregation push in the Pasco School district and former Whittier students were "bussed to schools...located in an area where almost no Blacks lived [and] with that the kids took with them their knowledge that background, their likes, their dislikes, their misunderstandings and there was some racial problems that occurred in their schools."[36] For Wally Webster, segregated educational facilities like Whitter Elementary represented the kind of inferior education he had received in Alabama. Upon arriving in Pasco in 1962, Webster tried to enroll in Columbia Basin College (CBC) where he was told his education "was not up to par" because he was educated in the South, and as president of CORE, he began to suspect that children in East Pasco may be stigmatized in the same way:

> I went to a segregated school [and] when I went to CBC, they told me that I was not up to par with my education. Something said to me that these kids are probably not up to par, either. Well, I know that a few of the parents were comfortable sending their kids to Whittier because it was close to home [and] they were afraid if—because I was advocating to close the school down...it would drop the property value, also. But I was able to prevail in the thought and we pressed upon the school board, we marched, we demonstrated with enough parents, and they made the decision to close Whittier School.

Wally Webster did eventually attend CBC, graduating with degrees in business and applied science, going on to achieve a master's degree. With this education, he was able to create a successful banking career in Seattle.[37] Outside of the acute problems with de facto segregation at Whittier Elementary, Black school-age children faced educational barriers ranging from a lack of Black role models to active stigmatization of Black students. Bessie May Williams-Fields grew up in East Pasco, graduating from Pasco High School in 1958. Williams-Fields believed that she "did not have a lot of support; I didn't have a lot of encouragement in terms of what I should do with my mind. I was always told that I had good dexterity, which I was real good in my fingers, and I was encouraged to be a beautician."[38] Williams-Fields did not let this lack of encouragement stymie her potential; she later earned a doctorate in educational administration. By 1968, various workforce programs had opened up limited jobs at Hanford and certain trades, but college was still seen as too aspirational for Black students. Aubrey Johnson couldn't recall hearing about going to college; "it was try to go to high school and get a high school diploma so that you can go and get a job working in various work forces out here in the area...there was no Black people [here] with a higher education."[39]

Figure 5.6 Aubrey Johnson.
Courtesy of the Hanford
History Project.

African Americans in Pasco faced other barriers in addition to those in education. A 1965 master's thesis by a Washington State University sociology student surveyed Pasco and found many of the same conditions and attitudes that his predecessors had found almost twenty years earlier. The student found Blacks received much less schooling than whites—only 30 percent of Blacks completed high school while over 80 percent of whites had a high school diploma. Part of this educational discrepancy had to do with unequal facilities like Whittier Elementary.[40]

The student's survey also found that living conditions had not improved greatly for Blacks since the late 1940s. In 1965, Blacks were more dissatisfied than whites with economic opportunity, police, sanitation, streets, recreational facilities, medical facilities, and schools. While 44 percent of Blacks believed the police department performance was fair to very good, 65 percent of whites felt the same way. Only 26 percent of Blacks, compared to 73 percent of whites, rated adult recreational facilities as fair to very good, and only 34 percent of Blacks, compared to 70 percent of whites, rated youth recreational facilities as fair to very good. Finally, over twice as many (24 percent of Blacks, vs. 11 percent of whites) viewed city government as poor or very poor compared to whites. These responses were undoubtedly rooted in realities. While the city had made several recent improvements in much of Pasco, East Pasco had been ignored.[41]

Table 5.1 Quality of Police Department Performance

	Good or very good	Fair	Poor or very poor
Black responses	34%	10%	36%
White responses	37%	28%	25%

Table 5.2 Quality of Adult Recreational Facilities

	Good or very good	Fair	Poor or very poor
Black responses	10%	16%	74%
White responses	42%	31%	27%

Table 5.3 Quality of Youth Recreational Facilities

	Good or very good	Fair	Poor or very poor
Black responses	16%	18%	66%
White responses	43%	27%	30%

While many conditions and attitudes remained similar to twenty years earlier, some things in Pasco had begun to change. Blacks and whites were interacting at a slightly higher rate. In 1965, 16 percent of whites responded that they had contact with Blacks in organizations (PTA, churches, unions, etc.) compared to 3 percent in 1948. Blacks responded with a higher rate of interaction—22 percent in 1965 compared to 0 percent in 1948. In 1948, only 32 percent of whites believed segregation existed in Pasco, despite abundant signs of Jim Crow. By 1965, 52 percent of white survey respondents acknowledged that segregation was a fact of life in Pasco. In 1948, less than half (48 percent) of survey respondents believed that segregation was opposed to principles of American democracy; by 1965 almost 80 percent of white respondents answered affirmatively to the same question. Efforts by African Americans and local civil rights organizations in the Tri-Cities and the influence of the national civil rights movement had obviously made some inroads regarding the attitudes of at least some white Pasco residents.[42]

The conclusions drawn from the survey, though, were decidedly mixed. Due to the results of the survey, the student rightfully concluded that African Americans in Pasco had "not made progress toward being accepted by the community of Pasco. The housing discrimination that occurred during the rapid growth in the area has still remained in effect." While arguing that "Negro and white attitudes toward each other have changed considerably in Pasco during the last seventeen years," the study also concluded, "Negroes still feel the effects of discrimination and segregation."[43]

Many of the changes in Pasco were the direct result of the actions by organizations like CORE, the NAACP, and the East Pasco Improvement Association (EPIA). In fact, Cowles considered the Tri-City chapter of CORE "one of the most militant and aggressive organizations in the state." The Tri-Cities CORE chapter was a real collaboration between white civil rights allies in Richland like the Brouns and Millers, and dedicated Black civil rights leaders in Pasco like Wally Webster, Jim Pruitt, and Dallas Barnes, to name a few. Wally Webster and Dallas Barnes were quick to point out the abilities of the "white people of quote-unquote high stature with very high moral commitments who gave their time and talents and financial resources to bring about change."[44] These organizations were inspired by national civil rights activities, but focused on issues that affected Blacks locally—primarily all types of segregation—from housing to schools to public places.[45]

Dallas Barnes went to work for US Testing at Hanford as a result of civil rights legislation in the mid-1960s that opened up jobs in federal projects for African Americans. Barnes was part of a new generation of Black Hanford workers who had an "inside job" (as opposed to unskilled labor jobs that occurred outside) with equal pay to his white counterparts. However, equal pay did not mean equal respect. Barnes remembered a conversation with his boss where he was praised for his scientific talent but realized a glass ceiling in terms of advancement in the company—that he would be good at sales "but we can't do that. Because white folks won't buy from you, your product is marketable; you're not."[46] Although Barnes felt a good deal of support from his employer to expand his scientific career, he eventually left US Testing to join the Community Action Committee and the War on Poverty, for in his own words: "The calling for social involvement was a much louder call. You can't have kids out there taking a beating while you're sitting in a lab titrating some damn sample."[47]

The Tri-Cities' progress on civil rights throughout the rest of the 1960s continued with mixed results. Segregated housing continued to be a reality for many African Americans in the Tri-Cities, particularly in Kennewick, despite the resolution creating the Human Relations Commission. In fact, a state report released in 1968 on population by races in Washington noted, "Kennewick... is conspicuous by the absence of Negroes."[48] In addition, Black residents in the Tri-Cities continued to face discrimination by local police and employers, and few to no Blacks were represented in city or local government. African Americans, though, would organize other protests, demonstrations, and boycotts into the 1970s to challenge that discrimination.[49]

At the Hanford Site the contractors that served the Atomic Energy Commission made significant efforts to increase diversification in their workforces, bringing in educated Black professionals as opposed to earlier migrations of lower-skilled workers. Dan Carter (no relation to Randolph) was one of the new waves of migrants. With a bachelor's degree in chemistry from Southern University, Carter was recruited by General Electric in early 1964 as an analytical chemist to work in Hanford's 300 Area, a fuel fabrication and research area of the site. John Abercrombie was another recruit, hired in 1967 by Isochem to work as a chemist at PUREX (the Plutonium Uranium Extraction Plant) in the Hanford 200 Area. Abercrombie was recruited as a graduate from Livingstone College in North Carolina, a historically Black college and university (HBCU), and in Richland he faced barriers in renting a home as an African American.

> We would see an ad for a house, we'd call, 'oh you're the first person to call!' And, 'we'll meet you there in thirty minutes!' And we get there [and] you know, 'somebody just pulled up fifteen minutes ago and rented the house. Sorry about that.' I even had one gentleman tell me that I'd go bankrupt if I rented the house, buying furniture. [He] ended up working for me a while later, and I never mentioned it to him.[50]

All of those interviewed who came to work at Hanford after 1964 were hired in to skilled, technical, or professional jobs that were de facto off-limits to Blacks just a generation before. Certainly, the winds of change began to slowly diversify Hanford in the 1960s as affirmative action legislation reshaped the Hanford workforce.

In August 1964, the city of Richland created its own human rights commission to promote equality and oppose discrimination in education, employment, and housing. In the process of debating the creation of a human rights commission, the Richland City Council also debated the possibility of creating an open housing ordinance. Apparently, some of the inspiration for such an ordinance in Richland was the enactment of the first open housing ordinance in Seattle in October of 1963. That ordinance, however, faced stiff opposition and was overturned overwhelmingly by Seattleites in 1964, a result that may have convinced Richland city leaders not to pursue the open housing course at that time. Therefore, the open housing ordinance failed in 1964 in Richland, much like it did nationally, but would be reopened for consideration four years later.[51]

When the Richland Human Rights Commission decided to pursue an open housing ordinance in 1968, it did so on the heels of its first controversial protest. It had earlier publicly opposed the decision by the Mid-Columbia Symphony Guild to have its annual fund-raiser ball at the Pasco Elks Club because the Elks refused to allow Blacks into their organization. Richland's mayor, Fred Clagett, told the commission in a joint meeting that their actions were "way out of line." This was just the first hint of tension between Clagett and the Human Relations Commission. Later in the year, the Richland chapter of CORE accused Clagett of trying to terminate the Human Relations Commission by gagging audience participation at a joint city council–Human Relations Commission meeting and by showing a lack of concern for the grave problems experienced by minorities. Despite the tension between the commission and the council, commission members decided to push ahead with their plan for an open housing ordinance.[52]

On May 20, 1968, the Richland City Council unanimously passed one of the most comprehensive open housing ordinances in the nation. The law prohibited racial, religious, or ethnic discrimination in all housing in Richland. Those found guilty of housing discrimination would face a $300 fine. The ordinance also created a seven-member housing review board that would enforce the law. What made the ordinance so comprehensive was that it allowed for no exclusions. In addition to prohibiting discrimination by real estate agents and rental property owners, it also prohibited discrimination by property owners renting rooms in their homes, whether single family or duplexes. Duplexes were included in the ordinance because a number of duplexes had been built in Richland during World War II to house Hanford workers. While all seven councilmen voted in favor of the ordinance, the law's strongest proponent on the council was ex-mayor John Sullivan who argued that the intent of the ordinance was "to get rid of this moral evil of housing discrimination."[53]

Richland was the first of the Tri-Cities to pass an open housing ordinance and, apparently, part of its motivation was the lack of movement in either Pasco or Kennewick. Indeed, one local newspaper's headline in July 1964, when Richland first openly discussed such an ordinance, read "Richland's New Open Housing Missile Aimed Right at Kennewick." Although Richland's ordinance was not enacted until four years later, it still was the first in the Tri-Cities and well ahead of Seattle. Kennewick and Pasco continued to lag behind.[54]

Richland's Human Relations Commission remained active after its success with the open housing law. In 1969, the Commission responded to the state report, *Race and Violence in Washington State*. In their response to the state report, the Human Relations commission addressed all of the same areas—employment, housing, education, police relations, and social interaction. A thorough attempt to address racial issues, the report reflected Richland's continued lead in the Tri-Cities on racial issues. Of course, part of the reason for that lead may have been the small Black population in Richland compared to Pasco. With only 300 to 400 Black residents, Richland lacked the "threat" to its racial balance that whites in Pasco perceived.[55]

Pasco's progress on civil rights through the rest of the decade of the 1960s continued to be mixed at best. In 1968, WSBAD investigated charges of employment discrimination by Pasco construction firms, bias by the Pasco Police Department, both in hiring practices and in response to calls from Black residents, and discrimination versus Black athletes by Columbia Basin College, the community college in Pasco. Black athletes at the college were housed only in East Pasco and were not allowed to grow their hair into large Afros. At the same time, WSBAD praised the Pasco School District for its efforts to integrate schools and hire nonwhite teachers, like Clarence Alford. About the same time, the city council in Pasco established the Pasco Anti-Discrimination Commission (PADC) in response to pressure from civil rights organizations and from WSBAD.[56]

Relations between the Pasco Police Department and residents of East Pasco were fraught ever since the migration of thousands of African Americans to the Tri-Cities area during World War II and the early Cold War. As the 1960s progressed, the conflict between the police and the East Pasco community accelerated as East Pasco, perhaps emboldened by national civil rights activism, sought minority representation on the police force and an end to what they saw as harassment and racial profiling. CORE led many integration efforts as Wally Webster remembered. "Pasco City Hall was a totally white city hall that was supposedly serving the whole city. There was not a [Black] police officer, or anyone in public works, engineering or any of those places. So, we were marching on city hall for employment opportunities. The Pasco Police Department for example, had never had any people of color working. I applied for a grant that paid the salary of the first Black police officer in Pasco."[57] James Pruitt seconded: "We had no Black policemen, we had no Black lawyers in this town. We had nothing. And why not? Why not recruit some of these people? Because they were unwelcome." Pruitt's directness and courage would place him as a peacemaker in the middle of one of the most violent riots in Pasco history.[58]

Richland's open housing law had set an example for the other cities. It was not until after Richland enacted its law that either of the other cities seriously considered following suit. In August 1968, the Pasco City Council for the first time considered adoption of an open housing ordinance. The proposed ordinance was essentially the same as the one passed by the Richland City Council a few months earlier.[59]

These changes, though, were not enough to mollify many young Blacks in Pasco. Outraged by what they saw as token changes and inspired by the growing Black Power movement, in October and November, Black students at Pasco High School were involved in violent clashes with white students. Additionally, black students also led a march from the high school to the downtown area to protest continued segregation and discrimination. WSBAD conducted an investigation of the incidents and found a disparity in the treatment of white and Black students by faculty at Pasco High School, segregated housing, a lack of job opportunities for African Americans, a lack of interracial social contacts, and a lack of a feeling of power and security by many young Blacks in Pasco.[60]

James Pruitt had led marches in each of the Tri-Cities in support of civil rights causes, and in 1969 he was placed in the Police and Community Relations Department as the first Black employee of the city of Pasco. Pruitt became a liaison between the Pasco Police Department and the Black community in East Pasco after a near riot in Pasco resulting from one of these student marches. In 1969, a group of several hundred students gathered in front of the Franklin County Courthouse in downtown Pasco to protest conditions in the city.

> And police went down and they had four warrants. They went down and arrested four young men they was after for drugs. [And] Lieutenant Butnam hit a couple of girls with his night stick and he drew the crowd. And the kids came back the next day with rocks, rifles, shot guns—there was over 400 people in that park, young people. Those kids was out there fixing to get destroyed, because they'd come to destroy the police department. They'd torn over police cars and stuff up there in the street; they'd burned down the trees in front of the courthouse. I got on the wishing well and I cried like a baby. If those kids had pulled out those guns out there and start shooting at them police, they were going to destroy them. And I promised them, if they would just think about it and go back home, I said 'as long as there is blood in this body, I would never let this happen in this town again.' And the kids dispersed. I went down and put in my application after that.[61]

Pruitt's role in the Police and Community Relations Department was to investigate reports of police harassment. One of the first changes made to the police department was to remove the shot guns from the trunks of police cars, which had long been a symbol of intimidation used against African Americans. Several police officers left the department as a result of Pruitt's investigations and support from the mayor, city manager, and chief of police.[62]

Civil rights activists also responded to these situations by creating the East Pasco Neighborhood Council in 1969 to address issues of employment, housing, street repair, and police protection. Katie Barton headed the Neighborhood Council and was active in many local organizations, including the local chapter of the NAACP and the Community Action Committee, a War on Poverty organization begun in 1966 by Art Fletcher. In 1969, she became the first Black woman to serve on the Pasco City Council, winning a seat previously held by Fletcher, the "father of Affirmative Action," who had become Pasco's first Black resident elected to the city council in 1968.[63] As her son Keith noted, "she stood up for what she felt was right, and then she didn't want to take anything less."[64] Change remained slow, though, as it was not until 1984 that Pasco elected its first Black mayor, Joe Jackson. Jackson became the third Black mayor in the state of Washington.[65]

Over twenty years after African Americans first migrated to Pasco in large numbers, the city remained largely segregated and conditions, for the most part, were not improving. Local groups, such as the Elks, voted overwhelmingly to continue to exclude Blacks from their membership in 1971.[66] CORE led civil rights efforts to challenge the discrimination by the Pasco Elks, writing both to the national Elks organization in Texas to protest the policy and proactively contacting local groups that held events at the Elks Lodge, urging them to reconsider holding events there, given the exclusionary stance of the organization. On several instances between 1966 and 1971 the Tri-Cities chapter of CORE picketed the Elks Lodge. What made the Elks such an important point of protest was that "so much of the power structure of the Hanford groups would meet at the Pasco Elks Club" remembered Andy Miller. Andy's parents, Shirley and Richard, were active CORE members and Richard was in upper management for Hanford contractors. By picketing Hanford events at the Elks, Richard put his career in jeopardy by opposing the very events that his coworkers and even his bosses attended.[67]

By the late 1960s and early 1970s, a younger generation of civil rights activists began to take charge, focusing on the segregated housing, discrimination in employment, and police bias that remained part of everyday life for African Americans in East Pasco. For Aubrey Johnson there was a distinct difference between the younger generation and the

Manhattan Project generation who had left the South and found better and higher paying employment at Hanford and in the Tri-Cities. To him, the earlier generation may have overlooked various inequitable employment, educational, and living conditions that harkened back to the places they had left. "We had too many older people that was afraid. They brought the South here with them. Don't make waves, just go along with the program, go along to get along. Then the younger people had more of a radical view, and I among them, that is I'm not going to let it happen to me."[68] Wally Webster recalled the moment that galvanized him to do something in Pasco:

> I was sitting on a bar stool in my uncle's tavern (Jack's Pit and Grill in East Pasco), watching TV, and was watching the March on Washington. And I felt extremely guilty. I felt like I had walked away from the movement in Alabama. I should've been there. I should've been marching. I should've been, I should've, I should've never left, I should be there, contributing there, instead of here. What they talked about on TV in Alabama, I could see it in East Pasco. I could see it in Kennewick. I could see it in Richland.[69]

When asked about what was different about civil rights in the Tri-Cities, Webster, like Aubrey Johnson, pointed to the generation gap: "I think we [older Black residents of East Pasco] had been lured into a comfort zone. We had gotten somewhat complacent with what we had. That had a lot to do with that we were better than where we came. But to say we can still do better took a bit more convincing than I originally thought it would."[70]

In the early 1970s, members of the Black Student Union at Washington State University produced a booklet documenting living conditions in East Pasco. The students argued in the booklet that "despite Washington's claim to northern 'liberalism' the conditions that exist in Pasco, in many respects, are not unlike those of the South." The booklet noted that these conditions existed despite the high concentration of people holding PhD degrees in the Tri-Cities. At the time, one of the key issues for Blacks in East Pasco was urban renewal. As in many Black communities in the United States, urban renewal meant the destruction or dispersal of Black communities. In Pasco, seventy-eight Black homes were destroyed to make room for industry. Only eight were replaced. Only one African

American was hired by the new industrial firms located in East Pasco. The conditions of economic deprivation and social isolation still permeated the existence of African Americans in Pasco in the early 1970s.[71]

The Urban Renewal program was one that had high hopes in the East Pasco community, but it ended up fragmenting the physical and social fabric of that community. The City of Pasco tapped a Hanford draftsman, Webster Jackson, to lead the effort. Jackson (brother of Joe Jackson, the first Black mayor of Pasco) was a fixture of the East Pasco community, graduating from Pasco High School in 1952. He was the first Black man to complete a four-year apprenticeship program with the local carpenters' union.[72] Jackson's job was unenviable: purchase derelict properties in East Pasco with the eye on refurbishing, or more likely, demolishing them and finding new housing. Dallas Barnes served as the relocation officer for Urban Renewal, working with Webster Jackson, and as a whole considered the effort a mixed success: "the streets were paved and everything else…they had a rehab program where they would take some of the houses that were structurally sound and give people either grants or loans to fix them up…we had builders to come in and build some low income housing…but when Blacks moved out [of East Pasco] then white flight began."[73]

In April 1969, Wally Webster became director of the Community Action Committee (CAC), a federally funded program of the Economic Opportunity Act (EOA), the legislation that created the War on Poverty. A key element of that legislation was the creation of Community Action Programs, which were primarily concerned with creating neighborhood councils like the East Pasco Neighborhood Council. The CAC worked with the East Pasco Neighborhood Council to interface with the Urban Renewal program. Webster felt

> tension and conflicts from a program standpoint. The Urban Renewal program did not have a major component to it in terms of what was being renewed. We knew that they were buying houses that they considered to be dilapidated and moving people out, but there was no housing being developed to give people an option to stay in the neighborhood or another section of the neighborhood…and I believe to this day that was probably one of the biggest failures that I encountered in a sense that, for me, that we didn't see it through well enough to say if you buy

this house, you should have another affordable house to move in and hold the community together, as opposed to dispersing a community.[74]

For Aubrey Johnson, Urban Renewal forever took away the close-knit Black community, plagued as it was with substandard housing and services, that he had identified with growing up in East Pasco.

> We was a village; we were a family. That was a highlight of my life, living in East Pasco until the '70s when it was Urban Renewal came in and removed, replaced. I mean, everything to me was East Pasco. At one time there was four groceries stores in East Pasco. There was a dry cleaners and there was Kitty's Grocery Store, the East Side Market, there was the Tin Top and there was JD's. There was two night clubs, there was Norse's and King Fish Supper Club. I think there were probably about eight cafes: it was Squeeze-in Diner, Bobby's and Ray's, Haney's Café, Big Mike's, there was a café at the tavern, there was Belgian's Pool Hall, there was Avery's Café, there was a little record shop. It was like everything basically, that we needed was in East Pasco. I hated to see it when Urban Renewal came. Because what it did, it removed the Black people from the little shacks, they call them, the little homes they had to the projects. And then we lost everything that we had, because all of that was gone. We had no representation. They came in and the city—you had to sell it. They gave you nothing for it…there was no negotiation. That broke down our whole community.[75]

Aubrey Johnson still proudly resides in East Pasco.

Despite some of the challenges and problems caused by Urban Renewal, by the early 1970s African Americans in the Tri-Cities had made important gains. African Americans were no longer excluded from Richland, Kennewick, or West Pasco. African Americans were employed in significant numbers in all three of the Tri-Cities and in management positions at Hanford. All local schools were integrated. In addition, no more "we cater to white trade only" signs hung in stores anywhere in the Tri-Cities. In other words, the system of Jim Crow that had excluded Blacks from nearly every public venue—from theaters to churches to taverns to housing—was gone. Black activists like Dan Carter started the first Head Start program for Benton and Franklin counties and the Community Action Agency for the counties, which still provides community services like housing, weatherization, and other community support activities.[76] Indeed, a concerted and persistent effort by local African American and civil rights organizations and the influence of national developments had defeated Jim Crow in the Tri-Cities.

However, that these gains had to be fought for at all, that Black Tri-Citians had to struggle to join the social fabric of the community outside of East Pasco, was not lost on Dallas Barnes: "Not too many white folks had to go to school or get a job because of an Equal Opportunity Employment. You don't have to worry about getting a house because you're a Fair Housing Community or an Equal Educational Opportunity product. Everywhere a Black person tried to find—wherever they found themselves, there was always a special legal permission or allowance for them to be there."[77] When asked about civil rights era activities in the Tri-Cities, interviewees made it clear that while they were aware of the larger civil rights struggles, and may have been buoyed by the activism and courage of freedom riders and civil rights leaders in the South that were broadcast nationwide, they wanted to fix their own problems in their community.

Hanford and the Tri-Cities economy struggled through the late 1960s and most of the 1970s as plutonium production at Hanford slowed with the embrace of détente. A short burst of activity in the mid-1980s, the "Reagan Restart" of Hanford's production facilities eventually cooled with the ending of Cold War tensions and Hanford ceased production of plutonium in 1988, and in 1989 the "Tri-Party Agreement" was signed between the U.S. Department of Energy, the Environmental Protection Agency, and the State of Washington Department of Ecology, committing the three agencies to work on a comprehensive cleanup of the Hanford Site.[78] What did these transitions—urban renewal and the shift at Hanford from production to cleanup—mean for the Black community in the Tri-Cities and those workers at Hanford? Dallas Barnes summed it up thusly:

> I don't think of Hanford as Hanford because everything is so diversified right now—is doing anything. I don't even think that you can point to a minority community as such—a Black community. I don't think you can do that. I don't think you can say that there is an East Pasco anymore that's predominantly black. In fact, I know you can't. You can't do that. If you're going to say the blacks have been absorbed in the community, then you can't say that's the case, because we can't see their physical presence in your classroom, or on this campus, or distributed through

the mainstream or business community that you would expect, having them come through all of that. In terms of what Hanford did, I think Hanford made an effort during this day. But I think Hanford's efforts with Blacks, just like their efforts with the reactors out there: they're decommissioned. [*laughter*].[79]

This chapter reinforces scholarship, such as that by Quintard Taylor, which has explored the existence of segregation and civil rights activism in the Pacific Northwest. Many scholars have argued that we need to rethink our definition of the civil rights movement away from a single southern or national civil rights movement and toward an exploration of various Black freedom movements that took place throughout the country.[80] This chapter agrees with that argument and suggests the need for an understanding for variations within regions. The Tri-Cities' story demonstrates that segregation and civil rights activism did not happen only in the South or in large multiracial urban centers outside of the South, but also in smaller communities where inspired groups of African Americans challenged entrenched systems of Jim Crow and, despite continued challenges, won some significant gains.

Notes

1. Dr. Dallas Barnes Interview by Robert Bauman, February 12, 2004.

2. Katie Barton, Vanis Daniels, and Velma Ray, interview by Ellen Prendergast, October 4, 2001, Richland, tape, African American Contributions to the Manhattan Project Oral History Project, Accession number ELPVD100401, Hanford Cultural Resources Laboratory (HCRL) Oral History Program, Richland, Washington.

3. "Kennewick Negroes to Mark '54 Ruling," *Tri-City Herald*, May 1963; "NAACP Leader Finds Kennewick Treatment Fine," *TCH*, May 9, 1963.

4. Hawkins to D.A. Pugnetti, May 9, 1963, Jack Tanner Papers, Series B, Box 2, Folder 13, Washington State Historical Society.

5. Wallace Webster, interview by Robert Franklin, July 20, 2018, Richland, Documenting African American Migration, Segregation, and Civil Rights at Hanford, Hanford Oral History Project, Richland, Washington.

6. Dallas Barnes, interview by Robert Franklin, March 22, 2018, Richland, Documenting African American Migration, Segregation, and Civil Rights at Hanford, Hanford Oral History Project, Richland, Washington.

7. Jack Briggs, "No Illegal discrimination uncovered in Kennewick," *Tri-City Herald*, May 17, 1963.

8. *Washington State Board Against Discrimination Report on the City of Kennewick, July 1963.*

9. James Pruitt, interview by John Skinner, October 18, 2001, Pasco, African American Community Cultural and Educational Society, History and Recognition Committee.

10. Rickie Robinson, interview by Robert Franklin, February 16, 2018, Richland, Documenting African American Migration, Segregation, and Civil Rights at Hanford, Hanford Oral History Project, Richland, Washington.

11. Katherine Helen Brouns Schiro Harvey, interview by Robert Franklin, June 29, 2018, Richland, Documenting African American Migration, Segregation, and Civil Rights at Hanford, Hanford Oral History Project, Richland, Washington.

12. James Pruitt interview; Cornelius Walker, interview by Vanis Daniels and Leonard Moore, Pasco, African American Community Cultural and Educational Society, History and Recognition Committee.

13. Quote is from William Wiley in Jack Briggs, "Peaceful Demonstration Attracts 74 Marchers," *Tri-City Herald*, May 19, 1963.

14. Melvin B. Voorhees, "Negroes March: The Troubled Air in Kennewick," *Argus*, May 24, 1963, Box 2, Folder 13, Tanner Papers.

15. Beth Hennings to Tanner, May 11, 1963, Box 2, Folder 13, Tanner Papers.

16. Hennings to Jack Tanner, May 10, 1963, Box 2, Folder 13, Tanner Papers.

17. Hennings to Mayor and City of Kennewick Officials, May 10, 1963, Box 2, Folder 13, Tanner Papers.

18. See Belinda Robnett, *How Long? How Long?: African-American Women in the Struggle for Civil Rights*, (NY: Oxford Press, 1997); and Orleck, *Storming Caesars Palace.*

19. Katherine Harvey interview.

20. Ibid.

21. "Demonstrations are Contemplated in the Tri-Cities Area," *Spokane Spokesman-Review*, May 11, 1963.

22. Rosellini to Tanner, May 13, 1963, Box 2, Folder 13, Tanner Papers.

23. Bill Frist, "Probe Asked in Negro Ban at Kennewick," *Spokane Spokesman Review*, May 13, 1963; "Kennewick is Called Racial Birmingham," *Tri-City Herald*, May 13, 1963.

24. *Washington State Board Against Discrimination Report on the City of Kennewick, July 1963.*

25. "Negroes Live In Only One Tri-City Project," *TCH*, July 12, 1962.

26. Ibid.

27. "Kennewick Discrimination Implied," *Tri-City Herald*, July 9, 1963; *Washington State Board Against Discrimination Report on the City of Kennewick, July 1963.*

28. James Pruitt Interview.

Civil Rights in the Tri-Cities 165

29. "Racial Work in Tri-Cities is Praised," *TCH*, May 19, 1965.

30. "CORE Member Lashes Kennewick Councilmen," *TCH*, July 27, 1965; "State Official Applauds Kennewick Resolution," *TCH*, August 4, 1965.

31. Aubrey Johnson, interview by Robert Franklin, April 9, 2018, Richland, Documenting African American Migration, Segregation, and Civil Rights at Hanford, Hanford Oral History Project, Richland, Washington.

32. Vanis and Edmon Daniels, interview by Robert Franklin, May 7, 2018, Richland, Documenting African American Migration, Segregation, and Civil Rights at Hanford, Hanford Oral History Project, Richland, Washington.

33. James Pruitt Interview.

34. Barnes interview, February 12, 2004; Ralph Worsham, "East Pasco Conditions Poor, Says Official," *TCH*, April 19, 1966, 16; "Pasco Progress Noted in Civil Rights Field," *TCH*, April 20, 1966; *Race and Violence in Washington State: Report of the Commission on the Causes and Prevention of Civil Disorder*, Olympia, 1969. Images of Watts represented a powerful threat and were often used as such by African Americans in various locations across the country to negotiate civil rights and poverty program demands. For more information, see, Robert Bauman, "'The air was more filled with tension than smog': Race and the War on Poverty in Los Angeles"; William Clayson, "When Liberalism Incites Militance: The War on Poverty and Chicano Activism in Texas"; and Christina Greene, "'Someday, I Don't Know When...The Colored and White Will Stand Together': Low-Income Southern Women and the War on Poverty," Papers presented at "War on Poverty at 40" conference at Princeton University, November 21, 2003.

35. David Arthur Sever, "Comparison of Negro and White Attitudes in a Washington Community" MA Thesis, Washington State University, 1967, 27, 37–43, 69–70; Barnes Interview.

36. Clarence Alford, interview by Robert Franklin, May 17, 2018, Richland, Documenting African American Migration, Segregation, and Civil Rights at Hanford, Hanford Oral History Project, Richland, Washington.

37. Wally Webster interview.

38. Joe Williams, interview by Vanis Daniels and Leonard Moore, Pasco, African American Community Cultural and Educational Society, History and Recognition Committee.

39. Aubrey Johnson interview.

40. David Arthur Sever, "Comparison of Negro and White Attitudes in a Washington Community." MA Thesis, Washington State University, 1967, 27, 27–43.

41. Ibid., 69–70.

42. Ibid., 85–92.

43. Ibid., 31, 100.

44. Wally Webster interview, Dallas Barnes interview.

45. "Racial Board Man Advises Pasco CORE to Be Militant," *TCH*, April 19, 1966; Taylor, *Forging*, 190. Another civil rights group in the later 1960s and early 1970s was the BEAT, or Black Expressions of Art in the Tri-Cities, which focused on promoting Black culture and arts through workshops, speakers, and exhibitions.

46. Barnes interview.

47. Barnes interview.

48. "Richland's New Open Housing Missile Aimed Right at Kennewick," *The International Argus – Pasco*, July 11, 1964; Calvin F. Schmid, Charles E. Noble, and Arlene E. Mitchell, *Nonwhite Races – State of Washington*, Olympia: Washington State Planning and Community Affairs Agency, 1968.

49. Barnes Interview; Gale Metcalf, "A History of Struggle," *TCH*, May 21, 1989; "Pasco Blacks Vote Downtown Boycott," *TCH*, March 31, 1970; "Pasco Blacks Plan Shopping Boycott, Picketing," April 7, 1970.

50. John Abercrombie, interview by Robert Franklin, July 23, 2018, Richland, Documenting African American Migration, Segregation, and Civil Rights at Hanford, Hanford Oral History Project, Richland, Washington.

51. City of Richland Council Minutes, July 6, 1964 and July 20, 1964, Fred Clagett Collection, Box 2, Folder 7, Manuscript, Special Collections and University Archives, University of Washington; "Richland Human Rights Commission" undated pamphlet, Richland Public Library. For the story of the 1963–64 open housing challenge in Seattle, see Taylor, *Forging*, 204–206.

52. Web Ruble, "New Enthusiasm Arouses Human Relations Group," *TCH*, March 27, 1968; Jack Briggs, "Mayor's Pick No 'Yes' Man," *TCH*, December 22, 1968.

53. Like many of the open housing laws passed by localities, including Seattle, in 1968, Martin Luther King's assassination and the resulting violence played a crucial role. See Taylor, "A History," 261–263; Taylor, *Forging*, 208–209. See also, "Housing Ordinance Given Nod in A-City," *TCH*, May 8, 1968, 23; Web Ruble, "A-City Approves Fair-Housing Law," *TCH*, May 21, 1968; Richland City Council Minutes, May 20, 1968, Clagett, Box 2, Folder 11.

54. "Richland's New Open Housing Missile Aimed Right at Kennewick," *The International Argus – Pasco*, July 11, 1964; Calvin F. Schmid, Charles E. Noble, and Arlene E. Mitchell, *Nonwhite Races – State of Washington*, Olympia: Washington State Planning and Community Affairs Agency, 1968.

55. *Race and Violence in Washington State*, 4; Richland Human Relations Commission report to Richland City Council, August 6, 1969, Richland Public Library.

56. Kristi Henderson, "State Board Will Probe Racial Charges in Pasco," *TCH*, March 22, 1968; "Pasco Schools Praised for Integration Effort," *TCH*, March 22, 1968; Jim Philip, "Negro Says Police Use 2 Standards," *TCH*, July 17, 1968; "12 Named to Anti-Bias Unit," *TCH*, July 17, 1968.

57. Webster interview.

58. Pruitt interview.

59. "Pasco Mulls A-City Housing Law," *TCH*, August 28, 1968.

60. Walter Oberst, 171–172.

61. Pruitt interview.

62. Ibid.

63. Shu-Chen Lucas, "Katie D. Morgan Barton (1918–2010), May 24, 2010. Blackpast. org. Accessed 3/23/2019. https://www.blackpast.org/aaw/vignette_aahw/barton-katie-d-morgan-1918-2010/.

64. Marion Keith Barton, interview by Robert Franklin, May 1, 2018, Richland, Hanford Oral History Project, Washington State University Tri-Cities.

65. Oberst, 166–168; Esther Hall Mumford, "Washington's African American Communities," in *Peoples of Washington: Perspectives on Cultural Diversity*, Sid White and S. E. Solberg, eds., Pullman, Washington State University Press, 1989, 103; Shu-Chen Lucas, "Katie Barton"; Phyllis Fletcher, "Arthur Fletcher," www.blackpast.org.

66. "Tri-City Elks Reject Blacks," *TCH*, October 8, 1971.

67. Andy and Shirley Miller interview.

68. Aubrey Johnson interview.

69. Webster interview.

70. Webster interview.

71. "Pasco, Washington," undated pamphlet, MASC, Washington State University Libraries.

72. "Black Tri-Citians Reflect on Struggles, Progress" *TCH*, February 14, 2011.

73. Barnes interview.

74. Webster interview. For more on the War on Poverty and its implementation in local communities, see Robert Bauman, *Race and the War on Poverty: From Watts to East L.A.* (Norman: University of Oklahoma Press, 2008).

75. Aubrey Johnson interview.

76. Dan Carter interview.

77. Dallas Barnes interview.

78. Hanford.Gov, "Tri-Party Agreement," accessed 2/19/2019, https://www.hanford.gov/page.cfm/TriParty.

79. Dallas Barnes interview.

80. See, for example, Steven F. Lawson, "The Historiography of the Civil Rights Movement," *American Historical Review* (April 1991): 456–471.

CHAPTER SIX

Latino/as and the Continuing Significance of Race in the Tri-Cities

Robert Bauman and Robert Franklin

A s in much of the American West, Latino/as are the nonwhite group who have sustained the most growth and had the most significant social and cultural impact on the Tri-Cities in the past forty years. Those Latino/as who have arrived and settled in the region, largely since the 1970s, have found many of the same racial scripts and narratives that greeted other nonwhite groups in earlier years. Racial discrimination and segregation in housing and education have continued to dominate the experiences of Latina/os as they did African Americans, Chinese Americans. and Japanese Americans before them. And, as with the groups who arrived earlier in the mid-Columbia region, Latino/as in the Tri-Cities have adapted and challenged the ever-present discrimination and segregation and have built a strong and vibrant community. Since Latino/as have, for the most part, arrived in the mid-Columbia region since the 1970s and their migration was not directly related to the Hanford Site, the Hanford History Project has not, to this point, collected oral histories of Latino/as. Since this volume is focused on nonwhite groups with oral histories that are part of the Hanford History Project collection and whose migration has been directly connected to Hanford, this chapter provides a brief, but far from comprehensive, summary of the history of Latino/as in the Tri-Cities. That important work, central to the recent history of the region, remains to be done.

The first Latino/as to live and work in the mid-Columbia region were likely miners who came through the area in the 1860s and left by the 1870s. The Latinx population in Washington remained small for the next several decades. Only 450 Mexican Americans resided in the state of Washington in 1920. Some of those had arrived during World War I to fulfill the wartime labor shortage. Juan Ramon Salinas, who arrived in 1917, was probably the first Mexican immigrant to work in the Yakima Valley. Most of these laborers worked in the sugar beet industry. In the 1920s, additional Mexican workers migrated to the Pacific Northwest as track maintenance workers for the railroads. By 1929, Mexican laborers comprised almost 60 percent of railroad section gangs in the Pacific Northwest.[1]

During World War II, because of critical labor shortage (in part created by the internment of Japanese Americans), the War Manpower Commission urged the DuPont Company, the primary contractor for the Hanford Engineer Works, and the Army Corps of Engineers to hire Mexican Americans to work on construction of the site. Colonel Franklin T. Matthias, the commanding officer at Hanford during the war, initially balked at the idea of hiring Mexican American laborers, arguing that hiring Mexican Americans would "require a third segregation of camp facilities, inasmuch as the Mexicans will not live with the Negroes and the Whites will not live with the Mexicans." Eventually, Matthias relented to the commission's will and hired about 100 Mexican Americans, mostly from El Paso and Brownsville, Texas, who were housed in segregated housing in Pasco.[2]

Labor shortages during World War II also led to the bracero (day laborer) program agreement between the United States and Mexico which brought thousands of Mexican laborers to the Yakima Valley and mid-Columbia region as agricultural laborers from 1943 to 1947. Over 39,000 Mexican laborers were employed in the Pacific Northwest during World War II. In April 1943, the first group of 250 braceros arrived by train in Yakima. Labor camps generally consisted of one-room dormitories or tents with cots and wood-burning space heaters. Washington State College Extension Service noted that it would have been "impossible" to successfully continue crop production in the region during the war without Mexican laborers. Mexican agricultural laborers were also hired in Wenatchee, Prosser, Walla Walla, and Kennewick. Many of the Mexican laborers in Walla Walla were hired by canning companies. Expiring in 1947, the initial bracero law was replaced by a new law that contained administrative changes. These changes, along with labor protests, led Northwest growers to stop contracting braceros. Importantly, both the Mexican laborers brought to the mid-Columbia region as part of the bracero program and Mexican Americans hired to work at Hanford were temporary workers. Shortly after the war, most had left the Tri-Cities area.[3]

The first permanent Mexican American laborers in the Tri-Cities area began arriving in the late 1940s. Beginning in 1948, the canning and agricultural industries began hiring Mexican Americans. Labor contractors representing different agricultural interests traveled to Colorado and Texas recruiting Mexican American laborers. Another significant factor in the arrival of Latino/as to the mid-Columbia region in the 1950s was the Columbia Basin Project. In 1952, water reached the Columbia Basin Project canals in Franklin County for the first time. The project transformed Franklin County into an important agricultural region and created the need for a significant number of agricultural laborers. Many of these laborers came with their families and eventually established permanent residency in Washington. Thus, the establishment of Mexican American communities in the region originated during the 1950s.[4]

By 1970, the Latino/a population in the region had increased but was still small. Latino/as comprised approximately 5 percent of the Franklin County population in 1970 and a much smaller percentage of the Benton County population. In the early 1970s, Green Giant could not find workers for its expanded asparagus operations. As a result, it hired crew leaders from La Grulla, Texas, and Eagle Pass, New Mexico, to recruit workers. This active recruitment of Mexican American agricultural laborers created a connection between the mid-Columbia region and South Texas. Many families began annual migrations from South Texas to the agricultural fields early every spring for agricultural work that paid much better than at home. As a result, the school population in Franklin County would boom every March with the arrival of the migrant families. From the 1980s through the early 2000s, every February, Pasco School District employees traveled to South Texas to enroll students who came north in March.[5]

Eventually, some of these families stopped the annual migrations and decided to call the mid-Columbia region home. By the 1976–77 school year, Mexican American students comprised 14 percent of the students in Pasco schools. By 1980, the Franklin County Latinx population had reached 15 percent of the total population, and Latino/a students made up 20 percent of students enrolled in Franklin County schools. By 1987, that number had risen to 30 percent. By 1990, the Latinx population in Pasco was 40 percent of the total and Latino/a students comprised 50 percent of the elementary school population, 40 percent of middle school population, and 30 percent of high school population. By the 1980s, Latinos were the largest ethnic minority group in the state of Washington with a total population of 100,000.[6]

The dramatic increase in the Latinx population in the mid-Columbia region continued in the 1990s. By 1995, Latino/as comprised 19 percent of the mid-Columbia population—30 percent in Franklin County, 8 percent in Benton County, and 24 percent in Yakima County. By 2000, Benton County was 12.5 percent Latino and Franklin County was 47 percent Latino. In Richland, Latino/as comprised about 5 percent of the population, in Kennewick 15.5 percent, and in Pasco 56 percent. By the year 2000, Latino/as had become the majority population in small agricultural communities in eastern Washington, like Sunnyside, Grandview, and Othello.[7]

Like other nonwhite groups who arrived in the Tri-Cities region before them, Latino/as initially faced residential segregation, as they were steered towards housing in East Pasco, replacing African Americans who had often replaced Asian Americans. Although Latino/as have moved into the neighboring cities of Kennewick and Richland (indeed, Latino/as now comprise over 25 percent of the population of Kennewick), a significant majority of Latino/as in the Tri-Cities continue to reside in Pasco. The racial scripts related to housing in the Tri-Cities continued to impact nonwhites into the twenty-first century.

While Mexican Americans continue to comprise by far the largest percentage of the Latinx population in the mid-Columbia region, some immigrants from Central and South America have also migrated to the area for agricultural labor. While most of the region's Latinx population live and work in agricultural areas, increasingly Latinx businesses have thrived. In addition to the success stories of individual Latino/as who have become civic and business leaders in the community, Latino/as have strengthened and broadened the culture in the mid-Columbia region.

Like Asian American and African American migrants who arrived earlier in the twentieth century, Latino/a migrants and their families have formed community institutions and cultural celebrations and established successful businesses.[8]

One example of a family that began as agricultural laborers and became leaders in the local community is the Guajardo family. In 1957 José and Consuelo Guajardo brought their family to work in the fields in Franklin County. The Guajardos became one of first Latino families to settle in the Tri-Cities. When they first arrived, they lived in Campbell Cabins in Kennewick or Old Navy Homes in Pasco along with the other agricultural laborers. In 1966, José Guajardo, along with his brother Manuel and his colleague, Rosalio Armijo, formed the Tri-Cities Latin American Association, the first Latino organization in the region. In 1968 Armijo became the first Latino delegate to represent Washington State at the Democratic convention. By 1970 José Guajardo had saved up enough money to fulfill his longtime dream—owning his own restaurant. He and his family opened Guajardo's Café in downtown Pasco where it was one of the first Latino owned and operated businesses. Castillejas Bakery, which opened in 1968 in downtown Pasco, was the first.

Castillejas Bakery and Guajardo's Café were forerunners of things to come as more Latinx businesses followed their lead. In 1979 KDNA became the first Spanish-language radio station in the mid-Columbia region. Two years later, La Clínica opened the first migrant medical clinic to serve the burgeoning Latino community. In 1985, Simon and Anita Ochoa opened Tienda La Chiquita, the first Latino/a non-restaurant business in downtown Pasco. In 1989, Luisa Torres was appointed to the Pasco City Council, becoming the first Latina to hold that position. In 1992, Latino/a business leaders formed the Tri-Cities Hispanic Chamber of Commerce, which has been an influential cultural, economic, and political force since its inception. And, in 2007, Albert Torres started *tú Decides*, a weekly bilingual newspaper, published in the Tri-Cities.

In addition to involvement in business and politics, Latino cultural activities have had a profound influence in the mid-Columbia region. In 1990, Pasco held its first Cinco de Mayo festival and parade. It has since become a major regional and annual event. Other cultural events like Fiesta de Familia and the Fiery Food Festival reflect the influence of Latino culture in the Tri-Cities. A full exploration of the experiences and significance of the dynamic and considerable Latino/a population in the Tri-Cities requires a much longer analysis than can be provided here.

So, much like Chinese and Japanese immigrants in the late nineteenth and early twentieth centuries and African American migrants in the mid-twentieth century, Mexican American migrants and Latino/a immigrants have built a community in the Tri-Cities. But they arrived in a community with an already-established racial script. That script primarily limited nonwhites to East Pasco and to manual labor positions in the regional economy. Over the years, though, as their population has grown, Latino/as have challenged that script through establishing community institutions, businesses, and cultural and educational institutions. Indeed, a recent *New York Times* article on the racial divide between whites and Latinos in Yakima, Washington, roughly sixty miles northwest of the Tri-Cities, which highlighted the discrimination faced by local Latino/as and their challenges to that racism, easily could have been about Latino/as in the Tri-Cities.[9]

When George Yamauchi asked the question, "What is an American?" in 1943 and answered his own question by stating, "Is he white, black, yellow, red, or any other certain color? It is generally conceded that he is any one of these or a mixture of them all. That is one of the principles of our Constitution, is it not?" he was challenging the dominant racial narrative in the Tri-Cities. Other nonwhites over the years did the same, just in different ways. African Americans challenged the racial status quo by forming civil rights organizations, demanding better jobs, and marching through the streets of Kennewick and Pasco. And some, like CJ Mitchell, challenged those racial scripts by moving into places like Richland, which previously had been all white. Native peoples challenged that same racial script by insisting on regaining rights lost when the Hanford Site was constructed. The Yamauchi family took that narrative head-on by becoming business and community leaders, only to be told being quintessential Americans was not good enough, punished because they were of Japanese descent. But they continued to fight that narrative during and after the war. Most recently, Latinos have continued to question those racial scripts and narratives through challenging residential segregation and through the development of educational, economic, and cultural institutions.

Many of the stories and experiences of these nonwhite groups in the Tri-Cities reflect the experiences of nonwhites in the larger American West. The violent death of Henry Williams, the narrative of Native peoples removed from their land, Chinese and Japanese immigrants working on railroads and establishing successful businesses despite rampant discrimination, and, in the case of Japanese Americans, internment; the arrival of thousands of African Americans for wartime jobs and facing a version of Jim Crow not unlike that in the South; African Americans fighting for civil rights and an end to segregation; and the late twentieth-century arrival of Latino migrants and immigrants, primarily for agricultural and manual labor, are narratives that have happened in many places throughout the American West. The connection to the Hanford Site and the size and impact of the African American migration and Latino migration to a nonurban area in the West, though, make this story unique. The stories in this volume demonstrate both the familiarity and uniqueness of the experiences of nonwhite peoples in the Tri-Cities region. These stories demonstrate that these groups have helped make the region the dynamic, complex, and multiracial place it is today. Indeed, the Tri-Cities area is the fastest-growing region in the state of Washington, due in large part to its nonwhite population. In addition, the stories in this volume show the ever present and continuing significance of race, racial scripts, and challenges to these scripts in the region known as the Tri-Cities.

Notes

1. Richard W. Slatta, "Chicanos in the Pacific Northwest: A Demographic and Socioeconomic Portrait," in *Pacific Northwest Quarterly*, 70:4 (October 1979), 155–162; Carlos B. Gil, "Washington's Hispanic-American Communities," in *Peoples of Washington: Perspectives on Cultural Diversity*, eds. Sid White and S. E. Solberg. Pullman: Washington State University Press, 1989, 157–193.

2. Robert Bauman, "Jim Crow in the Tri-Cities, 1943–1950," *Pacific Northwest Quarterly* 96:3 (Summer 2005), 125–126.

3. Erasmo Gamboa, *Mexican Labor and World War II: Braceros in the Pacific Northwest, 1942-1942*, Austin: University of Texas Press, 1983; Erasmo Gamboa, "Mexican Labor in the Pacific Northwest, 1943–1947: A Photographic Essay," in *Pacific Northwest Quarterly*, 73:4 (October 1982), 175–181; Erasmo Gamboa and Antonio Sanchez, "Fruits of Our Labor: A Survey of the History and Heritage of Hispanics in Washington State" ca. 1990.

4. Gamboa, *Mexican Labor and World War II*; Gamboa, "Mexican Labor in the Pacific Northwest"; Gamboa and Sanchez, "Fruits of Our Labor"; Bruce E. Johansen and Roberto F. Maestas, "Washington's Latino Community: 1935–1980," *Landmarks*, Summer 1982, 10–13.

5. Johansen and Maestas, 10–13; U.S. Bureau of the Census, *Nineteenth Census of the United States, 1970 Volume 2: Characteristics of the Population* (Washington, DC: US GPO, 1973). For an excellent exploration of one family's migratory farm labor experience in the region, see Isabel Valle, *Fields of Toil: A Migrant Family's Journey*, Pullman: Washington State University Press, 1994.

6. U.S. Bureau of the Census, *Twentieth Census of the United States, 1980 Volume 2: Characteristics of the Population* (Washington, DC: US GPO, 1984); U.S. Bureau of the Census, *Twenty-First Census of the United States, 1990 Volume 2: Characteristics of the Population* (Washington, DC: US GPO, 1994).

7. U.S. Bureau of the Census, *Twenty-Second Census of the United States, 2000 Volume 2: Characteristics of the Population* (Washington, DC: US GPO, 2004).

8. For a brilliant article that establishes the connection between maintaining community and financial success in the United States by immigrants, see Tyler Anbinder, Cormac O'Grada, and Simone A. Wegge, "Networks and Opportunities: A Digital History of Ireland's Great Famine Refugees in New York," *American Historical Review*, 124:5 (December 2019), 1591–1629.

9. Dionne Searcey and Robert Gebeloff, "The Divide in Yakima is the Divide in America," *New York Times*, November 19, 2019.

Oral History Interviews

Ellenor Moore

*Interview conducted by Robert Franklin, March 21, 2018, in
Ellenor's home in Pasco, Washington*

ROBERT FRANKLIN: My name is Robert Franklin. I am conducting an oral
history interview with Ellenor Moore on March 21st, 2018. The interview
is being conducted at Ellenor Moore's home in Pasco. I will be talking with
Ellenor about her experiences living in the Tri-Cities. And for the record, can
you state and spell your full name for us?

ELLENOR MOORE: Yes. My name is Ellenor Louise Moore. It's spelled E-L-L-
E-N-O-R, middle initial, L, Moore, M-O-O-R-E.

FRANKLIN: Great, thank you so much. Where and when were you born?

MOORE: I was born in Louisiana.

FRANKLIN: Okay.

MOORE: In 1932. I'm 85 years old. So.

FRANKLIN: I'd like to talk about your life before coming to the Tri-Cities, so
I'm wondering if you could kind of—what type of environment was it to grow
up in Louisiana in the '30s and '40s?

MOORE: Well, you know, I was in the late teens when I came, when my father
got work here and came from Louisiana here to work. Growing up in Louisiana,
it was really—well, we went through part of the Depression, the big depression
and everything. But you know, everyone was kind of in the same conditions. So,
as a child, I didn't realize how bad it was. But it really was. It was bad. At that
time, we lived in the country. My father worked—he wasn't a farmer. He just
didn't like it; he never—he wasn't one. And he had grown up partly in St. Louis,
where his mother had lived. He came back to Louisiana.

The story is that he met my mother and then he was there and he stayed
there, but he didn't like it at all. He always had the idea he was going to get
away and he was going to go wherever he could go. During World War II, he

179

was thinking he wanted to go back to St. Louis. But housing and everything was so hard to get, he never did really do that. He wound up—he went out and worked in the defense, when they were building the army camps and stuff like that, back in 19—what would that have been? '41, '42? So that was the kind of work, he did that.

And then when he came back, of course he couldn't find anything to do except worked at a sawmill. We lived in the housing that was there, which was very poor. There was no indoor plumbing or anything like that. You grew up—I remember at like eight, nine years old, ten years old, it was really, really bad. So that was the only thing that kind—that kept us there. After the sawmill, we moved into the little town, which was Jonesville and that's where I went to school there. Then my dad got a job at a car—automobile franchise, I guess you'd call it. He worked there until he was able to leave and come here to work.

FRANKLIN: What year did your father come here?

MOORE: In 19—the early part of 1950.

FRANKLIN: And what did he come here to do?

MOORE: He came here to do whatever kind of work he could get. I mean, he wanted to get away. From my understanding, most of the people that came here, a lot of them, they just—they were looking for work. We heard about it from—well, my uncle had been in the service, and when he came back he was stationed in Bremerton. That's how we knew about, you know, the Northwest. I had never even heard about it. Here I was, I don't know how old I was; I was probably eight years old, and he came, he was stationed there, and then he was discharged and he came back home to Louisiana, but he stayed for a very short time, because he did not want to be there. He'd gotten—he had been overseas and stuff like that. And he came back and settled in Seattle.

Then my aunt came. I remember when he came back up here and he was saying that he was going to live up here. I remember my aunt saying to him, well, as soon as you can, send for me, because I don't want to be here either. And she came. Then my grandmother, they sent for my grandmother, my mother's mother. And they were in Seattle.

But it took a while before my father was able to get away from there. The way he got away is that my grandmother had met this man, Mr. Jones, that had worked at Hanford. He was talking about how they were hiring people and they wanted people to work and that's how my dad found out about it.

As soon as he could leave there, he did. He came here to live. It took him two years to save enough money to send for the family.

FRANKLIN: Oh, wow.

MOORE: What I remember about it is the living conditions and housing was just horrible.

FRANKLIN: Here or in Louisiana?

MOORE: Here! Here. Because there was no housing for Black people. You had to live in East Pasco. The housing wasn't adequate at all. We moved into—I remember when we came—I didn't come with—at that time, my grandmother had moved back to Louisiana, so when the rest of the family came, when my mother and the other two children came, I stayed with my grandmother, and they sent for me later on. But in the same year. My mother actually cried because of where they had to live when they first came here.

FRANKLIN: Really? Could you describe it? What kind of—

MOORE: Well, I can remember, it was like a little encampment over on, what, Idaho Street, I believe it was. It was owned by a family called the Haneys, and you probably—because they were here for many, many years and they still are here. They have grandchildren, all of them still here. And they owned some property and they'd put up some little shacks that people could rent. That's what I'd call them, they were little shacks. They were—no inside plumbing; they had like a public bathhouse on the property. All of that was just so foreign to us.

So my mother spent most of her time trying to find a place for us to move. I think we lived in that place about three months. And then she found a house over on—what was that? On Douglas Street. And so it was—that was just— we were all so glad to get out of that place where we were. So that's what I remember about it.

There was not very much—now, I never worked out at Hanford. My dad did. But that was the conditions. And by that time, I finished high school and my first real job, I got it at Our Lady of Lourdes. Sister Anthony Marie was my supervisor. I never will forget her, because when I applied for the job, I was just going to take any job. It wasn't any special job; I just wanted to work. I had finished high school, and I'd started to go to business college in Kennewick. It was very difficult, because I didn't have very much money or anything like that. But I needed to work, and I thought, well, I have to get a job.

I applied at Our Lady of Lourdes and I was hired. I was prepared to work wherever if it was cleaning up in the kitchen or whatever. Sister Anthony Marie hired me and trained me as a hospital aide. That was—at that time, the aides had to wear the white uniform, the white stockings and everything except the cap, as a nursing aide. So that was my first real job here. The pay was $120 a month. And I was glad to get it.

FRANKLIN: How would that have compared to the job back in the—to the similar type of job back in the South?

MOORE: Well, before we'd moved, my mother—it was two doctors in the little town where we lived. My mother got a job where she worked at that doctor's office. I think she was getting paid, maybe, $15 a week.

FRANKLIN: Oh, okay, so, $120 a month was quite a bit more.

MOORE: Yeah. And my first real job. Oh, I was very happy to get it. I worked a year and a half. Things had started to improve a little bit. That's when they started building some other housing in East Pasco. But I worked 15 months at Our Lady of Lourdes and then I moved on to Seattle, because my aunt and uncle and all lived in Seattle. I got a job as a hospital aide at the veterans' hospital, the new one that they opened that year. And so that's where I worked until I'd gotten married. You know, so it was a real journey.

But I also kind of wanted to go to school and it just seemed like I never did get a chance to do it. I had to work. And then I got married, and of course, three children, just one right after the other. And I worked a lot, but it was at home, taking care of kids. I married Thomas Moore.

Now he had been here since, I guess, 1949. He was a divorcé; he had two girls. So I had a family right away. And then, as I said, three children. It was five children. The girls were—when Tom and I got married, the girls were ten and five. So that was a nice experience for me. But I had helped raise—actually, at home, I was the oldest one. So my three brothers and—my three siblings, I'd always helped with them. So I knew how to take care of kids. [*laughter*]

FRANKLIN: Did you meet Thomas in Seattle, or—Thomas was from here? Or he had moved here?

MOORE: He had moved here. When he came here from what I've heard, from some of the things he said, he always wanted to be a businessman. He had a restaurant downtown near the overpass, you know that street that—what is that? The main street that comes through Pasco there. Lewis Street.

FRANKLIN: Lewis Street.

MOORE: Lewis Street. So he had—and, you know, at that time, it was kind of segregated in the sense that—but he went out of business with that. I don't know how long he had it. At the time I married him, he had a pool hall over in East Pasco. That was when he had the other restaurant, I think, that was when he was married to his first wife. And then when they were divorced, he still had that pool hall. But that—at that time, things had opened up. There was some housing where people of color could get housing—rent places near the railroad track on the east side. But that's about as far as they got. Took a while for people to be able to get decent housing.

FRANKLIN: Right, because Pasco was divided into—

MOORE: It was divided into East Pasco and North Pasco. The railroad track actually divided the community and—I have to get—I have hay fever here.

FRANKLIN: Oh, no problem.

MOORE: So I got to get my tissue.

I remember when working at Our Lady of Lourdes, I had to walk to work because I didn't have any transportation. And at that time, there was not—it was a lot of empty spaces over there in East Pasco. It wasn't that much housing, a lot of tumbleweeds, which I'd never seen in my life. I didn't even know what a tumbleweed was. [*laughter*] I can remember, one of the things that I remember, walking to work—and the wind blew a lot then—those tumbleweeds would just come rolling down the street, well the roads, mostly. You didn't want to get caught in that bunch, because they'd gather up as they'd come, and you don't want to get caught in that. [*laughter*] So I can remember, walking, trying to dodge tumbleweeds on my way walking.

And coming under that underpass, that always frightened me. I never wanted to do it, but I had to. You either did that or you walked across the railroad track. I was afraid to walk across the railroad track, because of trains. So, you know, going under that underpass was not easy for me. So anyway, that's some of the things that I remember about that.

It's just the hardships. Dad would come home from work sometime and he would say things like, oh, well, they had to hose us down today. What is that? Well, you know, they wash you off, because they could read that we had been in a hot place. Now, here's the thing. I don't think anyone, pretty much, that was working out there understood what that really meant. They didn't really understand. I mean, they didn't know how dangerous it was.

FRANKLIN: Yeah.

MOORE: And so—we didn't. I was the oldest one in my family, but I didn't really understand anything about that. I didn't know that it was really dangerous and it was something that he could've still had on him, on his clothing or whatever, when he came home, and I'm sure he did. But that happened a lot, where he was working, he said, we got into a hot area. They didn't really explain that to workers. They told them, but, you know? Who knew? I mean, most of the people, a lot of the people were just like my dad. They'd come from an area that nothing like that had ever happened. They didn't really know what it was all about.

FRANKLIN: What kind of education level did your dad have?

MOORE: My dad, I think he went to—let me see—he finished the eighth grade.

FRANKLIN: Okay. And when he got a job out at Hanford, did he ever talk about what he did? Was he like construction, or—?

MOORE: It was construction. He belonged to the labor union. And it was construction, and a lot of it, I guess, was clean-up stuff that they did. Cleaning up what, I have no idea. You know, we didn't know, and they didn't either. They just did whatever they were told to do.

FRANKLIN: Was he happy with the compensation of the job, like the pay, was it a good job for him, or was he still kind of looking unsatisfied, kind of looking for—

MOORE: Well, it was a good job for him. I mean, he had never been able to get a job that paid as much as it did. Yeah. I don't remember him complaining about the work; he was just glad to be working.

FRANKLIN: How long did he work out at Hanford for?

MOORE: Oh, let's see. Oh, he worked there until—in the '70s.

FRANKLIN: Oh, okay. So quite a while then.

MOORE: Yeah, so from 1950 until—I don't remember exactly in the '70s. Mother finally convinced him that she didn't want to live here, and they moved to Seattle. Mother—my mother never was satisfied here. She also got a job at Our Lady of Lourdes, the same year that I did. Because my oldest—my youngest brother was like two years old or something, three years old. So I worked the swing shift, and she worked days. So we kind of worked out the remaining—and in between us going, she coming from work and me going to work, there was a lady that we knew that my father had actually helped that family to come to Pasco, too. They were from Louisiana. The Wilkins. I don't know if you—

FRANKLIN: Was it a family that he knew personally?

MOORE: Yeah.

FRANKLIN: Is that how a lot of—

MOORE: Oh, yes.

FRANKLIN: Seems to me that's how a lot of migration into this area happened, was people tell family and friends and is that—

MOORE: Right, that's what happened, because from where we came from in Louisiana, I don't think there was anyone there that even had heard of Hanford. Didn't even know that much about Washington state. The thing of it is, you know, I remember the first time I noticed Washington state on something, during the '40s, we would get boxes of apples that they gave—I think they called it commodity or something, that the government—it was surplus fruit and stuff that was sent to help the people. Dad helped to distribute that stuff to families. We got a box of apples, and on the apple box it said Washington State. So that was pretty much what I knew about Washington state until I got into school and got to learn more about geography and everything. But yeah, that was my first knowledge of Washington state. We got a box of apples with what the government gave. And they gave things like—I don't remember getting any other fruit, but I remember the apples, we did get apples.

FRANKLIN: In Louisiana where you lived before you came here, where you lived was—was where you lived segregated?

MOORE: Oh, it was definitely segregated.

FRANKLIN: How deep did segregation go there? Did it go all the way to—

MOORE: [*laughter*] About as deep as it could get. We had separate schools. My first school that I went to, the very first I can remember, we lived about probably three miles from—well, it seemed like to me it was a very long way, being a young child. But I would imagine it was about three miles.

That's when we lived in the country. Daddy was working, at that time, he worked at the gin—gin cotton where they baled the cotton. We lived in the country in this little area. We had a house that they built on the plantation. It was a plantation. There was a plot of land just adjacent to the house that my mother would work in that. I remember her out there hoeing and stuff when I was very little.

I went to school. It was a church, a one-room church house. And one of our cousins was the teacher. And all the kids were in this one room. The big—she trained the kids that were in the fourth, fifth grade to help the young ones. So that was my first of going to school. I went to school. And believe it or not, we had a horse. His name was Shorty. Mother would put me on the horse and my brother was a baby at that time. She would hold the baby, and I'm sitting behind her on the horse and drive me to school.

FRANKLIN: Wow.

MOORE: And then come pick me up. That was—the part I remember about that was, I was so afraid the first day that I went to school because—the only thing that made me not so afraid, one of our cousins was the teacher. So I did know her, but I didn't know any of the other children. And we didn't live close, as I said, children—they were at least three miles away from me. So I didn't know any of them. And I was so afraid. I just did not want to be there. [*laughter*] I was so glad when Mother came and picked me up. But that was the beginning.

Then we moved—going back now, I'm kind of going back and forth, because we moved to another area that was close to the sawmill where Daddy worked. Because he'd work at the sawmill and then during the season when they were doing the cotton, he worked at the gin, baled the cotton. And it was other people did live closer to us then, because they had a house that there were several houses in the area where the sawmill was. The people that worked there lived in those houses. And then the school I went to was still another church house thing. So from the first through third grade, I went to a one-room church house school.

FRANKLIN: And these were segregated schools?

MOORE: Oh, of course it was segregated. The teachers were all Black. When we moved to town, that's when I actually got to go to a real school building. Because there was a settlement of Black people in that area. There were white people that lived across the highway. The highway ran through. They lived, they had different schools and everything. But in that—that's when I went to school in a real school and we had several teachers. It was, the high school was there, too.

So those were—that part was really good experience, and I remember feeling good about it. I was a very good student and the teachers liked me. I had friends and there were other kids there and everything. When I got in high school, I played basketball. That was nice; we'd go to the little towns to play the other teams and that type of thing.

So that, I enjoyed, even though it was segregated, but that's all we knew of, being segregated. I mean, when you went to the movies, we had to sit upstairs in the balcony. You had to buy your ticket from another window on the side of the building, and then you couldn't go into the front of the building in the lobby and buy the ticket. You had to—they had a window on the side and you went upstairs to the movie. But we would go, we'd go to the movies every week. [*laughter*] You know, every weekend, we went to see—I remember the only thing they played was Western movies. It was like Gene Autry—you probably don't even know who I'm talking about. [*laughter*]

FRANKLIN: No, believe it or not—believe it or not, I do. Yeah. I grew up with my grandmother and she was really into old Westerns.

MOORE: Yeah. So that was a real treat for us. The tickets cost $0.12 for children. So you should see me trying to save up my pennies during the week so I could go to the movies.

FRANKLIN: What about other elements of life in—like the store and restaurants and things? Were those also segregated establishments as well?

MOORE: Oh, yes. They were segregated here, too, when people first—when my husband first came here, as I said, the restaurant he had down there on Lewis Street, it was sort of segregated. I mean, it was segregated to the point to where Black people couldn't go to other restaurant—they had their own little restaurants and stuff, even over there in East Pasco.

FRANKLIN: Were there—

MOORE: There were a couple restaurants, and they were—

FRANKLIN: Were there signs here? Was it as formal as it had been in Louisiana? Or—?

MOORE: No. No, it was just subtle in the sense that you weren't going to get served or you just knew that you—you know. There's certain places you didn't go. There was no one—no Black people living in Kennewick. You couldn't—even when it got to the point here in Pasco when more and more Black people came in, and it sort of opened up, you could rent a house in some parts, as I said, the parts near the railroad track, on this side of the railroad track. But there was no Black people living in Kennewick. They wouldn't rent you a place.

FRANKLIN: Mm-hmm.

MOORE: So that was completely—

FRANKLIN: I wanted to ask, we talked a little bit about your coming here, but I wanted to ask, what were your—how did you—did you take a train here?

MOORE: I took a train. It took five days to come from Louisiana to Pasco.

FRANKLIN: What were your first impressions of Pasco when you got here?

MOORE: Oh, I was upset! Just kind of like my mother. My mother, as I said, she was still in tears. She just hated the place. [*laughter*] I didn't like it. I knew that—well, my dad was working, so we did have a roof over our head, and he was feeding the family and stuff.

So it was not that we didn't have that; we had—in Louisiana, after we moved out of the country, things weren't too bad. It was segregated, of course, but every—the Black part of town had their own restaurants and a couple stores, and they did have a big grocery store there in that part of the town where people go. Only one that I remember, one big sort of big grocery store. But you know, I kind of lost my thought now. Because I'm going back and forth. Is that okay to do that?

FRANKLIN: Oh, yeah, yeah.

MOORE: Because I'm remembering—

FRANKLIN: That's just the way our memories work and how life is.

MOORE: And when you compare some things.

FRANKLIN: Yeah.

MOORE: But you were asking about—you said if there was signs here?

FRANKLIN: Yeah. If the segregation was as formal, or—if formal's the right word. Because Louisiana's segregation, the South, there were signs, it was in the law. Here it seems to have existed but kind of outside the law or informally, and I kind of wanted to just get your memories of that.

MOORE: Yes. It was here. It was here, you felt it if you were a person of color, you definitely felt it, and you knew that—there were no Black people working at any of the restaurants or anything. There may have been some in the kitchen, but I don't remember because I didn't go to them anyway. But in my young adulthood, you just didn't, you didn't go. When you went to a restaurant—as I said, I don't remember ever seeing any signs, but there were only certain ones that you could go to. There were no Black people working in any of the restaurants where you could see them. As I said, there may have been some in the kitchen, working. But I don't know. When I got the job at Our Lady of Lourdes, as I recall, there were only three people of color working there, including myself.

FRANKLIN: And your mother?

MOORE: And my mother. But there was two—one lady worked in the kitchen at Our Lady of Lourdes, and then there was one that was—I don't know if she was an aide or not. She worked there for years and years and years.

FRANKLIN: How were you treated by your coworkers there?

MOORE: Very nice. I never had any problem with anyone. And it was a Catholic hospital, and I was Catholic, and the sisters, as I said, I remember sister Anthony Marie. She was just such a lovely, nice person. Because when she hired me, I didn't know what she was going to hire me for. I said I was ready for any kind of work. When she hired me, I really knew nothing about working in a hospital. So she taught me pretty much everything.

I didn't even know how to read a thermometer. I remember the first week that she gave me a thermometer and she taught me how to read it, and you know, the first few days, I could not even see the line in it. I would turn it and turn it, and I couldn't see the line. But once you learned how to do it, it's so easy. The minute you hold it up, you see the line. But she had a lot of patience and she taught me the terminology and everything that we did. I was soon on the floor, following the other aides at first for about a month, and the nurses. And I learned quickly, so within two months, I knew how to do the different things that they needed me to do.

FRANKLIN: Oh, wow.

MOORE: So it was nice.

FRANKLIN: Did you finish high school in Louisiana, or did you finish high school here?

MOORE: I finished in Louisiana. That was the year we moved, that Mother moved.

FRANKLIN: Okay.

MOORE: So when Mother and the other kids moved, then I came. But I had finished high school there.

FRANKLIN: What was the hardest aspect of life in this area to adjust to, moving from Louisiana?

MOORE: [*laughter*] As I said, the housing, the places where we had to live when we first came here. Because we had a nice little house in Louisiana, once we had moved to town. Yeah. And so, it was just—and the conditions. It was dirty, the wind blew all the time, sand was everywhere. During those days—and sand would get in; I don't care how you—everyday, you had to dust, you had to clean in the places where we were living, because sand would get through any little crack. And there were some cracks! [*laughter*]

FRANKLIN: Yeah, that's a common story, all around. Yeah, wow.

MOORE: Yeah, that was the worst part of it. And when I—after I'd started work, actually, within six—well, within six months, I had bought myself a little car, and I didn't have to walk in the wind blowing the sand. So that was—I was actually pretty satisfied until—I knew I didn't want to live here, though, and that's why I moved to Seattle.

FRANKLIN: When did you come back to the area from Seattle?

MOORE: I came back in '54—moved back in '54.

FRANKLIN: Oh, okay.

MOORE: So I worked 15 months here and then I went to Seattle and I worked almost two years.

FRANKLIN: What was it that brought you back, was it your husband?

MOORE: Mm-hm. I got married, and as I said, then I was stuck here, because—you know. He lived—he always wanted to have his own business. So the restaurant business and the other—a pool hall, I think he had, it didn't work out too well. So actually when we got married, he was a laborer, which he had never really done. And he had joined the labor union. He got a job working on Ice Harbor Dam when they were building it. We had one of the houses over there on California Street, which is facing the park over there, now. That park, they actually—that was all—that park was just all open field when we got married. But there was a row of houses. They dismantled and moved all those houses and then set that up as an industrial area, you know, from the area on over to the railroad tracks, I think, is all industrial.

FRANKLIN: That was part of the redevelopment? How did you feel about coming back to Pasco? Were you—

MOORE: Well, when you're young and you get married, and you're in love—it was okay. Because my husband was here and so it was okay. Evidently, it had to be okay because I lived here then thirty-something years, raised my kids here, anyway. But when they had divided that area and was redeveloping that area, see, my husband built a fourplex over there on Douglas and—I don't know if that's Wehe; I can't remember if that's Wehe or not. I don't even go over there anymore. I mean, I hated East Pasco so bad. [*laughter*] Since I've been back here, I've only been over that way about three times.

FRANKLIN: Oh, wow. Why is that? Just—

MOORE: It was because it was just such a horrible beginning over there, you know? I just didn't—I didn't like it. Now, there's nothing there, really. Now, my husband, see, he developed a business there. He finally went into build a wrecking yard, which is one of the biggest wrecking yards, I guess—it was at that time—right there on Wehe and A Street, on the other side of the railroad track. So that was the business that stuck with him, and the one that he was able to develop, and made it successful, and that's what we were able to raise our kids with, with that business.

FRANKLIN: How would you describe life in East Pasco and the community and what did you do in your spare time?

MOORE: I didn't do anything. There was no social life. As I said, I was lucky enough to get a job pretty soon after—within three months, I had a job. So I worked and I came back home. [*laughter*]

FRANKLIN: Any community events that stick out to you?

MOORE: There was a church that—I'm Catholic, so I'd come to church, but you know it was over here, Saint Patrick's. Once in a while, I'd visit some of those other churches over there. There was only a couple at that time. But there was really no social life.

FRANKLIN: What kind of role did church play in the community?

MOORE: Oh, it played a big role. It still plays a pretty big role for the people that belong to those churches. They play a pretty big role. The churches, always in the Black community, play a large role. Because the churches were there when there was nothing else. It's not only for their spiritual satisfaction; it's the social thing, too.

FRANKLIN: Do you recall any family or community activities or traditions or events that people brought with them from the places that they migrated from?

MOORE: I wasn't really involved too much—the church, as I say, was the— oh, well, now, you mean back then, or now? Over the years, yes, they brought some things with them. Like they celebrate Juneteenth which came from a Southern celebration.

FRANKLIN: Mm-hmm, the end of slavery, right?

MOORE: Well, when they found out about it was the end. It was June, it took until June, yes. So, yes, that's one of the celebrations that they have here.

FRANKLIN: Because that's now a pretty big pageant and community event all around the United States.

MOORE: Right. And it's because of Black people coming from the South and they brought that with them. That would be something, a celebration that they would have every year. And it has caught on. So, yeah, they do have it. And they celebrate Martin Luther King's birthday and stuff like that. And that's something, of course—it was people from the South really pushed that to happen. In the small communities.

FRANKLIN: Right, right.

MOORE: You see, when I came here, I had—there was nothing for me to do, except work and I would go to mass on Sundays, and then I worked and I'd go home. And I wasn't here that long, then. When I came back, and once my children got up, I didn't work until—I didn't go back to work until my youngest child was old enough to go to school. So, from the time my first child was born until then, I just took care of home and the children. I got a job at Safeway, which was the second Black person to ever work at Safeway. They had a little store downtown Pasco on 4th—or was it on 5th? And I worked there—I got that job in 1963, and I worked there—and I worked part-time; I didn't work full-time because my children were still young and I didn't want to be away from them that long. So they were very, very accommodating to me—

FRANKLIN: Safeway was?

MOORE: Safeway. Because I made arrangements with them that during the summer, they would hire a student to work in my place so I could stay home with my children. I didn't want them all summer without having me there. So, Safeway did that, and I worked with Safeway for 12 years.

FRANKLIN: Ah. You said you were the second—

MOORE: I was the second Black person to work there. The first Black woman, she's still here, Doris—I can't remember Doris' last name now. But they moved her to one of the stores, I think it was either Kennewick or Richland, that she went to work over there and they hired me in Pasco.

FRANKLIN: Where was the Safeway located in Pasco, was it in East Pasco, or was it—

MOORE: It was on 5th—no, it was on 5th and Clark, I think. Yeah. It's where that—it's a bank there now, used to be a bank. I haven't been over there since I've been back now.

FRANKLIN: Hmm, I don't know if I've been over there either.

MOORE: Yeah. But it was on 5th and Clark.

FRANKLIN: Were you treated fairly by the management and the patrons? Or—

MOORE: Well, the management was fine. The patrons, when I first, I would say the first week or the first two weeks I was in there, they would line up in the other checkstand. We had three—did we have three checkstands or two? We only had two checkstands, I think. It was a small store. And they would line up in the other stand and I'm just standing there at my checkstand, because—and pretty soon, they realized that, oh, yeah, if I can go through that checkstand, I can check out real quick and I'm gone. [*laughter*] So it took people about three weeks or two weeks to realize that, okay, it doesn't make sense for me to stand over here in this line when I can go on through the checkstand. And they did.

And I was a good checker. I learned to be a very good checker. At that time, it wasn't like scanning now, you scan through; we had to memorize the prices, and you keyed everything in, you subtotaled, you put the tax in and totaled, and you had to count out their change to them, because there was no automatic telling you how much change that was coming back and everything. Well, I've always been a real fast learner, so, as I said, within a month, I was a real good checker. I worked twelve years there.

A couple times, I went out—they sent me out to Richland, but after that—my kids were teenagers then, and I worked in the Richland store, out there. But I had no problems with people, because I treated everyone the same, I was courteous. At that time, we had to be nice and courteous when you worked in a store or something. Now people will check you out and won't even speak to you. You know, they scan the groceries across the thing and never even say a word to you sometimes. I was just very nice and courteous to people; I treated everyone the same. So, it worked out fine.

I actually enjoyed working at that store. I did, I had no problems. And I never did—at that time, the employment office was next-door to Safeway downtown. There was an employment office down there. That's when they had really started to hire people of color, minorities and Blacks, out at Hanford. I mean, other than just doing the labor work and stuff like that. So I was asked to take a test and go out to Hanford to work, and I refused, because I didn't want to be away from my children that much.

See, that was my thing. I worked. My family was more important to me than my job, really. And so I just—I didn't want to put in full-time work and having to travel out there and everything to work. So I never—that was one of the reasons I never did go. Several of my friends did, and they were trained to do clerical work and different things like that. So they'd opened up to where they were actually training people to—

FRANKLIN: Around what time was that?

MOORE: That must have been, let me see, I have to think back here. Oh, gosh. That had to be like in the late '70s?

FRANKLIN: Oh, okay.

MOORE: I think it was like in the middle to late '70s and early '80s when quite a few people that I knew went out to work. During the time my kids were growing up, I did volunteer work. My kids all went to St. Patrick's through to the ninth grade. I did volunteer work there and of course a cub scout leader and PTA and all that stuff. So I was involved in that type thing. Then my children, when they got into high school, I was appointed by Governor Evans to serve on the Washington State Women's Council. I did that for about almost three years. That was during the time when we worked for the equal rights amendment and different things like that.

I had always wanted to go back to school. I went to college, CBC, and at that time, I quit work for two years and I went to CBC. And then I got my two-year degree and I decided I wanted to go ahead and get my bachelor's. I did that through programs that were brought down from Eastern Washington. And I went back—oh, after that time—I'm trying to keep this in the right way, now. I was still working for—oh, when we had the big problem in the school district where they reassigned the high school principal which had been there for years and years and the town just went crazy and recalled the school board that was the school board at that time. And they recalled the whole school board.

FRANKLIN: What was that over?

MOORE: It was over not treating minority kids right at the high school. And all the schools, really. But the high school is where they had the biggest problem. That was during the time when the civil rights movement was everywhere and going on. So that year, they had recruited a Black music teacher that taught at the junior high school, and his wife was appointed— there was an opening on the school board, and she was appointed to serve on the school board. So, she actually saw what was happening, how the Black students were treated at the high school, and how if there was a disagreement between a white student and a Black student, the Black student wound up getting suspended; the white student didn't. Regardless of who started it and what it was about. And different things like that; it was just stuff going on. She and the other school board members started trying to do something about that, and bring about some equal treatments, wanting—

And the community—and so they thought the best thing to do was to reassign the principal that had been there for years and that was his little kingdom and he could do whatever he wanted to do. When they reassigned him to another job, he refused it, and said he was treated unfairly and that type of thing. He had his group of people that sided with him, and then the group of people that wanted to change things in the community. So the school board was recalled. I mean, they just recalled that whole school board.

They had also hired—while that school board was in together, and after they had started trying to make some changes—at that time, I really wasn't following it too much until they appointed—a new superintendent came in, a young man from—I don't remember where he was from—and he had brought in a group of people that was progressive, that wanted to make changes and stuff like that. So anyway the school board was recalled and the principal decided he wasn't going to take the job that they had offered him. He thought he could make them change and get his way.

I was one of the people that was appointed to be on the temporary—on the school board until—it was three of us, three people appointed to serve on the school board. One was a farmer from out in the blocks, and another one was a guy that worked at Hanford. So the three of us had to come in and serve on the school board and it was a learning experience for all three of us. I mean, we had not had that kind of experience. It was really some trying times going on.

They wanted to force us to hire the principal back at high school. And we said, no, we weren't going to do that. Our job was to appoint two other people; it was a five-member board, and our job was to appoint two other people to make up the board, and we did. We appointed a minister that was a minister in this part of Pasco, and then a businessman, too. So I was the only minority person on the board. I had to really be on my mark. I mean, I had to really learn as fast as I could about what was going—all three of us did—I mean, all of us did, really. To appoint the two other people, we had to be really careful who we appointed, because we had to be people that were open-minded and wanted to carry the school district forward instead of falling back into that same type of mentality that was before. So, it was very, very difficult.

We would have—when we'd have the first six months or the first year, the levy failed, because people were all upset and everything. So the levy would fail and they cut out a lot of the good programs, I mean enhancement-type programs, because they levy failed. My son was in high school. At that time, he was in the tenth grade, coming out of St. Pat's. He was on the debate team. That was canceled. And he was so upset, he lost interest in school. So that was a personal problem for me. [*laughter*] Trying to get him, you know, so he wasn't so upset about something that he really enjoyed doing. He was a very good debater, and that didn't work.

But getting back to the big problem, the school board problem, we had to really make up our mind what way we were really going to go with this. Three of us, we had to appoint two other people, which we did, the people that we picked, we thought they were people that would be open-minded. And at that time, also, they had very few, I think maybe there were three Black teachers in the whole district. So it was a real big problem.

I remember, our school board meetings would be so full, we had to move them to the auditorium at the grade school, McGee. No, was McGee over there? I think it was. In order to have room for everybody. And they were rowdy, and they brought cameras, and they brought recorders and everything, so they could record every word that we said in the meeting. How long—excuse me, I'm going to ask you a question. How long have you been around? Were you around during that time? You were there, so you know what happened.

Tom Hungate: I was over in Kennewick.

Moore: You were in Kennewick. I know you were, but I mean, the *Tri-City Herald*, every day there was a big article in the paper about everything, and people were making threats. I mean, I had phone calls where they'd threaten me that I'd better vote to hire back the principal that had been there, or either—whatever. So we had to make up our mind what we were going to do.

I had to really be on top of them when it came to choosing the other two people that was going to be on that board. Because the two guys that were on the board, as I said, they were both very good—they were good people, I liked them. The three of us kind of clicked. But we had to be careful who we appointed. Several times, I had to really just speak up and say, no, that person is not going to work, because of research I had done. I had to do research! The other two guys, they weren't thinking so—they had never been exposed to segregation or anything. I mean, these are two people who didn't know where I was coming from. I had to speak up and let them know what was really happening.

It worked out, and we had the other two people appointed, and we decided that we would offer this principal that had refused to—he started driving a potato truck to make people feel sorry for him, you know, the ones who were on his side. So they'd march around, we'd have people marching in front of the school district office and everything when we were in there having meetings. That was really something.

FRANKLIN: Sounds like a real circus.

MOORE: But within a year, we also had to hire—we had to hire a new superintendent, because he—that was all going on, so he decided it was best for him to leave and go somewhere else. So that was another big problem of hiring the right person. We had to interview all these people for superintendent, and we had to interview for people to fill in the place as the principal. We went through two people we hired, and one of them stayed for a year, and he was gone. He just couldn't take it. [*laughter*]

Because the high school was just—many of the teachers had been there for years, too. And they were used to what had been going on before. So that was difficult. We finally, within a year and a half, the levy—we got the next levy passed. That was the beginning of people trying, really getting together and doing what they needed to do. And it worked out. That was a real learning experience for me. I learned more in—I served on the board for three years. That was worth a college degree.

FRANKLIN: The experience?

MOORE: The experience was, it really was.

FRANKLIN: Do you remember the name of the first—the principal that had been reassigned, and what happened to him?

MOORE: You know, I don't.

FRANKLIN: Okay.

MOORE: I'm 85, okay? [*laughter*]

FRANKLIN: I understand.

MOORE: I really don't remember his name.

FRANKLIN: Does the name, last name Ferrari, does that ring a bell?

MOORE: No, that wasn't it.

FRANKLIN: Okay.

MOORE: No, it wasn't.

FRANKLIN: In preparation for this project, I went and did some research and looked through some of the records from the Congress of Racial Equality branch that was here in the Tri-Cities, the CORE movement, and they had mentioned this—the records were from the '60s to the early '70s. They mentioned this—what was going on in Pasco, at Pasco High School, and that there had been issues with the principal, that there had been issues with some students, that there was a fight between some white girls and Black girls.

MOORE: Well, that—yeah, that had started happening quite often, when everyone was all upset and everything like that. You know how teenagers act out? So there was quite a bit of that that would go on. You know, to bring order to all of that, it was really—it was something.

FRANKLIN: I bet, I bet.

MOORE: It really was. Thank goodness we did—we got things in pretty good shape.

FRANKLIN: Yeah. Thank you. I had taken a lot of notes about that, but I want to go back through that material when I get back. That should be a—it seems a good part of my research.

MOORE: Well, I'm going to tell you, I have to say this about the *Tri-City Herald*. They were really biased in some of the stuff they printed.

FRANKLIN: Okay, I'll look for that. Biased against who, or for who?

MOORE: They were biased against—well, I felt they like they were biased against the new school board in a sense, for what we were trying to do. Because it was overwhelmingly on that other side for a while. I mean, we had to work really hard to turn things around. We really did. And we had to do it in a way where we were trying to make everyone feel good about what was happening, you know?

FRANKLIN: Yeah.

MOORE: So it was a very difficult job.

FRANKLIN: Right, you needed that community buy-in.

MOORE: Yes, you definitely did.

FRANKLIN: And community support.

MOORE: But it didn't take—as I said, within two years, we had it so that the community was behind us—the majority of the community. There's still those holdouts that were there. [*laughter*]

FRANKLIN: Right, there will always be a few. How long did you serve on the school board?

MOORE: I served on it three years.

FRANKLIN: Okay, so you passed the reins when things had—

MOORE: Well, I was appointed, at first, for one year. Because they're staggered, so when we were appointed, I was appointed for one year. And then I was elected and served the next two years. And I would have gone on, but my husband started complaining I was away from home a lot. He was used to me being at home taking care of things. [*laughter*] But my kids were in high school and everything, and they were old enough to where I felt like I could go ahead. And it was such an important thing, I felt so obligated. I had to follow through with it. I had to try to help things to be better than what they were.

FRANKLIN: Do you feel like things did end up being better? Do you feel like you made progress there?

MOORE: I think we made progress, yes. I think we made a lot of progress. We also recruited a lot of Black teachers, smart people, some of them wound up being—at least three or four of them wound up being principals of schools here and then went on to other places.

Carl Peterson was one that we recruited. He was one of the assistant superintendents that had been here, the group that had resigned and went on at the beginning of—after that first year of going through all that turmoil. He was recruited to the Tacoma area, and he—I mean, he's retired now, but he went on to build two schools there. So when he was recruited to first go over there, he was principal of the school for one year, and then they assigned him to build a school. And then after he was there two years, they wanted him to build another school, be in charge of building and setting it up.

So when we recruited—but that was only because we were on that—I was on that schoolboard. I was on that schoolboard—I was the cause of them celebrating Black History Month. Okay, I have to say this. After I was on the schoolboard, I was also then hired to work in the school district. So I worked as a community liaison person in the school district until I left here and moved to Seattle. But I helped to organize, and all the time trying to recruit very good Black people to fill in some of the teaching positions, to have some Black aides in the school district, which they didn't have any before. So I did a lot of that type of thing. Which helped, because then you had people that could come in with some other ideas.

Here's the thing I find about—a lot of people do things out of ignorance, just because they don't know, and they haven't been exposed to minorities. And once they're exposed to minority people that's educated and interesting, they change their mind about a lot of their feelings. It opens them up. So, anyway, I thought recruiting and having Black teachers in the district and stuff like that really helped a lot of people. And it helped to make things different.

FRANKLIN: And it helped to reflect the population, too.

MOORE: Right, yes, it did. Of course the Black population anymore is very, very small. Because I think most—many of the people just moved away. Their children did. Their children didn't stay here. At one time, I think we had about, what, 5% of the population in the school district was Black. Now, I think it's about three. I'm not sure, but I think it's about three.

But at that time, see, when I first came here, there were no minorities hardly at all. Now we have a lot of Mexicans, too, in the school district. At that time, there wasn't. So all of that has helped to just—helped the area grow and the school districts to change their mind about the way they were doing certain things. So, I think it's better.

I'm not—I've been away from here, though, like I said, I moved. So I just came back, and I haven't been involved. I'm too old now to be involved with stuff. And then, plus, I'm sick. But I think we did a lot of good.

And I worked a lot on the different charitable organizations that were here. I served on the boards of probably seven of them and brought in some awareness. That helped, too, because all the charitable—many of the charitable organizations had no minority representation. And so, that was one of the things that I did. I helped them to realize how important it was to have that type of input. When I was gone, they would still have the input. So that was my idea of trying to do that. And I think that helped a lot. I served on the United Way board for years. Anyway, I tried to do my share of working in the community.

FRANKLIN: It sounds like you really did. I mean, that's wonderful.

Moore: I actually enjoyed it. You know, I enjoyed meeting people, I enjoyed bringing about some awareness. And you know what I would say is, I can't speak for everybody. I can't—well, it finally got so I had to turn down different things that I was asked to do because it was too much. People were acting as if I was a spokesman for the whole Black community, and I had to just let that—that couldn't be. I'm not a spokesman for them.

So it was—I enjoyed that part of my life, because I was involved with community, and we got some really good things done. I didn't have anything to do, much, with employment-type things that happened. I served on the planning board for the skills center that opened in Kennewick. I don't know what it's called now.

Franklin: Is it Tri-Tech?

Moore: Probably that is, the skills center?

Franklin: Tri-Tech Skills Center?

Moore: Yeah.

Franklin: They have like a radio station, and—

Moore: Well, they opened up with a lot of different beginning skill things that went on there. Training for carpentry, auto mechanics, what, I think they had a beauty school, radio-type thing, a lot of different things that the high school kids could be exposed to.

Franklin: Great.

Moore: So, you know, those were things that I thought, I was glad to serve on those commissions and things, to try to help them plan that.

Franklin: Great. I wanted to ask you, were there opportunities available here in the Tri-Cities that were not available where you or your parents came from?

Moore: Oh, absolutely. I mean, it came to be, as more people came in. I think maybe, back in the late '40s and stuff like that, that's when minorities started coming here to work. But Hanford was the thing that opened it up to get more people in. As that happened, then things grew to where people—there were opportunities.

Franklin: In what ways were opportunities limited because of segregation or racism?

Moore: Oh, I think so. You said where was it? Here, in this area, yes, they were.

FRANKLIN: In what ways were they?

MOORE: It was just very subtle. I think a lot of it was very subtle. I mean, I went to—oh, I tried out a lot of things. I went to put my application in at a lot of different places. And I knew it was just thrown in the wastebasket when I left. [*laughter*] You know, I mean, but that's the way it was. They didn't turn you down.

FRANKLIN: Yeah, you can laugh at it now, but—

MOORE: Yeah, they didn't turn you down and say, we're not going to take your application. That's what they would have done where I came from. They'd say, well, you're not—you can't be hired here, you're not going to work, we're not taking your application. They would take the applications, but nothing ever happened with it.

FRANKLIN: Right, they'd smile and take it and then probably—

MOORE: Yeah, right. I don't ever remember anyone being rude or anything like that. The only rudeness, and that wasn't really in this area, that must have been in 19—let me see, what year was that, maybe '78? We never got a chance to do any vacation or anything, but we did decide that year we were going to go camping, when the kids were big enough to where they could enjoy going camping. My husband and I, we had a trailer that we hooked up onto our car and we were going camping, we were going to go up into Montana.

And so the only trouble, the only rudeness we ran into, we stopped in Ritzville. I think it's Ritzville, between here and—yeah. We stopped there and we went in the restaurant, and we had food, and when we came out, my daughter, which was four, about four years old, she said, Mom, I need to go to the restroom. I said, okay, so there was a service station right there, and I said, we can go here, then. Because my husband and the boys were still in the restaurant. And I went, and it was locked. I asked if I could have the key, and he said, no. It's broken. It's out of order.

So as we were standing there waiting for my husband to come out, because there was another service one across the street, and I thought, well, we'll just go across the street over there and go. And we were standing there waiting, and I saw other people come and go in the restroom. So when my husband came out, I said, you know, we asked to use that restroom, and he said it was out of order. But other people are going there.

And my husband went over and said to him, oh, I see your restroom, you got it fixed, huh? And the—oh, that man just went all to pieces, started yelling at Tom and stuff like that. And then the ones across the street said, hey, man, are you having any trouble over there, you need help? And I caught my husband's arm, I said, don't argue with him, let's just go. Just go. But, you know, if he had continued, in my mind, I thought, they'd probably beat him up, throw him in jail. And so that was the only thing I'd ever had that kind of trouble with.

So when I came back, I just couldn't let it go. I had to write a letter about it. I wrote a letter to the *Tri-City Herald* saying how we'd been treated there. I didn't think any more about it. It was printed. And then in a few weeks—I was working at Safeway then. That's right, it was in the '60s, must have been in the late '60s. I had just started working at Safeway, and there was—people contacted me that worked for, what, the civil rights or something. But it was a white woman that came and interviewed me, and she asked me about it, and I told her what happened.

She said, well—at that time, we lived over there near the highway on Lewis Street. We had bought a house over there. It was right on Lewis Street. She said to me, be careful. You know, someone may decide that they may do something—hurt you or something about this. I hadn't really thought of it in that manner. But that was disconcerting, to have someone come and say that to me. But she came to find out, to see what they could do, if they could bring charges or something against them.

Then, about a week later, it was—was it Texaco? I think it was a Texaco station, representatives from the Texaco station came to my work at the Safeway to interview me. And I just told them what had happened, and I said they were so rude, and all I wanted to do was take my daughter to the bathroom, and I told them what happened. I did get a letter of apology from the company after that.

See, but that's the kind of things that happened, the kind of things that people go through that went through and may still go through in some places, I don't know. But I mean, it wasn't anything that we were doing wrong, it's just that, I guess Ritzville was one of those places they didn't see very many Black people. And they thought the restroom at the service station, you couldn't use it. That was the idea.

FRANKLIN: Yeah.

MOORE: So when you ask about that type of thing, it was sometime very real.

FRANKLIN: Yeah, yeah.

MOORE: You know?

FRANKLIN: That's an important story to tell, because I think it's—for folks that don't experience that, it's hard to imagine and I think people need to hear about things like that, because it happens.

MOORE: It happens. And as I said, something bad could have happened back there. And I just knew it, and I just—I just said, come on, let's go. Let's just go! Because the man that was talking to him had one of those big wrenches—I don't know what you call it—in his hand. I imagine, if my husband had kept arguing with him, he may have decided to hit him.

FRANKLIN: Right.

MOORE: You know? And if that had've happened, no telling what would have happened.

FRANKLIN: Yeah, that would've been bad.

MOORE: That would've been bad.

FRANKLIN: I wanted to—your father participated in Hanford's early Cold War history. I wanted to ask, what did you learn or know about the prior history of African Americans at Hanford during the Manhattan Project, and from your perspective, what were their most important contributions in the areas of work, community life, and civil rights?

MOORE: Well, I think at the beginning, they did most of the dirty work. They were put into areas—and as I said, no one understood; it wasn't explained to people what they were really getting into. I think the people that were in charge didn't really understand themselves. They didn't know the ramifications of what it could turn out to be. So, yeah. But I think most of the Black people—it was later on that I think Blacks were hired in more— that they recruited people with more education, people that had other skills and stuff. But I think, my feeling is that most of the Black people were hired at first, they did the labor work, the cleanups, the things like that.

You know, it's a lot of cancer in this area. I've been diagnosed with myeloma since I've been back here. I probably had it for—I remember about 30 years ago, actually a doctor when I went in for my regular checkup, and I was a very healthy person; I never was ill—but just doing my annual checkup, and he said to me, your white cells are kind of out of whack. And so, of course, I didn't know what that meant, and he did several tests. I went to him three times. Right here in Pasco. And I went to him three different times, and he finally told me, well, I've done everything. I've done run all these tests and I don't see anything wrong with you. White cells is to help combat any kind of infection or anything, but you don't have any. He said, you're healthy. I don't see anything wrong with you and the test doesn't prove that there is. So, I don't know anything to do about it, except just occasionally have a checkup. So it went on for years, and I never had any problems, so when I'd have my annual, no one else ever said anything about it, and it kind of just slipped my mind.

Okay, I got sick in California and I was having all this pain, all this pain, and I didn't know what it was. My primary doctor was a very good doctor. She sent me to all these specialists, and they did tests, and they did all these things, and they kept saying, well, we don't see anything wrong with you! You're in good health. I was just, I mean, before then, I was such an active person. I've always been active. I was going to exercise classes three times a week, I took up ballroom dancing, I was dancing twice a week. No sickness except the blood pressure. I had high blood pressure and taking medication for that. But I wasn't having any pain or anything. And I went to all these doctors; they all did every test you could think of, and they would say to me, well, I don't see anything wrong with you. There's not anything we can do for you.

So, then, when I started to getting so weak—and that's when I said—my son just kind of insisted that he didn't like me being there by myself. It took 12 different doctors before I got a diagnosis. I just got a diagnosis last year, here. My primary doctor here really paid attention to when I had my blood work done, paid attention to what was going on with my white cells and sent me to an oncologist. He went through my medical records and everything and there he said, I think I know what's wrong, but I'm going to have to do two more tests to be able to diagnose it. So, he did a bone marrow exam and did complete skeletal scan. And so it's multiple myeloma. So, see, it's something that could be in your body for years and years and years and then finally show up.

FRANKLIN: Yeah, yeah, yeah.

MOORE: But then that made me think about my dad coming home saying, well, they had to hose us down today. Yeah.

FRANKLIN: Yeah. We talked quite a bit about civil rights activities in Hanford and Tri-Cities and you mentioned your work on the school board. Were there any other major civil rights issues for African Americans at Hanford and in the Tri-Cities during your time here?

MOORE: Well, let's see. I don't know about Hanford, because I never worked there, you see. I never did work out there.

FRANKLIN: Right.

MOORE: I just knew it from my friends that worked out there and my dad that worked out there. But—

FRANKLIN: What about here in the Tri-Cities?

MOORE: Oh, in the Tri-Cities, major—well, as I said, it was just kind of subtle. You knew it was there and there were things that happened that you didn't feel you could get hired by certain things because—Hanford actually opened it up for people to be hired, for minorities to be hired, because otherwise there wasn't—my stepdaughter was the first person of color to be hired at a bank here. It just hadn't—it wasn't happening. They weren't hiring people there. But she was hired. So I think the work, it just evolved after everything else surrounding we were doing—things had opened up in other places and stuff, and bringing in new people, people from all over the world have come here. I think that has helped a lot.

FRANKLIN: What action was being taken to address these issues in unemployment and in living, and African Americans being able to live outside East Pasco? How did that situation—

MOORE: Well, you know, different laws and stuff were passed, too. I've always thought that Washington State was—actually, when you think about it, I think it's a very good state that tried to be fair. As more and more minorities came in here, I think—there was other people coming, too, so it was people with—more progressive-type people.

FRANKLIN: How did the larger national civil rights movement influence civil rights effort here at Hanford and the Tri-Cities?

MOORE: Well, I don't know, I'm sure it had a big influence. It had a big influence. It was kind of slow catching on, but it had a big influence.

FRANKLIN: From your perspective and experience, what was different about civil rights efforts here?

MOORE: Well, oh, let's see. They started hiring more people and recruiting minority people to come in and work—

[*video cuts out*]

FRANKLIN: I think, and then we'll wrap up, because, yeah, it's been a long interview. It's been a great interview. A long interview is always a good interview.

MOORE: Well, when you edit it and everything, it'll be okay.

FRANKLIN: Yeah. Okay. So, I wanted to ask, and these—Tom gave me a couple great questions here. I wanted to ask, why were you appointed to be on the school board? Who reached out to you and why? Because you would've been a stay-at-home mom at the time, right?

MOORE: Well, no. Well, I think it was because there weren't very many Black people in the community that was—well, I wasn't—see, even when I was a mom, I still did things with the schools.

FRANKLIN: Oh, okay, yeah.

MOORE: So I was active in that. And I was outspoken. [*laughter*] That's kind of one of the things. I was always—I wasn't afraid to give my opinion about anything, so I think that's probably what happened. But I'm trying to think of who—it was this other Black lady that had—oh, it was Virgie Robinson, that's who it was. She worked for the school district—

FRANKLIN: Yes.

MOORE: —at that time. She said to me, they're looking for someone to have minority representation on the Washington State Women's Council, from this area. And she said, I was telling them about you. So she told somebody that was connected; I don't know. They called me and asked me if I would be interested in serving on it, and I said, yes, I would. So that was a good experience. That was for the—you know. That was before we had equal rights here in Washington State. So I served on that for, what, two years, I believe it was. Governor Evans was the one that appointed me, and then after then, I guess I might have served on it more than two years, yeah.

FRANKLIN: That's great.

MOORE: You know, I was being—I'd have to go to like Seattle and Olympia sometimes when they'd have meetings over there and that type of thing.

FRANKLIN: Another question, earlier on you mentioned that your grandma, who had come out here, went back to Louisiana. And why? Why'd she do that?

MOORE: Well—oh. Oh, I told you about—I think I said that she had met this man, Mr. Jones, she married him. And they split up. And she just decided she didn't want to be here, out here. So she moved back to Louisiana. Now, that was before my father moved out here. See, that was a couple years before he moved out here.

FRANKLIN: Gotcha, okay.

Moore: Then after I was here, and married and everything, I sent for her. So I had her here with me.

Franklin: Oh, so she came back out.

Moore: She came back with me for—and she stayed with me for—I fixed her a little place, and she stayed with us for about three years. And then her daughter, my aunt, in Tacoma, she went over to live with them, and she passed over there.

Franklin: Gotcha, okay. That makes sense.

Moore: My grandmother was a very—I think she was kind of my hero. Because she was not afraid to just get out and do new things. She's a very independent woman. Yeah. I learned a lot from her. [*laughter*]

Franklin: That's really wonderful. How were opportunities different for your children here in Tri-Cities than had been for you in Louisiana?

Moore: Oh, my goodness. It was a lot of difference. Oh, yes. I mean, it's so different. By the time my children graduated, things had changed a lot. They had the opportunities were there. You just had to take advantage of it. Yeah, oh, yes. Just like daylight and dark. When I went—when I graduated from high school in Louisiana, I wanted to go to college, but of course we had no money to go to college. The only way I could've gone, I would've had to— they had 4-H. I belonged to the 4-H club. I don't know if you know what that is.

Franklin: I was also in 4-H.

Moore: Oh, you were in 4-H?

Franklin: I grew up in a farm, yeah.

Moore: Oh, okay, 4-H Club. So, they had those clubs and they had scholarships. You could get a scholarship, but you had to go into farming stuff. Agricultural-type thing. And that was not for me. I had no—I was in the club in high-school, but it was just a social for me. I just wanted to be with the other kids. I had no idea about staying on a farm and doing—so I passed that up. I didn't want to do it.

The only other opportunity was to go into the service, which some kids did. I just thought, no, that's not for me, either. You know, they'd go into service and then you'd have to go off to college. Most of the only opportunities was what they trained for. I know a lot of the boys, they actually went and they took agricultural as their—that was their major, that's what they majored in. And then there was teaching, you could either get to be a teacher, you know, and I didn't really want to be a teacher.

So, I actually had no opportunity—I was so glad when my dad left and came and I had a chance to leave there. What I wanted to do was go into business. I did actually start business school here, but I had to work, so that kind of went out the window. But I always wanted to go to college. And I did it. My kids, my youngest child was a senior the year I went back to school.

FRANKLIN: Oh, wow. And did all your kids go to college as well?

MOORE: No, they didn't. My son that lives here, he worked with his dad and he still runs the business, Tommy's Steel and Salvage in East Pasco. He started working with his dad when he was like 12 years old down there. So he went to CBC for one year, and then he was still—he worked with his dad everyday.

FRANKLIN: That's Leonard, right?

MOORE: Leonard, yeah!

FRANKLIN: You're talking about Leonard?

MOORE: Yeah, Leonard. So that's what he went into. My other son went to Western for one year, and it was just—he couldn't get a job, and we just didn't have—it hadn't been long—my husband had just started the business; we just didn't have the money, and he didn't. So then he came back home and he got into the electricians' apprentice program. So he went through that. He worked out at Hanford for a little bit, but he said, Mom, I don't like it out there. I just don't want to work out at Hanford. Because he realized the dangers of them crawling around in these places. So he went to—where did he go next? He went to Colorado and he worked there for a while, and then he wound up in California. He got a job at the University of California there, as an electrician. He worked his way up to management and he took classes the whole time he was there so he could get his certificates and everything for management. So that's what he does now, and he does, as I said, now he's working at San Jose State, and he's the building—I can't remember exactly what it's called, but what he does is he's in charge of the building and remodeling at the school, whatever they do there. So that's what he went into. And my daughter was a model and she actually was the first Black Miss Tri-Cities.

FRANKLIN: Oh, wow.

MOORE: She wound up in Chicago and she married an attorney and she had modeled for several years, she traveled to Europe and places like that. And then she came back, as I said, and she lived in Chicago. And she got married and they have twin boys that will be 16 years old this year. And she's been a stay-at-home mom. [*laughter*] She decided she didn't want to—she stayed at home and raised her kids.

FRANKLIN: Yeah. So my last question is, is there anything else you'd like to mention related to migration, work experiences, segregation and civil rights, and how they impacted your life in the Tri-Cities?

MOORE: No. Well, I've always wanted to take advantage of opportunities, and I tried to get my kids to do that, too, look for opportunities that's out there. After they opened up, well, you had some opportunities. We didn't have that much at first. But I felt like my kids had opportunities, and they didn't always take advantage of what I wanted them to do, but they did okay. They all doing fine. I actually enjoyed working with the school district, because I was able to be in contact with young people, to try to encourage them, and that's not an easy job sometimes.

FRANKLIN: No, it's not.

MOORE: I mean, they'll look at you, and it just goes in one ear and out the other. But that always has been my goal, to try to encourage people of color that I was around—or anybody, actually—because I've worked where there are no minorities at all. Many of my jobs have been that way. It doesn't matter. It just doesn't matter to me about that, because I just love to see young people try to do the best they can do, and take advantage of the things that are there for them. It really hurts when you see many of them don't do that, or don't even try. I just—it's upsetting.

FRANKLIN: Well, great, Ellenor, thank you so much for taking the time to interview with us today. It was a wonderful interview.

MOORE: Well, I thank you for coming.

Wallace (Wally) Webster

*Interview conducted by Robert Franklin, July 20, 2018, campus of
Washington State University Tri-Cities*

ROBERT FRANKLIN: We ready? Okay. My name is Robert Franklin. I am
conducting an oral history interview with Wally Webster on July 20, 2018.
The interview is being conducted on the campus of Washington State
University Tri-Cities. I'll be talking with Wally about his experiences living in
the Tri-Cities and working at the Hanford Site. And for the record, can you
state and spell your full name for us?

WALLY WEBSTER: Wallace Webster. I go by Wally. That's W-E-B-S-T-E-R, is
the spelling of my last name.

FRANKLIN: And what about the first name?

WEBSTER: The first name is W-A-L-L-A-C-E.

FRANKLIN: Great. Thanks, Wally.

WEBSTER: Okay.

FRANKLIN: So, tell me how—well, let's talk about, let's start by talking about
your life before Hanford. When and where were you born, and where did you
live before coming to the Tri-Cities?

WEBSTER: Okay. I was born in a small town east of Mobile, Alabama, called
Theodore. And if you go down there, they say The-do. But I graduated
from high school. I immediately left Alabama and made a very quick stop in
Oakland, California, and then headed for Pasco, Washington.

FRANKLIN: And what—

WEBSTER: So I've been here since 1962.

FRANKLIN: 1962. And what year were you born?

WEBSTER: I was born in 1944.

FRANKLIN: Okay. And what—so you said you had graduated—went to school in Theodore, Alabama. I wonder if you could talk about your education there, back in Alabama and kind of the prevailing situation there.

WEBSTER: Okay. That's a good point, because it lends to my activities in Pasco. I went to school in a segregated school system. I graduated from high school. It was still segregated at that time. So, when I graduated from high school, I knew then that there was a better place that I could live. I didn't know where that was, so I went to Oakland, California, for a short period of time to live with my brother. Then I get an opportunity from my uncle to move to Pasco. In fact, he asked me to help him drive to Pasco. When I helped him drive to Pasco, I didn't go back to Oakland. So that's how I got here. And again, I was very, very familiar with segregation whether it was de facto or institutionalized. When I got to Pasco, I was surprised at the de facto segregation that I found in Pasco, which was very, very similar to what I experienced in Alabama.

FRANKLIN: Really?

WALLACE: Yes.

FRANKLIN: More similar to Alabama than in Oakland?

WALLACE: Yes. I didn't stay in Oakland very long, so I can't speak a lot to Oakland. But when I got to Pasco, all the Black people, or 90% of the Black people living in East Pasco. The schools that—the elementary school was Whittier School. It was completely Black, with the exception of maybe a few white students that came from the north side of Pasco. That didn't seem right. I thought I was leaving that behind me when I took the Greyhound bus and left Alabama. Matter of fact, it was somewhat disturbing after a while and learning the city, that I became very active—and some people would say an activist—but I became very active in helping, or doing something about breaking down that system.

FRANKLIN: Yeah. What did your parents do in Alabama?

WEBSTER: My mom was a stay-home mom. My dad was a laborer and a minister. He worked at an air force base. It's closed now. It's called Brookley Field Air Force Base in Mobile, Alabama, which was about ten or twelve miles east of Theodore.

FRANKLIN: What was your father—what were your parents' levels of education?

WEBSTER: My dad was quite literate but he only went to the eighth grade, and my mom was probably the sixth or seventh grade. They had five kids and four of the five got advanced degrees from universities. And the older one, he left home and became a construction laborer and became a journeyman painter and drywaller. Of the five of us, as I said earlier, we all got advanced college degrees and they insisted on us getting an education and doing better in life than what they were doing.

FRANKLIN: Was Theodore—so Theodore was a segregated town as well?

WEBSTER: Yes. And it was segregated from the standpoint of all Black people lived in one section of Theodore and all the whites lived in another section. Sometime that may have been across the road, but there was a dividing point. When I was going to school, a school bus would pick up the white students that lived down the road from me, but we all had to walk to school. So I saw that kind of discrimination all of my life.

The one thing that I will point out is you become acclimated to that condition after you've lived in it a long time, and it became another way of life—or a way of life. You don't really understand it until you go someplace else and see the difference. Maybe the first eye-opener I had was the very short time I lived in Oakland. It was more integrated than where I lived in Theodore. Then when I came to Pasco, I was more shocked, because I could see identically to what I saw and experienced and lived in, in Alabama.

FRANKLIN: Yeah, yeah. You mentioned your uncle asked you to help drive a truck up here. Did you have family in the area?

WEBSTER: In this area?

FRANKLIN: Yeah.

WEBSTER: He was my only.

FRANKLIN: And how did he get here?

WEBSTER: As I understand it, and I think I'm probably 90% accurate, when he got out of the military, out of the Army, he joined the labor movement. At that time, the labor movement, or migration, was from the Oakland military installations down there up to Hanford, where they were constructing all kinds of buildings and programs here. And then they migrated on up to Anchorage, Alaska, and worked there during the summer months and then they came back to this area. He decided that he no longer wanted to migrate with the construction industry. He worked construction here for a while. But he built a building and in it he housed three businesses. One was a restaurant, the other one was a pool hall, and the other one was a beer tavern.

FRANKLIN: Was this in East Pasco?

WEBSTER: In East Pasco.

FRANKLIN: Okay. Do you remember the names of these places?

WEBSTER: Yes, it was Jack's Grill and Pit, was the name of it.

FRANKLIN: And that was, the three businesses were Jack's Grill and Pit?

WEBSTER: Yeah, and they were all under that title. And they had separate walls and separate buildings. When he came down to Oakland, it was about October, I think, and he came down to the World Series, as a matter of fact. I think the Giants and the Dodgers were playing at that time. And then I came back up here with him.

FRANKLIN: Wow. What were your first impressions when you arrived in Pasco?

WEBSTER: Well, I liked the city, I liked where I lived. Like I said earlier, once I got here, I never did go back to Oakland. So I liked it a whole lot better than I did Oakland. But as I got to learn the city, I became more aware that it was not much different from where I came. And as I studied it more, and got to know more people, those individuals came from the same states and cities that I was familiar with: Alabama, Texas, Oklahoma, Louisiana. They had come here, also, with the labor migration. I couldn't understand for a long time why all of the Black folks was concentrated east of Pasco, which was on the other side of the railroad tracks. So as I got to talk to more people and got to learn about them, I quickly learned that many of them were very pleased to have a job and to work and make a living for their families, and accepted the housing that was available. That housing was in East Pasco.

FRANKLIN: Right. And they kind of accepted—for a time, accepted the de facto segregation.

WEBSTER: Oh, absolutely, yes, yes.

And I'll tell you, the thing that I liked about East Pasco, a great deal, which was similar to where I lived in Theodore, we all knew each other and knew each other very well. I don't know if there was a person in Pasco at that time that I didn't know them and they didn't know me, after I'd been there for six or eight months or so. So that's how I got to know who they are, where they came from, who their families were. And then it became obvious that something was wrong.

And a little bit more about myself, when I first got to Pasco and enrolled at Columbia Basin College, on the way up, my uncle was talking to me about my goals and opportunities and what I wanted to do in life. We had thirteen, fourteen hours together to do that. And I said I wanted to go to college, because that's something my dad and mom had popped into our head. But I left home before I enrolled in college. So he took me to Columbia Basin College in January, that was the beginning of the quarter. After meeting with counselors and talking to them, I was told that I was not college material. That my education was not up to par, and they didn't think I could make it through college. That was very disappointing to me.

I met a gentleman that I admire to this day. He heard my story. He was an administrator or coach or something at Columbia Basin. He talked to me about majoring or taking accounting. He explained it this way: he said, it can take you three hours to work a problem; it could take the next person 30 minutes. But if you come up with the same answer, what difference does it make? As long as you have the fortitude to stick with it and get it done. You also can check it to make sure it's accurate. That's what steered me into accounting, finance. And I spent 30-some years in banking and finance.

FRANKLIN: Do you remember his name?

WEBSTER: His name was Sig Hansen.

FRANKLIN: Sig?

WEBSTER: Yeah, S-I-G. I never will forget his name the rest of my life. He was probably one of the most inspirational individuals, from an education or career that I've met in my life.

FRANKLIN: And did you graduate from CBC?

WEBSTER: Twice. [*laughter*] They didn't have a WSU campus out here at that time.

FRANKLIN: Sure. What did you get degrees in?

WEBSTER: Well, one was applied science and the other was business, with a business emphasis, yeah.

FRANKLIN: Oh, that's great. What was the first place you stayed in after you arrived here?

WEBSTER: It's no longer there, but I stayed at 725 South Hugo Street in East Pasco. It was A Street going towards Sacagawea Park. That's where my uncle, not only had he built a business with three entities in it, he also had built an apartment building on the hill up there that had three or four apartments in it. The one apartment, he built especially for himself to live in. So I lived with him.

FRANKLIN: Your uncle sounds like quite the entrepreneur.

WEBSTER: Yes, no question about that. He left here after Urban Renewal purchased his property, and went to California. He went to Oakland because we had a lot of relatives in Oakland. He went there and opened a couple of businesses. So, yes, he was definitely an entrepreneur.

FRANKLIN: So it was basically an apartment.

WEBSTER: Yes, it was an apartment.

FRANKLIN: An apartment in a building that he owned.

WEBSTER: Yes, yes. It was an apartment building with four units in it, and he lived in the major unit in that building.

FRANKLIN: Gotcha, gotcha. What was the hardest aspect of life in this area to adjust to?

WEBSTER: Well, after I started Columbia Basin College, I never will forget for the rest of my life—this. I was in a business class, a business machine class. I had never operated a full-key add machine at that time. So I'm struggling. And this young lady sitting behind me came over to help me put my hands on the right home keys on this machine. She just came over, and she leaned over, and her hair fell kind of on my shoulder. A white female. And I can remember—I became so petrified that I could not move. My whole body froze. Because I was conditioned in Alabama that not only didn't you look at a white woman, especially, but to have her hair hanging over your shoulder, across, is tantamount to being lynched. That was an absolute no-no. And I never will forget. It frightened her, it frightened me. We remained friends for a long time after that, but that was one of the things that helped me understand that I had been preconditioned to something that I had to get over.

The second thing was—I mentioned Whittier School. I went to a segregated school, and I knew you can get comfortable. And I knew that when I left there and I went over to CBC, they told me that I was not up to par with my education. Something said to me that these kids are probably not up to par, either. So there has to be a reason why all Black kids are going to school here and all white kids are going to school someplace else. Well, I know that a few of the parents were comfortable sending their kids to Whittier because it was close to home, they were afraid that if—because I was advocating close the school down, as opposed to bussing white kids in. They felt that it would drop the property value, also. Not only convenient as having their kids going down the street, but property values. But I was able to prevail in the thought and we pressed upon the school board, we marched, we demonstrated with enough parents, and they made the decision to close Whittier School. Later they tore the building down. But I just did not feel that they could get the right education.

And then in this process, I learned that a lot of people were not registered to vote. This is a story—I guess the statute of limitations is expired now. But I was only, at that time, I was 17 or 18. But I was not old enough to vote. The voting age at that time was still 21. Went to a couple of the—well, the two major parties, the democrats and republican parties to get a voter registration going. The democrats in this case said I was too young to register people to vote. I learned from that experience. I went to the republicans and they agreed that I could register people to vote, but I could not sign the application as the registrar.

So I took it upon myself at that point to conduct a voter registration drive, and we registered more people—I would basically hang out where my uncle's business was and went in the community some organizations. I don't recall this day how many people we registered, but it was definitely in the hundreds. That was one way of getting people engaged in changing the environment in which we lived.

In Alabama, you could vote, but you had to play a poll tax. You had to pass an exam, then pay a poll tax to vote. And here all you had to do was go down and fill out the application and then turn it in.

FRANKLIN: I think that the poll tax and the exam is something that's so foreign to a lot of people these days, especially younger generation. Could you talk about in a little more detail about what that was, and how that stopped Black people from voting?

WEBSTER: Yes. Think of it in the context of your earnings, number one. Even if you were educated enough, or learned enough about the exam through some basic classes to pass it, they impose this tax. This tax was compounded. So they'll look at your age, for an example, and say, oh, you're 50 years old, so we're going to charge you a dollar a year since birth. Now your tax is $50, for an example. So before you could get your voter registration approved, you had to pay the $50. And it increased every year thereafter. Well, if you're only making enough to put bread on the table and pay the rent, that wasn't your number one priority. So it discouraged—and it was intended to discourage. Each county kind of set their own tax levels. Some may be $.50; some may be $2 a year. But they raised it to a level that it discouraged African Americans from voting.

FRANKLIN: And there was no poll tax on whites.

WEBSTER: There were—now, I'm going to assume there were poll tax on whites. I don't know the answer to that, to tell you the truth.

FRANKLIN: Okay. And what about the exam? Was it—what kinds of, from your knowledge, what kinds of questions and things were asked of people?

WEBSTER: Yeah. As I recall from listening to my father and others that took the exam, it was more white history. You learned about General E. Lee, you learned about the Civil War and why it was fought, but not that it was a war that was fought to end slavery; it was a war that was fought to preserve the economy of the South. So it was more, if I may use the term, white history, than who were governors at this point in time, the legislators, the senators, as opposed to African American history.

FRANKLIN: Mm-hm. It must've been—I can't imagine the feeling of being Black and having to answer questions about why the Civil War was fought in order to vote.

WEBSTER: Yeah, yeah. And I'll tell you another thing that—you just triggered a thought. We would always get our books and materials and school buses and everything else, they were kind of the hand-me-downs. They came from the whites. Those books that had anything in it about Black history, those pages were torn out before we got the books. I can remember, some people in the community would go and order books directly from the publisher. But we didn't take those books to school; we took the books that had the N-word written all through it and everything else. Drawings of lynchings on front pages of the book, on the blank sheets of it. Those are the books that we learned from. So after a while, you just kind of—it just kind of rolls off.

FRANKLIN: Right, it becomes normalized.

WEBSTER: Yes. Exactly, exactly.

FRANKLIN: Yeah, that kind of terror. Wow. You'd mentioned earlier that when you came here and you started to talk to people, there were people from Texas and Louisiana and Oklahoma. Were most of the people—African Americans you met in East Pasco—were they all recent migrants from the South?

WEBSTER: There had been somewhat recent, but generations came with parents. Because, mind you, I came in 1962. A lot of those people had worked at Hanford for 40 years at that time, or longer. But if you stop and think about it, if you have a family, and you have migrated to Pasco, and you're working every day, and you're earning two or three times more than you were earning when you were in Louisiana or Texas, and you were able to bring your family, you felt pretty good about it.

FRANKLIN: Yeah.

WEBSTER: And you got pretty comfortable. And you did not necessarily think about upsetting the apricots, so to speak. So they became conditioned. It was nothing—you didn't take a second thought about having to go shop at Grigg's Department Store to get what you want, and you go underneath a railroad track and up to go to Grigg's. You just did it. And you earned enough money to be able to go to the department store.

FRANKLIN: And you didn't have to go in a separate entrance.

WEBSTER: That's exactly right.

FRANKLIN: But if you went to Kennewick, you could go during the day, but you couldn't go at night.

WEBSTER: Yes, yes. Yeah, Kennewick was branded at that time by one of the regional NAACP/civil rights leaders as the Birmingham of the Northwest. Locally it was referred to as the sundown town. You could be there during the day, but by sundown you had to be out. It was basically, for all practical purposes, it was segregated. Just like Birmingham. It didn't even have an East Pasco. It was white almost 100% all over.

FRANKLIN: Right, because covenants had kept—

WEBSTER: Yes, yes.

FRANKLIN: Had kept African Americans from purchasing a home.

WEBSTER: Until the Fair Housing Act was passed, they had these covenants of first right of refusal. So if I was selling to—if one of the owners decides to sell to a Black person, someone could step in and say I'm exercising my right of first refusal and buy the property. But if they were selling it to a white person, they would not exercise that right. So they used that as a means to keep it segregated.

FRANKLIN: Yeah, it wasn't until the mid- to late-'60s, right, where the first African Americans—

WEBSTER: Yeah, right.

FRANKLIN: The Slaughter family.

WEBSTER: The Slaughter family, yeah. And that was done a little bit as a challenge to the covenants, to see if the Fair Housing Act would be enforced. So it was kind of a demonstration to that, a challenge to that.

FRANKLIN: Did you meet any Manhattan Project—people who had worked on the Manhattan Project that had come up for construction and had stayed in Pasco?

WEBSTER: I met a number of them that have passed on now, of course.

FRANKLIN: Of course.

WEBSTER: And had an opportunity to interact and talk with and, matter of fact, two or three of the individuals who were my—I consider my strongest supporters, had come up through the Manhattan act.

FRANKLIN: Who were they?

WEBSTER: One name, E.M. Magee. He was head of the NAACP. Another one was Luzell Johnson. He was a very, very quiet, unassuming man, but very powerful. When he spoke, people listened.

FRANKLIN: He helped found Morning Star.

WEBSTER: Yes, yes, exactly right.

FRANKLIN: Right? In his home with his wife.

WEBSTER: Very wonderful, wonderful, wonderful man. Another one, his name was Ray Henry. When I call these names, a lot of times, these may not be the formal names on their birth certificates, but these are the names we got to know them by very affectionately. But I'm pretty sure his name was Ray Henry. E.M. Magee, Luzell Johnson, I'm pretty sure those are their correct names. Those three individuals were very, very helpful in keeping me grounded as a youngster.

FRANKLIN: What did you know or learn about the prior history of African American workers at Hanford?

WEBSTER: Well, I knew that there was a shortage of labor, and I knew that they went to the states where there were high populations of African Americans and brought that labor to Hanford. Subsequently, I learned from some of the declassification of information back relating to that time, that there was a systematic strategy to get the work done, but not to bring social justice along with it.

What do I mean by that? When they brought African Americans here, they maintained the segregation. They maintained the separate chow halls and eating facilities and living facilities. They would post signs, this particular chow hall is for Negroes and this for whites. And they basically kept whites as supervisors. So they brought the segregation system, picked it up and moved it here intact. Because, as I understand it, they wanted to build buildings as opposed to do social engineering. So that's another reason why Blacks were in East Pasco, is that's where they each agreed that they could go and live, as opposed to Kennewick, and Richland, which was a government town. There were a few Blacks in Richland, but very, very few that met the criteria for living in Richland.

FRANKLIN: Right, and that criteria was a job with AEC—

WEBSTER: At a certain level.

FRANKLIN: —at a certain level, which would've been a challenge to say the least, for most African Americans to have that education and to prevail on the standard hiring practices of the 1940s and 1950s.

WEBSTER: That's exactly right. There was not the predominate number of people coming in from the labor supply that they were looking to build the plants out there.

FRANKLIN: But there were several Black families in Richland, is that right?

WEBSTER: Yeah. Yeah.

FRANKLIN: Could you name them?

WEBSTER: You know, I don't know all of their names. I think the Wallaces were one. I don't know names, but I do know there were several Black families. I did not know them personally, to be honest with you.

FRANKLIN: Sure, sure, sure. Let's see here. We kind of—oh, I wanted to—from your perspective, thinking about the African Americans that came during World War II to help build Hanford and who stayed, what were their most important contributions in the areas of work, community life, and civil rights?

WEBSTER: Well, number one is, this does not necessarily relate to civil rights, but I saw a very, very strong sense of family, a very strong sense of community. Even though by my perception, it was a segregated community. But there was a very strong sense of community. There were a lot of African Americans who worked at Hanford after it was built, and they were part of the downwinders. I don't know if you got into that a whole lot, but they were part of the folks who were contaminated and were actually compensated for their illnesses from working out there.

FRANKLIN: Was that because of the location of East Pasco, or were they—was it due to exposure on the job?

WEBSTER: Both the job and where they lived.

The one other thing that I really appreciated, even though they went to an elementary school that was segregated—and it's part of this family values— there were siblings who their kids were encouraged to go to the high school— which, Pasco then only had one high school. And was encouraged to go on to college. There were Pasco-ites that went on to the NFL and there's some wonderful things as a result of the experience that they got here at Hanford.

So, I don't mean to say that the quality of life was so bad that they couldn't overcome the challenges. But I saw challenges in my generation that I thought was not necessary. And I thought we had overcome in other parts of the world.

FRANKLIN: Did you feel that—you'd mentioned how Pasco kind of surprised you that Pasco was so much like Alabama. Did you think, leaving Alabama, that you were leaving that kind of segregation behind?

WEBSTER: Oh, no question. When I left Alabama, I was so determined to leave—and I was very young and I can think back now how my parents must've felt with me saying I'm leaving home. I had a fried chicken in a cardboard box, my mom cooked a pound cake, and I bought a loaf of bread. That was my meal. And then when I bought my ticket at the Greyhound bus station from Mobile, Alabama, to Oakland, California, I had $29 left. With those kinds of resources, going from one part of the world that you'd never been in before, going to another part of the world you've never been before, it took some determination and something to say you have the motivation to leave here. I guess from TV and other places, I decided to pack up and leave. Then when I got here, and again I found the same thing that I was experiencing in Alabama, I thought, my goodness, why did I make the sacrifice?

But I could see, just because I was able to go over to Columbia Basin College, and the fact that I could walk in the front door and go in the registrar's office—even though the counselor told me I would never ever matriculate in college. That was an incentive. And I'll tell you something else, when I got my master's degree, I went over and I took a photocopy of it and I left it in his office. He wasn't there, so I just left it in his office. But the thing that I appreciate most is arriving in this town of Pasco, the east side, and getting the level of support that I had as a newcomer. But I think they saw me as a teenager, as a youngster, who wanted to do something. And all the folks just said, let's get behind him and do something, because he's trying to do something positive. Yeah.

FRANKLIN: That's great. Kind of still a segregated environment, but one that maybe had more opportunity than the South for you, and for others?

WEBSTER: Yeah, but you know, in the South, there's one thing, at least when I was growing up: you had an opportunity to go to college, but you went to, again, a segregated college.

FRANKLIN: To an HBC?

WEBSTER: To an HBC. You had an opportunity in many times to be a professional, whether it was a school teacher or an administrator. You didn't have the options of being a medical doctor unless you went to another school in another state. Like in Alabama, my brother wanted to go to medical school and back in the days, they would pay you—the state would pay, if you would accepted in medical school, let's say in Tennessee or something, to an all-Black school. They would pay the tuition, because they didn't want you going to University of Alabama, for an example. So they would pay your out-of-state tuition to go there.

FRANKLIN: Why would that be?

WEBSTER: To keep it segregated. It was segregation. "Segregation today, segregation tomorrow and segregation forever." You've probably—

FRANKLIN: George Wallace, right?

WEBSTER: That's exactly right. So to keep it segregated, they would pay for you to go to another state. So it was—people who lived here were aware of that. And I think they just needed someone to be an advocate for change.

FRANKLIN: Yeah. Did you attend church?

WEBSTER: Here?

FRANKLIN: Yeah.

WEBSTER: Yes, yes, yes, yes. I was a member, active member of New Hope Baptist Church, which was right up the hill from Morning Star.

FRANKLIN: Right. How long did you go there for?

WEBSTER: I'm going to say probably ten years.

FRANKLIN: What role did church play in the community?

WEBSTER: The church was the foundation of the community. Almost everything positive came out of the church. I'll give you an example. I felt that in order—it's kind of going back to England and where they have piazzas, the places you can go and congregate and community, things like—I thought that Pasco needed a place, a neutral place, where people could go and they could call it a community center. And I could see the value of people gathering. We had a little place over in East Pasco called Kurtzman Park. It was a little building there. And I thought that we could do better.

So I studied up and found that HUD had what they call block grants. They would give block grants for certain amounts of dollars depending on your application. I worked and worked and worked and got the city, the city manager, Mar Winegar, one of the finest city managers I think that ever held a city manager job anywhere, agreed to work with me in helping to complete an application. We completed a HUD application and got some $440,000–$450,000 to build what is now known as the Martin Luther King Center in East Pasco. The central labor council owned the land where that building is. We worked with them, and they deeded that land as part of the in-kind contribution to match the HUD block grant. We were able to put that together.

The way that we—part of Mar Winegar's help and assistance—we were able to work out a strategy where the Pasco Parks and Recreation would somewhat manage the building. But to get the revenue, we went to get the various state agencies and other organizations to rent space in the building to help maintain it. So DS&HS, I think, had a small office there. Employment, security, had a small office there. Central Labor Council had a small recruiting office. So there were different offices in this building to help maintain it.

And it became a community center. And not only did the community need the services of the agencies that were there, but it became a—but to answer your question, all of that came out of the basement of Morning Star Baptist Church. Reverend Allen was the pastor at that time. So I think if you point to almost any significant accomplishment, the genesis of it came from the spiritual and religious community.

FRANKLIN: It functioned as a meeting place.

WEBSTER: Yes.

FRANKLIN: In the community.

WEBSTER: That's where the people went. I mean, when you wanted to do something, you go where the people are. On Sunday morning, that's where you're going to find them, and that's where you make your point. You convince the pastor that it's worthwhile, and then they'll let you get up and make announcements and talk to the congregation where you've got a captive audience. That's how you got your message across. So it was—because you didn't have a newspaper or TV channel or radio station or any of those, except for a routine newscast or something. But if you wanted to tell your whole story, you had to go to the church.

FRANKLIN: Right. How would you describe life in the community, in East Pasco?

WEBSTER: It was probably one of the best lives that I have lived. And I say that because everybody cared for one another. People lived in harmony. Didn't have much, so it wasn't economically driven; it was more social- and spiritual-driven. Everyone was treated with respect. You'd hear very few disagreements. You didn't have what they have today with solving disagreements, you know, with violence. It was probably one of the best places I've lived in my life.

FRANKLIN: What did you do in your spare time?

WEBSTER: Now, or then?

FRANKLIN: Then.

WEBSTER: Then? I didn't have any spare time, because I was going to college at the time, and I was also very active in the community. I was president—I went on to become president of CORE, the Congress of Racial Equality. I was president of the Tri-City chapter although I was very young, but again—

I want to make this point, something that I did not experience in Alabama. There were white people of quote-unquote high stature with very high moral commitments to help bring about this change. When I say that, I'm talking about lawyers and educators and scientists out here on the project who helped to bring about this change. You know, if I named—if I started naming like the Ed Critchlows—I don't know if you've—the Critchlow, Williams and Ryals law firm, I think, is still in existence here in Richland. A guy named John Sullivan was a lawyer. Dick Nelson was a scientist here in the Project. I mean, there were just a number of people who migrated to this area from other places, highly educated, technical backgrounds, could see the same thing that I saw and was willing to give their time and knowledge and energies to bring about this—the Brouns, Dick and Nyla Brouns. They gave of their time and talents and financial resources to help bring about this change. That was one of the better learning experiences I've had.

FRANKLIN: And you said that was different from Alabama.

WEBSTER: Yes. I mean, I never saw, in my generation, and certainly years later where there were whites in the North that was part of the Freedom Ride and other movements, Martin Luther King's movement, that came to the South. But you didn't find folks that lived in Theodore, Alabama, helping to bring about a change for Black folks in Alabama. So that was my first opportunity to work shoulder-to-shoulder with white people to bring about this change.

When we were marching on Pasco, for an example. Pasco City Hall was a totally white city hall that was supposedly serving the whole city. There was not a police officer, or anyone in public works, engineering, or any of those places. So, we were marching on city hall for employment opportunities. The Pasco Police Department, for example, had never had—at that time, had not had any people of color working. I applied for a grant that paid the salary of the first police officer in Pasco, on the Pasco Police Department.

FRANKLIN: There were also some issues between the Pasco Police Department and residents of East Pasco. There was some tension there, in that relationship in the '60s?

WEBSTER: As I recall, not to the extent that you have today, and not for the same reasons that you have today. I don't recall any shootings of unarmed black people or anything like that. I look back and I think there probably was some collusions on the part of the police department and some of the elicit activities that were going on, you know. Because some of these things operated in broad, open daylight, that if you had a police department that was cracking down on them, it wouldn't have been possible.

FRANKLIN: I was just looking back on an old interview with James Pruitt. I don't know if that name is familiar to you.

WEBSTER: Yeah, Jim Pruitt? Yeah.

FRANKLIN: He had been—Jim, yeah, sorry. In the interview, the interviewer keeps calling him James, and he's like, Jim, my name is Jim.

WEBSTER: Yeah, yeah, yeah, yeah.

FRANKLIN: He had been—he was appointed as a liaison between East Pasco and the police department, because there had been some excessive force arrests or something to that nature—or, it just seemed like there was a relationship that was a little rocky there for a period of time that would've warranted a liaison, right? Or was it just that maybe there was no interface between city government and East Pasco?

WEBSTER: I think it was more that than—I'll be honest with you, I don't recall. I just don't recall where there were racial tensions or anything like that between the police. I just don't recall that. And I do—I know Jim well—knew him well. It was more during the Urban Renewal and when that was going on. I think you may have talked to Webster about that. It was more during that time, when we were looking at bridging the gaps, the communications gaps and all that, because Jim was a liaison, I think, at the time that I got the grant to hire our first police officer. So I don't recall that it was racial tension as we know it today.

FRANKLIN: Sure, sure, sure. But there's certainly—a big part of your efforts was a big push to make the city more representative of its citizens.

WEBSTER: Yes. Streets and sidewalks were an example. Things that we didn't have that the west side had. Education, where kids could go to school and get the same quality of education that the west side got. Those were kind of— jobs where they could—not just the labor jobs at Hanford, but jobs working in the City of Pasco, whether you were working for the surveying group or— as a matter of fact, I think I went to work for a while as a member of a survey team in city hall, going out surveying streets and looking at improvement districts and stuff like that. So it was that kind of—but we had to push city hall and city management to move on those areas.

FRANKLIN: Right.

WEBSTER: And that was pushed with a lot of leather on the streets.

FRANKLIN: And you mentioned that you had been president of CORE, the Tri-Cities chapter of CORE.

WEBSTER: Yes.

FRANKLIN: And CORE was a pretty young organization at that time, right?

WEBSTER: Correct.

FRANKLIN: And did it draw from all the three cities?

WEBSTER: Yes. Oh, yes. Matter of fact, a number of our meetings were actually held in Kennewick. A lot of the organizing and strategizing meetings were held in Kennewick. And many of the folks that was part of it came from

Richland as well. And a number of them worked on the Hanford Project in very professional managerial roles.

FRANKLIN: Yeah, yeah, I've interviewed several folks who were involved with that. You mentioned the Brouns and then we had interviewed the Millers here—

WEBSTER: Yes.

FRANKLIN: And Jim Stoffels who was secretary.

WEBSTER: Right, right, right. The Millers, especially. They were involved as a family. I guess so with the Brouns. But I can remember the Millers were involved as a family. They were right there every day, working side-by-side. And we organized marches. We went from Pasco to Kennewick to emphasize the sundown.

FRANKLIN: Over the bridge?

WEBSTER: Over the bridge, over the bridge.

FRANKLIN: Was that the green bridge?

WEBSTER: Yes, it was. It's kind of comical now when I look back. We were marching over, arm-in-arm and walking across, and there some cars on the other side of the bridge, they were standing there with the rebel flag on them, and they were raising the engine, and you can hear the engines roaring. I was arm-in-arm with Jack Tanner, who was the regional NAACP president at that time out of Tacoma, very influential lawyer at that time, and went on to be a federal court judge. I looked over at Jack. I said, Jack, what are we going to do? Because we thought they were revving up these engines to just run the cars. And he looked at me and said, can you swim? [*laughter*] I never will forget that. I said, no, I can't swim in that water! Across the Columbia River. And he said, well, let's keep on marching then. Okay, so we just kept marching and went on to the other side.

FRANKLIN: Wow. How did that feel to see that symbol, which you must've grown up seeing the Confederate flag all over the place. How did it feel to see that in Kennewick and Pasco, in Washington State, where—

WEBSTER: I'll tell you. By that time, I was somewhat sensitized to what's happening here and learned about. But it took me way back. I mean, it took me to the guys that was riding around on horsebacks with hoods over their heads with same flags. I mean, the only difference was that these individuals were in muscle cars with flags on them. But it was scary. It was scary.

FRANKLIN: That symbol was meant to—

WEBSTER: Intimidate.

FRANKLIN: —intimidate you, right?

WEBSTER: Intimidate, no question about it.

FRANKLIN: They weren't showing up to promote Southern heritage.

WEBSTER: No, oh, no, no, no. It was to intimidate. But it was intended, in my judgment, to say to us, we're going to keep Kennewick white. That's what—and we're going to challenge you on it. And, not in our backyard.

FRANKLIN: You know, if I could share an anecdote real quick with you, a few weeks ago I went to the march for immigrants here in Richland.

WEBSTER: Mm-hmm?

FRANKLIN: And we were marching right by the courthouse, did a big loop around Howard Amon Park. And a gentleman in a truck—I thought this was really interesting—with a Confederate flag and an American flag, was rolling down the street revving his engine, yelling obscenities, flipping us the bird. Which, to see those two together is strange enough, but then to use that as a symbol of intimidation against immigrants. It still is clear as day what the intent of that symbolism is.

WEBSTER: Right. And in the South, I think even to this day, the Civil War was just like it was fought last week.

FRANKLIN: Yeah.

WEBSTER: I mean, with the rebel flags and the sentiments and beliefs and values is just like it was yesterday. And how those kinds of feelings can be carried forward for generations is just amazing. It's amazing to me.

FRANKLIN: Yeah. Do you remember any other particular community events, from—during those years in East Pasco?

WEBSTER: You know, we had a number of—I'm trying to, you know, there's—it's kind of coming back to me now. I can't remember the incident, but we had a number of meetings in Kurtzman Park that was very tense meetings. As a matter of fact, what used to happen is Carl Maxey from Spokane, prominent civil rights lawyer in Spokane, other lawyers from Seattle, would come to Pasco, because we didn't have any African American lawyers here at that time, and help us with civil rights issues. I remember I was having a meeting in Kurtzman Park where it got pretty heated, just among the—I don't remember the issues, but there was one bombing that took place here in East Pasco. It was this gentleman, who lives in Richland, had built a business—

FRANKLIN: Right. I interviewed him. Oh, shoot.

WEBSTER: Carter.

FRANKLIN: Yes, Dan Carter.

WEBSTER: Had built a business, janitorial business as well as he had a ceramic store. And somebody set off a bomb. We were all in Kurtzman Park, having a big powwow when that happened, because everybody jumped and ran. Not to say there were not some very tense times back in those days, but I don't remember any killings or anything like that that were associated with our movement or anything.

FRANKLIN: When I interviewed Dan and a couple others, they had alluded to—there was a disconnect or a tense relationship between African Americans in Richland and African Americans in East Pasco. And sometimes the two—not that they didn't see eye-to-eye, but that people in East Pasco kind of felt that those in Richland or from outside the area who were trying to help were kind of outsiders or maybe they didn't understand the Pasco issue. Would you say that's the case?

WEBSTER: I would say that's somewhat true. There was this feeling that African Americans that came to Richland came after the African Americans in Pasco had really built Hanford. So they were being recruited for the best jobs, and they had the best quality of life. And often did not relate very well to the people of East Pasco. And, yes, that's when this intra conflict started to exist. Although there were individuals in Richland that related very well. But it was more of an economic divide, and a social divide than a racial divide.

FRANKLIN: Right, right. Kind of a class thing.

WEBSTER: Right, that's exactly right. Right, right.

FRANKLIN: Related to kind of violence or destruction of property, I had heard in an older oral history, someone said that Luzell's daughter had tried to move to Kennewick and someone had—the house had burned down.

WEBSTER: Yeah, there were a number of incidents that happened right after the—and before the Civil Rights Act. I remember one individual—excuse me—who moved to Kennewick and it was Jones. Her last name was Jones. And they moved to Kennewick. She worked for the telephone company in

Pasco. Pacific Northwest Bell Telephone had an office right on Lewis Street. At night, we would take turns driving immediately behind her from the time she got off at Bell to the time she walked in the front door. So somebody would be with her. We would not let her go home by herself, because of all the threats and stuff like that.

FRANKLIN: Wow. Like phone, telephone and mail?

WEBSTER: And notes left on her car, and you name it.

FRANKLIN: Wow, wow.

WEBSTER: Yup. Rocks thrown against the doors of her house. They were trailblazers, in a sense, like the Slaughters, some of the first ones to live in Kennewick.

FRANKLIN: Right. Wow. I guess kind of a happier shift, do you recall any family or community events or traditions, including sports and food, that people brought from the places they came from?

WEBSTER: [*laughter*] Yes. We had some big events in the park and folks had their specialties, whether it was their black-eyed peas or their fried chicken. You know, there was another business that we had that she would always provide the chicken. There was the chicken shack.

FRANKLIN: Virgie's?

WEBSTER: Virginia's. Virginia.

FRANKLIN: Virginia's Chicken Shack.

WEBSTER: And then, believe it or not, she was in a building. She lived in one portion and the Chicken Shack was on the front. She didn't start serving chicken until maybe 10:00 or 11:00 at night and would go all night because of folks that went to the tavern and everywhere else that would go there after hours, right? But then across the A Street, down further in almost like a private home was another lady, her name was Sally. I can't tell you what her last name was, but it was Sally's, and that's where you went and got all the barbecue. I mean, this lady would barbecue for days. So all of those things would come to the park. And then we would have the Juneteenth gathering. You probably got the history on that, on Juneteenth, but that was a time to come to the park, celebrate, put the benches out, bring your best dish, and people just kind of congregated, just from everywhere in the Tri-Cities.

FRANKLIN: That was the celebrating the arrival of the news that slavery—

WEBSTER: That's correct, had ended. Two years after the Emancipation Proclamation.

FRANKLIN: Right. And that was not exclusively but primarily a Texas event, right?

WEBSTER: Yes.

FRANKLIN: But there were a lot of—

WEBSTER: Some in Oklahoma, but mostly in Texas, yeah.

FRANKLIN: Right, because there was a pretty big contingent of families from, especially from Kildare that had moved up and—

WEBSTER: Mm-hmm, you got it.

FRANKLIN: —and brought that tradition with them.

WEBSTER: Yes, yes. And it's kind of celebrated throughout the African American community to this day. But the point is that that was a major day in the park that people got together and brought their foods and their specialties there.

FRANKLIN: Okay. So we talked a lot about opportunities. You—so I wanted to shift kind of to some of your work—I don't exactly know your timeline, so I don't know where to start, but I wanted to talk about your work at Hanford, but also your work with the Urban Renewal. So I don't know which one of those is a better one to start with first.

WEBSTER: Well, Urban Renewal was first.

FRANKLIN: Okay. Let's talk about that first.

WEBSTER: It was going on at the time that I was the executive director of the Benton-Franklin Community Action Committee, which was in the late '60s, '69, probably, to '73, somewhere in that timeframe.

FRANKLIN: You were doing all of this in your late 20s, huh?

WEBSTER: Oh, oh yeah.

FRANKLIN: Like 20s and early 30s.

WEBSTER: Oh, yeah, and my teens.

FRANKLIN: And your teens.

WEBSTER: Yeah, early teens and early 20s. As director of the Community Action Committee—the Bi-county Community Action Committee, that was more of a continuation of some of the work that I had done as a teen in

Pasco. As a matter of fact, I was offered a job almost the day I—I left as a teen because I got inducted into the military at the time—the draft. I should say, I got drafted into the military.

FRANKLIN: Right, for the Vietnam War.

WEBSTER: Vietnam War. And then when I got out and came back to Pasco, discharged and came back to Pasco, I was immediately offered this job as the executive director of the Benton-Franklin Community Action Committee.

FRANKLIN: What years were you gone?

WEBSTER: I was gone from '65 until '69.

FRANKLIN: Okay.

WEBSTER: Yeah. So in April of '69 I became director of the Community Action Committee and again, continued some of the work that I was doing. Of course, that program was federally funded; it was part of the Economic Opportunity Act in the Johnson Great Society program. So you were limited in terms of how you could get involved in partisan politics, but city government and all those things were not considered partisan. They were considered non-partisan so I could be very active in those activities and working with the various organizations. So we created neighborhood councils and we were trying to get neighborhood councils to address issues in their specific neighborhoods.

One of the neighborhood councils that I worked closely with was the East Pasco Neighborhood Council. And there, we worked closely with the Urban Renewal, which, Webster Jackson headed that. There was tension and conflicts there from a program standpoint. Not necessarily from individuals running these programs, but from a program standpoint. The Urban Renewal program did not have a major component to it in terms of what was being renewed. We knew that they were buying houses that they considered to be dilapidated and moving people out, but there was no housing being developed to give people an option to stay in the neighborhood or another section of the neighborhood. So all those people who were in East Pasco next to the railroad track and somewhat west of Oregon Street or west of Wehe Street were being, property being purchased under the Urban Renewal program, like I said. But there was no replacement housing. So it became more and more industrial. We were kind of fighting to get housing.

Matter of fact, as part of that, Mister Romney, George Romney's dad who ran for vice president or ran for president—

FRANKLIN: Oh, right, George Romney—for Mitt Romney.

WEBSTER: From Michigan. Mitt Romney's dad physically came to Pasco—

FRANKLIN: Really?

WEBSTER: —to meet with us. Yes, yes, I've got photos with him. Because we were concerned about that displacement.

It just so happened that that program lasted longer than I did, and I didn't see it through. But I believe to this day that was probably one of the biggest failures that I encountered in the sense that, for me, that we didn't see it through well enough to say if you buy this house, then you should have another affordable house to move in and hold the community together, as opposed to dispersing a community. A lot of people went to rentals and moved out of the area and so the neighborhood that we knew as East Pasco was basically, from a homeownership standpoint, was basically cut in half, if not more.

FRANKLIN: Wow. Yeah. I had heard that from a couple others that had been involved in Urban Renewal.

WEBSTER: It's all big industrial stuff now.

FRANKLIN: Yeah. But it'd succeeded in getting rid of some of the very questionable and dilapidated housing, but it'd fragmented the community.

WEBSTER: Exactly.

FRANKLIN: And didn't replace that with better housing.

WEBSTER: Right, yeah. Yeah, because a lot of people had taken—I wouldn't say a lot, but some had taken their railroad cars that had been surplused I guess, and got them hauled in and joined them together. And they were putting them on cinder blocks and they were living in some of these places.

FRANKLIN: Wow.

WEBSTER: Very warm and nice and comfortable inside, but very limited space. But it was home.

FRANKLIN: Right, it was a home, and they fought to—it's not like the government was allowing them to get home loans. But now the government was coming in and saying, well, you know, you got to get rid of this.

WEBSTER: And buying it out, but no real place to go.

FRANKLIN: Was there pushback? From people in East Pasco?

WEBSTER: There was pushback, but not from an organized pushback that I would've liked to have seen or that I think would exist today.

FRANKLIN: Mm, it was just individuals?

WEBSTER: Yes. And again, I was a young kid, you know? I didn't quite understand the whole dynamics and everything that was going on, so I couldn't provide what I feel today is the leadership that that issue should've gotten to get the results that you were looking for.

FRANKLIN: Right, right. That's a sad but kind of common story in American cities with Urban Renewals, is describing that same effect, is a lot of the attention is paid to the clearing-out but very little is paid to—

WEBSTER: The building-up.

FRANKLIN: And finishing the program.

WEBSTER: That's correct, that's correct.

FRANKLIN: And then what did you do—you mentioned you didn't finish with the Community Action Council, or you didn't finish with the program, what did you move on to?

WEBSTER: Well, when I left there, I worked for a while after I got out of the CAC on completing the application and providing the infrastructure and the funding for the community center. I guess it's called the Martin Luther King Community Center now. Got that all completed, got the construction.

But at that time, I moved on to Central. As I mentioned, I got two AAs from CBC. Then I had an opportunity to move on to Central and finish undergraduate and graduate there. And after I left Central—and I also worked at Central. I was their first community affirmative action director, in helping to bring about diversifying their faculty. That went well.

Then I came back to Hanford and worked at Boeing Computer Services as a employment manager. And had the opportunity to work there for quite a while, before I moved to Seattle and went into the banking business, and that's where I retired.

FRANKLIN: You said at Boeing you were a—

WEBSTER: Employment manager.

FRANKLIN: Employment manager. What's—

WEBSTER: HR.

FRANKLIN: And was your job, was it a similar, for affirmative action type job?

WEBSTER: That was included, but at that time, we were on an employment build-up. I had the authority, with the limitations of security clearances, et cetera, to offer jobs to individuals onsite as we went around the country interviewing. We had selection criteria of course, and if we felt that a person—and the competition drove a lot of that as well. Because if you've got to come back and wait to explain and help a manager understand why this person is good, someone else has hired them and they're gone and no longer available. But we had the authority to offer the jobs right onsite, whether it was in San Francisco or Texas or wherever we were recruiting.

FRANKLIN: Were there many African Americans in similar positions to yours at Hanford, or was the workforce becoming more diversified?

WEBSTER: Yes. At Hanford, the workforce was becoming more diversified, because I think that was driven a lot by the Department of Energy. There were two gentlemen, well, actually, three, that worked in the human resources area at Department of Energy. And these individuals were also active in the community, who drove a lot of that. I don't know if you've heard the name Bob Hooper? Bob Hooper, Fred Rutt. I'll get Chandler's last name—first name here in a minute. But Fred Rutt, Bob Hooper, were in the employment area for Department of Energy. They influenced these contractors to do the same thing. As a matter of fact, Bob and Fred were also involved in community, like CORE and the Central Labor Council, which we worked very closely with in apprenticeship programs and recruiting there.

Then after I left, I left Boeing and went to—at that time, Rainier Bank, and I went into Rainier Bank in Affirmative Action. They were operating under a consent decree. But I had an agreement, after reading the consent decree and talking to executive management, that if I can meet the requirements—get the company to meet the requirements of this decree, which had to be signed off by a judge—that I would be able to go into the mainstream banking. We had a handshake on that. And the president of that bank, when the judge signed off on the decree, which was about two, two and a half years later, I moved right into the mainstream of the bank. That's where I stayed until I retired.

FRANKLIN: Wow, wow. I wanted to ask you—you sent me a few newspaper articles, by mail, and thank you very much. There's one of you receiving an employment application. Do you remember that photo? I wish I had brought it.

WEBSTER: I think that was where I was leading a group to get employment applications.

FRANKLIN: I think at the city.

WEBSTER: At the city. That's where we marched down to city hall and, as I mentioned to you, the city did not have people of color working. And in a challenge, they would tell me that we don't have anybody working because no one ever applies. So I went and gathered up about ten people and we all went down to city hall at the same time to make applications for jobs that they had available. That's when the photo was taken of us at the counter, applying for jobs, yeah.

I was—whether you're talking about a voter registration drive, whether you're talking about unemployment, whether you're talking about school desegregation, I always thought there had to be an endgame. There had to be tangible results to say that you've done something. It wasn't enough to march from Pasco to Kennewick or march around city hall or go to a schoolboard meeting and have placards in your hand. I had to be able to see African American teachers being hired. I had to see students going into a different class and graduating. I had to see people getting a job.

Man, I'm trying to remember the name of the company. It was a company when you go out to West Richland that relocated. They were processing potatoes and potato chips and all this—

FRANKLIN: Lamb Weston?

WEBSTER: Yeah. I went out there and was talking to the manager and he said, we don't discriminate. We've got x number of jobs, and if you bring the people, we'll hire them. The next day, I showed up with a carload of people and they walked in, and they did just what they said they would do. They hired them. And those folks had jobs. So, that's how I tried to measure my success: on the results, as opposed to the activities.

FRANKLIN: Right. If you had to summarize the major civil rights issues for African Americans at Hanford and in the Tri-Cities during your time here, what would they be?

WEBSTER: Summarize the activities?

FRANKLIN: Issues.

WEBSTER: Issues.

FRANKLIN: Yeah.

WEBSTER: I would say, number one would be at the top of the list would be education for younger people in the elementary level. Second would be jobs, more than just minimum wage kind of jobs. I worked very closely with Hanford to do that. Bob Hooper, Chuck Chandler—I remembered his name—and Fred Rutt were very helpful in paving the way. A guy named Ralph Eckerd who headed up an electrical company here, but also sat on a labor board, was very instrumental in helping to get apprentice employed on the way to journeyman. Being able to become a journeyman, not just in electrical, but in any other field. Matter of fact, they were instrumental in having an office in that neighborhood center in East Pasco to be able to recruit. And then they hired an African American guy to head that office to go out and do the recruiting for them. So employment was another major factor.

I also think the voter registration and the participation in civics played a major role that resulted in both an African American woman being appointed and an African American man being elected to the Pasco City Council. Then after that, another African American man being elected and then becoming mayor.

FRANKLIN: That was Joe—

WEBSTER: That was Joe. And so I think the voter registration and the awareness of the political scene and what you can do if you have representation in the right place. And the right place was not on the street; the right place was where the decisions were being made, sitting on the council. And I think that was important. I also pushed very, very hard to have an African American appointed to the board of directors of Columbia Basin College.

As a matter of fact, as part of this whole political theme, and the Republicans giving me the opportunity to go out and do some registration—and this decision was based solely—solely—on the individual—I opened the first Republican campaign office in East Pasco. That office was for Dan Evans, when he ran for governor. Like I say, I don't know of a politician today, bar none, that was more honest and more fair, more equitable, than Dan Evans.

FRANKLIN: Did that early experience with Republicans—or did that—are you a lifelong Republican?

WEBSTER: No. And that is—you know, I just told you that I'm from Alabama and grew up and the r-word down there—if you're African American, you may as well leave town, because you have tar and feathers all over you. So I'm probably as Democratic as anybody can ever get from the bottom of my foot to the top of my head. But that was not—and I went to the Democratic party first, to register people. When they turned me down, I went to the other alternative with the Republicans, and that's what gave me the opportunity to register people to vote.

But in Dan Evans' case, he was political in the sense that he was running as a Republican governor. But I was not. I was looking strictly at the individual. And the integrity that he brought to the process, and what I felt that he could do. I was never disappointed in that. And I—yes, I took some heat from, even in the African American community, for supporting a governor—well, you show me somebody that's better. And I believe that to this day that that was the right decision.

FRANKLIN: I was just curious.

WEBSTER: Yeah.

FRANKLIN: More than anything.

WEBSTER: Oh, yeah.

FRANKLIN: What were, in your opinion, what were some of the notable successes of some of the civil rights activities in the Tri-Cities?

WEBSTER: Well, I think, number one, is probably the biggest one outside of jobs and having individuals, like heading up the lab in Richland—

FRANKLIN: Oh, Bill Wiley.

WEBSTER: Bill Wiley. I think, if I had to pinpoint what I consider the biggest, was the ability to enforce the Fair Housing laws and get African Americans living in Kennewick. And there are individuals in Kennewick now—and this is our fault, as an African American community—have no idea, when they come to town, they just go right over to Kennewick and rent an apartment and live without any repercussions whatsoever. They don't have any idea—no—but bringing that about, don't need the credit. You just need to know that it's happening, is the most gratifying thing as far as I'm concerned. That they can go and live anywhere in the Tri-Cities that you want to live. All you got to do is be able to pay your rent or pay your house note, and you can live there.

FRANKLIN: What were some of the biggest challenges, or maybe failures?

WEBSTER: Again, I think the biggest challenge that I saw was getting the right people to rally around a cause that—I'm going to use the word "I" at this point—that I felt was most critical at that moment in time. That's where the Luzell Johnsons of East Pasco came in, to get the right—I call him Junior Smith, he was another one, too—to get them rallying around you and supporting you.

I think the biggest challenge—the other biggest challenge was breaking the barrier between Pasco city government and Pasco residents who were

African American. If you just stop and think about it, East Pasco was kind of like a throwaway place. Y'all or they or whoever, you can live over there. The streets were all dirt roads, there were no sidewalks, nothing, you know. They had some sewer and water, but no sidewalks.

FRANKLIN: Well, it didn't even have sewer or water originally.

WEBSTER: For a long time—originally, yeah. But my day, when I came along, it was pretty much. But there were hardly anyone investing or developing except for down near the railroad tracks when the industrial went in. And to say that we're part of the city. We want to work, we want to live, and we want to play in this city. And we pay taxes, and we deserve streets, sidewalks, curbs, gutters, et cetera.

FRANKLIN: Yeah.

WEBSTER: And we deserve employment in the city that we live. Those were the—making that connection was a huge challenge.

FRANKLIN: I had Pastor Wilkins describe it—he described it as, you could tell what the city thought of the Black residents in East Pasco because they were on the other side of the tracks, and then he said there was, like, a dump and a highway and then a stockyard.

WEBSTER: Yeah.

FRANKLIN: And that's what they thought of us, because that's where they put us, was next to the trash and the—

WEBSTER: Yeah, and whichever direction the wind was blowing, you knew it. Yeah, the big stockyard was directly across the street from where I lived. I mean, directly across.

FRANKLIN: Yeah, those don't smell pleasant.

WEBSTER: No, they don't. No, they don't. So we were, like I say, we were the throwaway part of the city. To bring about the sensitivity to change that mindset was a challenge.

FRANKLIN: Yeah. How did—oh, sorry.

WEBSTER: I was going to say one of the things, one of the other elements or factors that played a role was WSU. Glenn Terrell, I don't know if you heard that name or not. But Glenn Terrell was the president of WSU. He made many trips down and worked with us in East Pasco. He also—I shouldn't say he, but the Department of Sociology also sent students down to help us formulate ideas and do research and make sure our positions were strong and backed up with supporting data and reasonableness. So, that was before you had an extension or a campus or whatever they call it now, here at Hanford.

FRANKLIN: Yeah. I've seen some of the theses produced by the sociology students.

WEBSTER: Yeah, and we worked closely with Bill Wiley who was also a trustee at WSU, right? To help bring to bear some of the resources—human capital. Not necessarily money, but human capital to help us overcome some of the difficulties we were having here at the—

FRANKLIN: How did the larger national civil rights movement influence civil rights efforts at Hanford and in the Tri-Cities?

WEBSTER: Well, I mentioned that I was from Alabama.

FRANKLIN: Mm-hmm.

WEBSTER: I marched a couple times with Dr. King.

FRANKLIN: Really?

WEBSTER: I've heard him preach two or three times. My wife is from Montgomery. And I'm from Mobile. But when I would go up there, we would go and hear him preach. But what really moved me was I was sitting on a bar stool in my uncle's tavern, watching TV, and was watching the March on Washington. And I felt extremely guilty. I felt like I had walked away from the movement in Alabama. I should've been there. I should've been marching. I should've been, I should've, I should've never left, I should be there, contributing there, instead of here. That was also that connection, and that connection with CORE, getting James Farmer's information. All of that was part of the eye-opening experience here. What they talked about on TV in Alabama, I could see it in East Pasco. I could see it in Kennewick. I could see it in Richland. Those were all connected, in terms of the motivation to do something.

FRANKLIN: Wow. From your perspective and experience, what was different about civil rights efforts here?

WEBSTER: I think we had been lured into a comfort zone. We had gotten somewhat complacent with what we had. That had a lot to do with that we were better than where we came. But to say we can still do better took a bit more convincing than I originally thought it would.

FRANKLIN: Like, you maybe felt that some people—like, it was better, so it was good enough?

WEBSTER: Yeah, it was—you know, you and I probably have to really get our heads around the same thing. I'm doing 50 times better than my dad, so maybe I'm doing enough. And so, I'm comfortable. And I don't need to get involved with Black Lives Matter. I don't need to get involved with some of the immigration fights that's going on now. I've done that before. I've been there, I've done that. Now it's their turn. There are all kinds of ways of justifying being in your comfort zone. And there's something that's got to kick you out of that comfort zone and say, you need to be involved today. As long as you're breathing, you need to be helping to move things forward. And that's a challenge sometime, depending on how long you've been in that comfort zone and your motivation to do something.

FRANKLIN: Yeah. Well said. So, when you left, you left Boeing to move over to Rainier Bank, how come you left the area that had been your home— why'd you move over to the west side?

WEBSTER: That's a good question, and the answer is not as logical as you might think. We had purchased our first home. We had our—we have two kids, and the baby, my wife was literally nine months pregnant with the second. And here I come home saying that we're moving.

But what happened was, as part of my employment management job at BCSR, Boeing Computer Services Richland, we interfaced with certain jobs with our professional recruiters. This recruiter called me up one day and said, Wally, I have a client that's looking for—and he described this Affirmative Action job in banking in Seattle—do you know of anyone? I said, no, I don't know of anyone. I said, but send me a copy of the description, and I will pass the word around. It was just that; conversation over.

About three weeks later, he calls me up and said, Wally, you remember I talked to you about that Affirmative Action job? I said, yeah, I said, I don't— you didn't send me the description and I don't have anybody. He said, well, we were thinking about you. I said, oh, no, I don't want to move. That's not for me. I don't want to live in Seattle; I'm doing well right here in Richland. He said, what would it take for you to just go over and talk to them? I said, well, I'll tell you what it would take. Send me over on a Thursday night, I interview on Friday, I get to spend the weekend in Seattle and come back Sunday night. He said, deal.

So I went over and interviewed on Friday. The guy called me up and said, we would like to hire you. Would you consider coming? And I said no. And then about a day or so later he called me up again and said, how much would it take for you to come? And I'm being a smart-butt. I just threw out a number. And the first thing he said, you got it.

FRANKLIN: [*laughter*]

WEBSTER: And what do you do? I mean, you've made a commitment, right? And he met it. So now I'm—not only that, we'll do this, we'll do this, we'll fly you home every weekend until you have your baby, and then while she's recovering, you can go home every week, and you can do this, and we'll buy you a house, and we'll move you, and we'll put you up for 90 days while you find another house, and we'll provide you with a mortgage on your new house and—I moved.

FRANKLIN: Yeah. Yeah, that makes sense. How were your experiences in Seattle different from Tri-Cities?

WEBSTER: That's a very good question. As a matter of fact, I've thought about that a little bit. I'm not as involved in social organizations as I was here. But I've tried to make change from the inside based on my experience. I went through a succession of bank changes. So I sat on Seafirst Bank Foundation, for an example, to advocate for change through grants and stuff like that going. I currently sit on the chief of police advisory committee of the chief in Lynnwood where I live, to help bring about the communications and changes there. I've kind of learned that if you're at the table when the decisions are being made and you can influence them at that point in time, is that you can be more effective than reacting and waiting for the decision to come down and then going to react to it.

Governor Locke appointed me to the Legal Foundation of Washington. At that time I was the only non-lawyer on that foundation. And then Governor Gregoire re-appointed me to the foundation. They distributed $15, 16, 17 million a year to legal aide organizations throughout the state. Being able to influence that, and being able to determine the kind of organizations that would get money to carry out the legal aide for civil issues as opposed to criminal, and who got how much. Like Northwest Immigration Project was one of the major ones that's now helping to fight the immigration laws that's being—to be able to be a part of that, to me, is how I have been functioning. And that's how it's different from when I was here. I was on the outside, working from the outside. Now I find myself on the inside, working from the inside. If that makes sense.

FRANKLIN: Yeah, it makes perfect sense. And, yeah, because you kind of— you went into that world.

WEBSTER: Yes, yes.

FRANKLIN: Yeah. What surprised you, if anything, when you moved?

WEBSTER: Well, a couple things. Number one, contrary to what most people think, Seattle doesn't have a "Black community." They think of the central district as the Black community in Seattle. But if you walk through the central district, it's just as diverse as anywhere else you can go. That's not to say that a lot of Black folks don't live in central district, but a lot of Black folks live in south Seattle as well. So that kind of surprised me.

I worked on a campaign of several African Americans, like Mayor Rice, the first African American mayor of Seattle. Matter of fact, he was at Rainier Bank when I went to Rainier Bank. We worked together at the bank before he left to go to run for councilor and then the mayor. So the politics is a lot different.

And it's different from the standpoint that I don't think even to this day, that I am part of the nucleus of the political power in the Black community in Seattle. I'm still an outsider. Whereas in Pasco, three weeks after I got here, I was inside of the political structure of the Black community, if there was such a thing, and able to go and meet with the mayor even though they might disagree, or the chief of police, or the captain of the police department.

FRANKLIN: Well, you know, when I started this project, everybody was like, oh, you got to talk to Wally Webster, you got to talk to Wally Webster. It's almost like you were still here.

WEBSTER: Yeah. Well, I think that's because I was involved in so many things at such a young age, and like I said, I measured myself on progress. Whether it was the first Black police officer, or whether it's the East Pasco Neighborhood Council, or whether it's the voter registration drive, whether it's the hiring processes in Hanford and with the apprenticeship programs in labor unions, taking somebody out to Lamb Weston to go to work there. I just believed that you go based on results.

I want to brag a little bit and just say the other thing is—not that the other way was bad, and it takes both—but I was not a—and still to this day, I'm not a militant person. I don't try to threat to get the results that I'm looking for. I kind of use the analogy of water. You may get to the bottom of the cliff, but you can take the path of the least resistance to get there. So you try to manoeuver your way—it may take a little bit longer, but eventually you get there. You get there with less roadkill. And to me, I've always—I learned early, it's not always just the what, but it's also the how. So I treat people that way. That might be another reason why.

Even though I've been in Alabama and faced segregation and grew up going to the other side, stepping off the sidewalk, and keeping my head down, and going to inferior schools—which you didn't know you were going to an inferior school until you got someplace where you were challenged, right? In spite of all of that, I'm not bitter. I think all of those situations made me who I am today. And I think that made me a better person today. So I don't know if that's why, but that's what I think.

FRANKLIN: Yeah. What would you like future generations to know about working at Hanford and living in Tri-Cities during the Cold War?

WEBSTER: I think the most important thing for them to know is why they are here and what happened. There was one incident I didn't talk to you about, and this is—when they were building the Federal Building, we went to talk to the Federal Building to see how many African American jobs were going to be there, and we couldn't get anybody to talk. Couple of us just sat right down in the middle of the—you know the gates that they put around the building when they're doing construction and they open them up in the daytime for workers to go in and out? Dozers and everything. We just sat right down in the middle of the street, in the middle of the gateway, demanding to see somebody to tell us how many jobs going to be in this building. Not while it's in construction, but after it's finished.

So I would like for them to know, especially those that are associated with Hanford, what went before them to create an awareness that got them there. It wasn't just their education, the school that they graduated, and the degree that they hold, because there are a lot of people with those kinds of degrees that don't have a job like they have at Battelle. But somebody paved the way. And they're standing on the shoulders of somebody. And they just need to know that, as my dad used to say, if you see a turtle sitting on a fencepost, somebody helped him get there. And they got to know that they're a turtle on a fencepost. They got to know that somebody helped you get there. You didn't get there all by yourself. Because your legs are too short to wrap around a fencepost, you know?

FRANKLIN: I want to just—that's an interesting story. So you sat down—you kind of blocked the construction way. What did you find out about the jobs there? Was there a direct action from that, or a result from that action?

WEBSTER: To be honest with you, there were direct actions from the construction employment. But I didn't get immediate knowledge of a direct from the folks who occupied the office—occupied the building. I didn't get direct results. But I will tell you that after working in the community with

Hooper and Rutt, after coming to work in that building as employment manager for Boeing Computer Services and interacting with everyone there, I was able to influence. I was able to influence who worked there.

FRANKLIN: Was that—

WEBSTER: And there are people working today on this project, that I was telling you that I had the ability to recruit and hire on the spot, whether they were at Southern University or whether they were at Grambling State University or whether they were at some other school in Atlanta, Georgia, when we went to the Consortium of Historically Black Colleges down there, or we were in LA and hiring people there. Competing with Lockheed and others and when they were having layoffs. So I know people on both sides of the outlet today working at Hanford that came from my signing off a piece of paper, make them an offer, here's an offer, subject-to.

FRANKLIN: Yeah.

WEBSTER: Yeah.

FRANKLIN: Right on. Is there anything else you would like to mention related to migration, work experiences, segregation and civil rights and how they impacted your life at Hanford and in the Tri-Cities?

WEBSTER: I think I've said it all that I can recall, but I would like to say that, again, that the Tri-Cities is where I grew up, where I matured as a man and as a person. It shaped my life. It gave me the incentive to do, not only more for myself, but it demonstrated to me what you can do for others, if you just take the time to do it. I am extremely pleased that my uncle plucked me out of Oakland and drove me to Pasco. Very, very pleased and happy that that happened.

FRANKLIN: Right on. Well, Wally, thank you so much for coming and taking the time to interview with us.

WEBSTER: This was a pleasure.

FRANKLIN: Same here.

WEBSTER: Thank you so much. I appreciate the opportunity.

FRANKLIN: Yeah, awesome.

Contributors

Laura J. Arata is Assistant Professor of History and Director of Public History at Oklahoma State University. She received her PhD from Washington State University in 2014, specializing in Public History and the American West. She served as co-principal investigator for the Hanford History Project in 2013-14, and her chapter, "Orchards and Open Arms: Women in the Priest Rapids Valley, 1863–1943," appears in the first volume of the Hanford History Series, *Nowhere to Remember: Hanford, Richland, and White Bluffs to 1943*. Her recent articles include "Terror and Tourism: Lynching, Legend, and the Montana Vigilantes," and "Mickey Mouse Cowboys: Memory, Authenticity, and Disney's Wild West." Her first book, *Race and the Wild West: Sarah Bickford, the Montana Vigilantes, and the Tourism of Decline 1870–1930* (University of Oklahoma Press, 2020) traces the life and legend of a former slave who became sole owner of a public utilities company and an active promoter of tourism in Virginia City, Montana.

Robert Bauman is Professor of History at Washington State University Tri-Cities. Bauman is an award-winning scholar whose research and teaching interests are in twentieth-century U.S. social policy, religion, and race in the American West. He is the author of a number of articles and book chapters and two books, *Race and the War on Poverty: From Watts to East LA* (University of Oklahoma Press, 2008), and *Fighting to Preserve a Nation's Soul: America's Ecumenical War on Poverty* (University of Georgia Press, 2019). He also is co-editor and co-author of *Nowhere to Remember: Hanford, White Bluffs, and Richland to 1943* (Washington State University Press, 2018). His article, "Jim Crow in the Tri-Cities, 1943-1950" won the Charles Gates Award for the best article published in the *Pacific Northwest Quarterly* in 2005.

Robert Franklin is the Assistant Director and Archivist of the Hanford History Project, Director of the Hanford Oral History Project, and history lecturer at Washington State University Tri-Cities. The Hanford History Project focuses on preserving the WWII and Cold War history of the Hanford Site by managing the Department of Energy's Hanford

Collection. He brings a variety of public history skills to preserving and interpreting the history of the Hanford Site, partnering with a number of universities, nonprofits, federal government agencies, and cultural heritage organizations to tell Hanford stories. A true public historian, he is also the president of the B Reactor Museum Association and a docent with the Manhattan Project National Historical Park tour program. He also is co-editor, and co-author of *Nowhere to Remember: Hanford, White Bluffs, and Richland to 1943* (Washington State University Press, 2018).

Thomas E. Marceau is a North American archaeologist who has developed regional experience and expertise over forty-six years working first in the Northeast, then the Rocky Mountains, and most recently in the Pacific Northwest. Since his retirement in 2016, he has served as an adjunct faculty member in the Department of Anthropology at Washington State University Tri-Cities, where he teaches classes in archaeology. He worked on the U.S. Department of Energy (DOE) Hanford Site in Richland, Washington, for twenty-two years advising project management of their obligations to protect cultural resources on the site as cleanup progressed, and involving Native American Elders in project planning, review, and implementation activities to ensure that Tribal Treaty rights and interests were factored into all project decisions. His extensive experience as an archaeologist in the region, his collaborative working relationship with area Tribes, and his wide-ranging interactions with pre-Hanford residents as well as Hanford Site workers all contribute to his understanding of the broad cultural context of the Hanford Site, from prehistoric to contemporary communities.

Bibliography

ATOMIC HERITAGE FOUNDATION, VOICES OF THE MANHATTAN PROJECT

Bohnee, Gabriel. Interview by Cynthia C. Kelly and Thomas E. Marceau. Richland, Washington, September 2003. http://manhattanprojectvoices.org/oral-histories/gabriel-bohnees-interview. Accessed August 6, 2018.

Buck, Rex, Jr. Interview by Cynthia C. Kelly and Thomas E. Marceau. Richland, Washington, September 2003. http://manhattanprojectvoices.org/oral-histories/rex-bucks-interview. Accessed August 6, 2018.

Jim, Russell. Interview by Cynthia C. Kelly and Thomas E. Marceau. Richland, Washington, September 2003. http://manhattanprojectvoices.org/oral-histories/russell-jims-interview. Accessed August 6, 2018.

Taylor, Veronica. Interview by Cynthia C. Kelly and Thomas E. Marceau. Richland, Washington, September 2003. http://manhattanprojectvoices.org/oral-histories/veronica-taylors-interview. Accessed August 6, 2018.

HANFORD HISTORY PROJECT ORAL HISTORIES

Interviews conducted by Robert Franklin

Abercrombie, John. July 23, 2018.

Alford, Clarence. May 17, 2018.

Allen, Rose. January 12, 2018.

Barnes, Dallas. March 22, 2018.

Barnes, Dallas; Jackson, Webster; and Albert Wilkins. May 31, 2018.

Barton, Marion Keith. May 1, 2018.

Bell, Donald Sr. April 4, 2018.

Brown, CW. June 12, 2018.

Carter, Dan. February 19, 2018.

Curfman, Liz. July 16, 2018.

Daniels, Edmon and Vanis. May 7, 2018.

Fite, Mae. April 5, 2018.

Guice, Gordon. January 23, 2018.

Harvey, Katherine Helen Brouns Schiro. June 29, 2018.

Jackson, Emmitt. March 23, 2018.

Johnson, Aubrey. April 9, 2018.

Martin, Wayne. April 5, 2018.

Miller, Andy and Shirley. June 26, 2018.

Mitchell, David (Duke). March 2, 2018.

Mitchell, Greg. April 23, 2018.

Moore, Ellenor. March 21, 2018.

Moore, Vanessa. May 11, 2018.

Peoples, Emma. May 2, 2018.

Rambo, Bryan. March 23, 2018.

Rambo, Rhonda. March 23, 2018.

Robinson, Rickie. February 16, 2018.

Slaughter, John. February 28, 2018.

Sparks, Bobby. May 8, 2018.

Sparks, Jeannette. May 5, 2018

Stoffels, Jim. July 13, 2018.

Webster, Wallace. July 20, 2018.

Interviews conducted by Robert Bauman

Barnes, Dallas. February 12, 2004.

Mitchell, CJ. October 30, 2013.

Interview by Robert Bauman and Robert Franklin

Kupfer, Brenda, Roy Satoh, Linda Yamauchi Adkinson, and Bruce Yamauchi (Yamauchi Family Interview). September 18, 2018.

AFRO-AMERICAN COMMUNITY, CULTURAL AND EDUCATIONAL SOCIETY (AACCES) INTERVIEWS

Interviews by Vanessa Moore

Ash, Edward. August 25, 2001.

Crippen, Virginia. May 13, 2015.

Moore, Thomas. June 23, 2001.

Ray, Velma. October 6, 2014.

Sparks, Jeannette. May 5, 2015.

Interviews by Vanis Daniels

Haney, Benny. 2001 or 2002.

Richmond, Olden. June 21, 2001.

Interviews by Vanis Daniels and Leonard Moore

Walker, Cornelius. 2001 or 2002.

Williams, Joe. 2001 or 2002.

Interview by Vanis Daniels, Vanessa Moore, and Leonard Moore

Johnson, Luzell. February 18, 2002.

Interview by John Skinner

Pruitt, James. October 18, 2001.

HANFORD CULTURAL RESOURCES LIBRARY (HCRL) ORAL HISTORY PROGRAM

Interview by Ellen Prendergast

Barton, Katie, Vanis Daniels, and Velma Ray, October 4, 2001.

ADDITIONAL ORAL HISTORIES

Buck, Frank. Interview by Robert W. Mull. In S. L. Sanger, *Working on the Bomb: An Oral History of WWII Hanford*. Portland: Portland State University, 1995.

Daniels, Willie. Interview by S. L. Sanger. In Sanger, *Working on the Bomb*. 116–117.

BOOKS AND ARTICLES

Allen, John E., Marjorie Burns, and Scott Burns. *Cataclysmic Floods on the Columbia: The Great Missoula Floods*. Revised Second Edition. Portland: Portland State University Press, 2009.

Alt, David. *Glacial Lake Missoula and Its Humongous Floods*. Missoula, MT: Mountain Press Publishing Company, 2001.

Ames, Kenneth M. "Review of the Archaeological Record: Continuities, Discontinuities and Gaps, Cultural Affiliation Report," National Park Service, U.S. Department of the Interior, Archeology Program, Washington, D.C. In *Report on the Non-Destructive Examination, Description, and Analysis of the Human Remains from Columbia Park, Kennewick, Washington*, edited by Francis P. McManamon, Washington, DC., 1999. https://www.nps.gov/archeology/kennewick/ames7.htm. Accessed on May 21, 2018.

Anbinder, Tyler, Cormac O'Grada, and Simone A. Wegge. "Networks and Opportunities: A Digital History of Ireland's Great Famine Refugees in New York." *American Historical Review*, 124:5 (December 2019), 1591–1629.

Asaka, Megan. "'40-Acre Smudge': Race and Erasure in Prewar Seattle." *Pacific Historical Review*, 87:2, 231–263.

Bauman, Robert. "The Birmingham of Washington: Civil Rights and Black Power in the Tri-Cities." Unpublished paper, n.d.

———. "Jim Crow in the Tri-Cities, 1943–1950." *Pacific Northwest Quarterly* 96:3 (Summer 2005), 124–130.

———. *Race and the War on Poverty: From Watts to East L.A.* Norman: University of Oklahoma Press, 2008.

———. "Teaching Hanford History in the Classroom and in the Field." *The Public Historian*, 29:4 (Fall 2007), 45–55.

Bauman, Robert and Robert Franklin, eds. *Nowhere to Remember: Hanford, White Bluffs, and Richland to 1943.* Pullman: Washington State University Press, 2018.

Bjornstad, Bruce. *On the Trail of the Ice Age Floods: A Geological Field Guide to the Mid-Columbia Basin.* Sandpoint, ID: Keokee Books, 2006.

Blankenship, Anne M. *Christianity, Social Justice, and the Japanese American Incarceration during World War II.* Chapel Hill: University of North Carolina Press, 2016.

Bretz, J. Harlen. "The Channeled Scabland and the Spokane Flood." *Proceedings of the Academy and Affiliated Societies*, Geological Society of Washington, 423d Meeting, Washington, DC, 1927.

Brown, Kate. *Plutopia: Nuclear Families, Atomic Cities, and the Great Soviet and American Plutonium Disasters.* New York: Oxford University Press, 2013.

Chatters, James C. "The Recovery and First Analysis of an Early Holocene Human Skeleton from Kennewick, Washington." *American Antiquity* 65:2 (2000), 291–316.

Chin, Art. *Golden Tassels: A History of the Chinese in Washington, 1857–1977.* Seattle: Art Chin, 1977.

Daniels, Roger. *Concentration Camps, U.S.A.: Japanese Americans and World War II.* New York: Holt, Rinehart and Winston, 1971.

———. *Prisoners Without Trial: Japanese Americans in World War II.* New York: Hill and Wang, 1993.

Dudziak, Mary L. *Cold War Civil Rights: Race and the Image of American Democracy.* Princeton, NJ: Princeton University Press, 2000.

Faulkner, Susan Davis. "Thoroughly Modern Mary." *Franklin Flyer* 47:1 (March 2014), 1–6.

Fecht, Karl R., et al. "Late Pleistocene- and Holocene-Age Columbia River Sediments and Bedforms: Hanford Reach Area, Washington, Part 1." *Geological Atlas Series*, BHI-01648, Rev. 0. Richland, WA: Bechtel Hanford, 2004.

Fecht, Karl R. and Thomas E. Marceau. "Late Pleistocene- and Holocene-Age Columbia River Sediments and Bedforms: Hanford Reach Area, Washington, Part 2." *Geological Atlas Series*, WCH-46, Rev. 0. Richland, WA: Washington Closure Hanford, 2006.

Findlay, John M. and Bruce Hevly. *Atomic Frontier Days: Hanford and the American West.* Seattle: University of Washington Press, 2011.

Franklin, Robert. "Alphabet Houses." In Gabrielle Esperdy and Karen Kingsley, eds., *SAH Archipedia.* Charlottesville: University of Virginia Press, 2012. http://sah-archipedia. org/buildings/WA-01-005-0019. Accessed 2019-05-30.

Gamboa, Erasmo. "Braceros in the Pacific Northwest: Laborers on the Domestic Front, 1942–1947." *Pacific Historical Review,* 56:3 (August 1987), 378–399.

———. *Mexican Labor and World War II: Braceros in the Pacific Northwest, 1942–1947.* Seattle: University of Washington Press, 2000.

———. "Mexican Labor in the Pacific Northwest, 1943–1947." *Pacific Northwest Quarterly,* 73:4 (October 1982), 175–81.

Gamboa, Erasmo and Antonio Sanchez. "Fruits of Our Labor: A Survey of the History and Heritage of Hispanics in Washington State." n.d.

Goodloe, Trevor. "Roslyn, Washington." https://www.blackpast.org/african-american-history/roslyn-washington/. Accessed November 10, 2019.

Griffey, Trevor. "The Ku Klux Klan and Vigilante Culture in Yakima Valley." *The Seattle Civil Rights and Labor History Project.* University of Washington. 2007. http://depts. washington.edu/civilr/kkk_yakima.htm.

Harvey, David W. "An Oasis in the Desert? White Bluffs, Hanford, and Richland, The Early Years." In *Nowhere to Remember: Hanford, White Bluffs, and Richland to 1943,* edited by Robert Bauman and Robert Franklin, 13–35. Pullman: Washington State University Press, 2018.

Hildebrand, Lorraine Parker. *Straw Hats, Sandals and Steel: The Chinese in Washington State.* Tacoma: The Washington State American Revolution Bicentennial Commission, 1977.

Hinnershitz, Stephanie. *Race, Religion, and Civil Rights: Asian Students on the West Coast, 1900–1968.* New Brunswick, NJ: Rutgers University Press, 2015.

Huckleberry, Gary, et al. "Recent Geoarchaeological Discoveries in Central Washington." In Terry W. Swanson, editor, *Western Cordillera and Adjacent Areas.* Boulder, CO: Geological Society of America, Field Guide 4, 2003, 237–249.

"Indigenous Flood Stories from over 14,000 Years Ago," *Ice Age Flood Institute,* http:// iafi.org/indigenous-flood-stories-from-1400-years-ago. Accessed March 23, 2018.

Ingerson, Alice E. "What Are Cultural Landscapes?" The Arnold Arboretum of Harvard University, Institute for Cultural Landscape Studies. 2000. www.icls.harvard.edu/ language/whatare.htm.

Johansen, Bruce E. and Roberto F. Maestas. "Washington's Latino Community: 1935–1980." *Landmarks* (Summer 1982), 10–13.

Kirk, Ruth and Carmela Alexander. *Exploring Washington's Past: A Road Guide to History.* Seattle: University of Washington Press, 1990.

Lee, Erika. *The Making of Asian America: A History.* New York: Simon & Schuster, 2015.

Lemke-Santangelo, Gretchen. *Abiding Courage: African-American Migrant Women and the East Bay Community.* Chapel Hill: University of North Carolina Press, 1996.

Limerick, Patricia Nelson. *The Legacy of Conquest: The Unbroken Past of the American West*. New York: W.W. Norton, 1987.

Lipsitz, George. *How Racism Takes Place*. Philadelphia: Temple University Press, 2011.

Lucas, Shu-Chen. "Katie D. Morgan Barton (1918–2010)." Blackpast.org. https//www.blackpast.org/aaw/vignette_aahw/barton-katie-d-morgan-1918-2010/. Accessed 3/23/19.

Martínez-Matsuda, Veronica. "For Labor and Democracy: The Farm Security Administration's Competing Visions for Farm Workers' Socioeconomic Reform and Civil Rights in the 1940s." *The Journal of American History* 106:2 (September 2019), 338–361.

Matthias, Franklin T. "Diary and Notes of Col. Franklin Matthias, 1942–1945." U.S. Department of Energy Public Reading Room, Consolidated Libraries, Washington State University Tri-Cities.

Molina, Natalia. *How Race is Made in America: Immigration, Citizenship, and the Historical Power of Racial Scripts*. Berkeley: University of California Press, 2014.

Murray, Alice Yang. *Historical Memories of the Japanese American Internment and the Movement for Redress*. Stanford: Stanford University Press, 2008.

Native American Rights Fund. "'We Also Have A Religion:' The American Indian Religious Freedom Act and the Religious Freedom Project of the Native American Rights Fund." *Announcements* 5:1, Boulder, Colorado. 1979.

Ng, Wendy L. *Japanese American Internment during World War II: A History and Reference Guide*. Westport, CT: Greenwood Press, 2002.

Nomura, Gail M. "Washington's Asian/Pacific American Communities." In Sid White and S.E. Solberg, eds., *Peoples of Washington: Perspectives on Cultural Diversity*, 113–155. Pullman: Washington State University Press, 1989.

Oberst, Walter A. *Railroads, Reclamation and the River: A History of Pasco*. Pasco: Franklin County Historical Society, 1978.

Okihiro, Gary K. *American History Unbound: Asians and Pacific Islanders*. Berkeley: University of California Press, 2015.

Okihiro, Gary K. and Joan Myers. *Whispered Silences: Japanese Americans and World War II*. Seattle: University of Washington Press, 1996.

Omi, Michael and Howard Winant. *Racial Formation in the United States from the 1960s to the 1980s*. New York: Routledge Press, 1986.

Orleck, Annelise. *Storming Caesar's Palace: How Black Mothers Fought Their Own War on Poverty*. Boston: Beacon Press, 2005.

Parker, Martha Berry. *Kin-I-Wak, Kenewick, Tehe, Kennewick*. Fairfield, WA: Ye Galleon Press, 1986.

Race and Violence in Washington State: Report of the Commission on the Causes and Prevention of Civil Disorder. Olympia, 1969.

Rasmussen, Morten, et al. "The Ancestry and Affiliations of Kennewick Man." *Nature* 523 (2015), 455–458.

Reidel, Stephen P., et al. "The Columbia River Flood Basalts and the Yakima Fold Belt." In T.W. Swanson, ed., *Western Cordillera and Adjacent Areas*, 87–105. Boulder, CO: Geological Society of America Field Guide 4, 2003.

Riddell, F. A. "Smohalla's Village." Department of Anthropology. Pullman: Washington State University. 1948.

Sanger, S.L. *Working on the Bomb: An Oral History of WWII Hanford.* Portland, OR: Portland State University, 1995.

Searcey, Dionne and Robert Gebeloff. "The Divide in Yakima is the Divide in America." *New York Times*, November 19, 2019.

Sever, David Arthur. "Comparison of Negro and White Attitudes in a Washington Community." MA Thesis, Washington State University, 1967.

Sides, Josh. *L.A. City Limits: African-American Los Angeles from the Great Depression to the Present.* Berkeley: University of California Press, 2003.

Slatta, Richard. "Chicanos in the Pacific Northwest." *Pacific Northwest Quarterly*, 70:4 (October 1979), 155–62.

Stoffle, Richard W., David B. Halmo, and Diane E. Austin. "Cultural Landscapes and Traditional Cultural Properties: A Southern Paiute View of the Grand Canyon and Colorado River." *The American Indian Quarterly* 21:2 (1997), 229–249.

Stoffle, Richard W., et al. "Risk Perception Mapping: Using Ethnography to Define the Locally Affected Population for a Low-Level Radioactive Waste Storage Facility in Michigan." *American Anthropologist* 93:3 (1991), 611–635.

Takaki, Ronald. *Strangers from a Different Shore: A History of Asian Americans.* Boston: Little, Brown and Company, 1998.

Taylor, Quintard. "A History of Blacks in the Pacific Northwest, 1788–1970." PhD Dissertation, University of Minnesota, 1977.

———. *The Forging of a Black Community: Seattle's Central District from 1870 through the Civil Rights Era.* Seattle: University of Washington Press, 1994.

———. *In Search of the Racial Frontier: African Americans in the American West, 1528–1990.* New York: W.W. Norton, 1998.

Valle, Isabel. *Fields of Toil: A Migrant Family's Journey.* Pullman: Washington State University Press, 1994.

Van Arsdol, Ted. *Tri-Cities: The Mid-Columbia Hub.* Chatsworth, CA: Windsor Publications, 1990.

———. "The Yamauchis in the New World." *The Franklin Flyer* 20:2 (July 1987), 1–9.

Washington State University, General Extension Service. "A Community Survey of the Pasco-Kennewick Area, November 1949." Pullman: Washington State University, 1949.

White, Richard. "Race Relations in the American West." *American Quarterly*, 38:3 (1986): 396–416.

Wilkinson, Isabel. *The Warmth of Other Suns: The Epic Story of America's Great Migration.* New York: Random House, 2010.

Zedeño, Nieves, et al. "Landmark and Landscape: A Contextual Approach to the Management of American Indian Resources." *Culture & Agriculture* 19:3 (1997), 123–129.

THESES AND DISSERTATIONS

Wiley, James T., Jr. "Race Conflict as Exemplified in a Washington Town." MA Thesis, State College of Washington, 1949.

Williams, Melissa E.E. "Those Who Desire Very Much to Stay: African Americans and Housing in Vancouver, Washington, 1940 to 1960." MA Thesis. Washington State University Vancouver. 2007.

GOVERNMENT DOCUMENTS

Advisory Council on Historic Preservation. *Memorandum of Understanding Among the U.S. Department of Defense, U.S. Department of the Interior, U.S. Department of Agriculture, U.S. Department of Energy, and the Advisory Council on Historic Preservation Regarding Interagency Coordination and Collaboration for the Protection of Sacred Sites*. Washington, DC, 2012.

American Indian Religious Freedom Act, Public Law No. 95-341; 92 Stat. 469, 42 U.S.C. 1996, Washington, DC, 1978.

American Indian Writers Subgroup (AIWS). "American Indian Perspectives on the Yucca Mountain Site Characterization Project and the Repository Environmental Impact Statement." Consolidated Group of Tribes and Organizations, American Indian Resource Document, DOE-Nevada. 1998.

Archaeological Resources Protection Act, 16 U.S.C. 470aa–470mm; Public Law 96-95, Washington, DC, 1979.

Birnbaum, Charles A. "Protecting Cultural Landscapes: Planning, Treatment and Management of Historic Landscapes," *Preservation Briefs No. 36*, Technical Preservation Services, National Park Service, Washington, DC, 1994.

E.I. Du Pont de Nemours & Company, Inc., "Construction, Hanford Engineer Works, U.S. Contract No. W-7412-ENG-1, Du Pont Project 9536, History of the Project." Wilmington, DE: Du Pont, 1945.

Executive Order No. 13007. *Indian Sacred Sites*. The White House, Washington, DC, Federal Register, 61:104, (1996), 26771–26772.

Lyng v. Northwest Indian Cemetery Protective Association, 485 U.S. 439, U.S. Supreme Court, Washington, DC, 1988.

Marceau, Thomas E. "Historic Overview." In Thomas E. Marceau, et al., *History of the Plutonium Production Facilities at the Hanford Site Historic District, 1943–1990*. DOR/RL-97-1047. Hanford Cultural and Historic Resources Program, U.S. Department of Energy, Richland, Washington. 2002.

McManamon, Francis P. "The Initial Scientific Examination, Description, and Analysis of the Kennewick Man Human Remains." In Francis P. McManamon, editor, *Report on the Non-Destructive Examination, Description, and Analysis of the Human Remains from Columbia Park, Kennewick, Washington.* National Park Service, Department of the Interior, Washington, DC. 1999. www.nps.gov/archeology/kennewick. Accessed May 21, 2018.

McManamon, Francis P., et al. "Examination of the Kennewick Remains – Taphonomy, Micro-Sampling, and DNA Analysis." In *Report on the DNA Testing Results of the Kennewick Remains from Columbia Park, Kennewick, Washington.* 2001. www.nps.gov/archeology/kennewick/fpm_dna.htm. Accessed May 21, 2018.

Native American Graves Protection and Repatriation Act. Public Law 101-601, 25 U.S.C. 3001 et seq., 104 Stats. 3048. 1990.

National Historic Preservation Act, Public Law 89-665, 16 U.S.C. 470 et seq. 1966.

National Park Service. *Historic Landscape Initiative.* Washington, DC, 1999.

Opinion and Order (Civil No. 96-1481-JE). United States District Court for the District of Oregon, Portland, Oregon. 2002.

Parker, Patricia L. and Thomas F. King. "Guidelines for Evaluating and Documenting Traditional Cultural Properties." *National Register Bulletin 38,* National Park Service, Washington, DC, 1990.

Protection of Archaeological Resources, 43 CFR 7, 49 FR 1027, as amended at 60 FR 5260, 5261(1995). 1984.

Sharpe, James J., and Thomas E. Marceau. *Archaeological Excavation Report for Extraction Well C3662 in Support of the 100-KR-4 Pump-and-Treat Project,* BHI-01556, Rev. 0. Bechtel Hanford, Inc., Richland, Washington. 2001.

Treaty with the Nez Perce, 1855, 12 Stats. 957.

Treaty with the Walla Walla, Cayuse, etc., 1855, 12 Stats. 945.

Treaty with the Yakima, 1855, 12 Stats. 951.

U.S. Bureau of the Census, *Nineteenth Census of the United States, 1970 Volume 2: Characteristics of the Population.* Washington, DC: US GPO, 1973.

U.S. Bureau of the Census, *Twentieth Census of the United States, 1980 Volume 2: Characteristics of the Population.* Washington, DC: US GPO, 1984.

U. S. Bureau of the Census, *Twenty-First Census of the United States, 1990 Volume 2: Characteristics of the Population.* Washington, DC: US GPO, 1994.

U.S. Bureau of the Census, *Twenty-Second Census of the United States, 2000 Volume 2: Characteristics of the Population.* Washington, DC: US GPO, 2004.

U.S. Department of Energy. DOE O 1230.2. *American Indian and Alaska Native Tribal Government Policy.* U.S. Department of Energy, Washington, DC: 2000.

U.S. Department of Energy, Richland Operations Office. *Hanford Cultural Resources Management Plan,* DOE/RL-98-10, Rev. 1. U.S. Department of Energy, Richland Operations Office, Richland, Washington. 2003.

Index

Other Books in the Series

NOWHERE TO REMEMBER
Hanford, White Bluffs, and Richland to 1943
Edited by Robert Bauman and Robert Franklin

Hanford Histories Volume 1

Drawn from Hanford History Project personal narratives, *Nowhere to Remember* highlights life in three small close-knit eastern Washington agricultural communities—until 1943, when the Manhattan Project forced a permanent, mandatory evacuation. Early chapters cover settlement and development, examining the region's past within the context of American West history. The volume also details the tight bonds between residents, women's early twentieth century experiences, removal stories, and reactions to the loss.

LEGACIES OF THE MANHATTAN PROJECT
Reflections on 75 Years of a Nuclear World
Edited by Michael Mays

Hanford Histories Volume 2

Covering topics from print journalism, activism, nuclear testing, and science and education to health physics, environmental cleanup, and kitsch, essays collected by the Hanford History Project illuminate facets of the Manhattan Project earlier scholars left unexplored and reveal how its legacy lives on.

Other Books on Hanford

AMERICA'S NUCLEAR WASTELANDS
Politics, Accountability, and Power
Max S. Power

America's Nuclear Wastelands presents an expert, yet straightforward overview of this complex topic, including nuclear weapons history and contamination issues. The author also explores the current institutional and political environment, demonstrating the critical role of public participation for present and future generations.
"As eye opening as it is readable."
—Public Library Association
2009 Best of the Best from the University Presses, American Library Association

ATOMIC GEOGRAPHY
A Personal History of the Hanford Nuclear Reservation
Melvin R. Adams

Thoughtful, often surprising vignettes from one of Hanford's first environmental engineers sift through its rubble, abandoned documents, factories, and surroundings, recalling challenges and sites he worked on or found personally intriguing.

"For a book about nuclear waste cleanup, paradox and irony figure prominently—*Atomic Geography* is an intelligent, probing, and strangely poetic read."
—*ForeWord Magazine*

2016 ForeWord Magazine *Top Ten University Pick*

MADE IN HANFORD
The Bomb that Changed the World
Hill Williams

At an isolated location along the Columbia River in 1944, the world's first plutonium factory became operational, producing fuel for the atomic bomb dropped on Nagasaki, Japan during World War II. Former *Seattle Times* science writer Hill Williams traces the amazing, tragic story—from the dawn of nuclear science to Cold War testing in the Marshall Islands.